WHERE THE HORNBEAM GROWS

WHERE THE HORNBEAM GROWS

A Journey in Search
of a Garden

BETH LYNCH

WEIDENFELD & NICOLSON

First published in Great Britain in 2019 by Weidenfeld & Nicolson
an imprint of The Orion Publishing Group Ltd
Carmelite House, 50 Victoria Embankment
London EC4Y 0DZ

An Hachette UK Company

1 3 5 7 9 10 8 6 4 2

A CIP catalogue record for this book is
available from the British Library.

ISBN (hardback) 978 1 4746 0688 2
ISBN (trade paperback) 978 1 4746 0689 9
ISBN (ebook) 978 1 4746 0691 2

Typeset by Input Data Services Ltd, Somerset

Printed and bound by CPI Group (UK) Ltd, Croydon, CR0 4YY

www.orionbooks.co.uk

For Shaun

. . . comment nous nous enracinons, jour par jour,
dans un 'coin du monde'

. . . how we take root, day after day, in a 'corner of the world'

Gaston Bachelard

Contents

Contents

A Note on Names

The naming of plants is an open-ended business. Besides its botanical Latin name, of which there may also be an obsolete version, a single plant might have a common English name or two, or several, not to mention vernacular names in other languages. Then there are the abbreviated names – 'montana', 'moyesii' – by which individual gardeners might know favourite plants, and the names personalised by association with people or places in a gardener's life: 'Burton's Blue', 'Milton's Geranium', 'Swaledale'. I know people for whom 'montana' means *Clematis montana*; when I say 'montana', though, I have *Centaurea montana* in mind.

If I were writing a gardening book, my plant nomenclature would be standardised in some way. But this is a different kind of book, a memoir: it speaks my own language, which is far from standard. Like most people, I learned and still learn the names of plants in many different ways: accidentally, osmotically, serendipitously, sometimes systematically. Because my mother spoke of aquilegias and euphorbias when I was young, I do not know them, though you might, as columbines and spurges. What you may think of as an ipomoea, on the other hand, is a morning glory for me.

When a plant crops up in the following pages, I have used the name by which I know it – sometimes botanical (aquilegia), sometimes common (morning glory). If that plant's presence is substantial I have also mentioned its chief alternative name (columbine and ipomoea respectively) to aid recognition or identification. Full botanical names (*Aquilegia vulgaris*), where they appear, are italicised in keeping with convention.

The names of some people have been changed.

Prologue

I always knew that the garden was of the woods. The trees across the lane filled the frame of my bedroom window, and on summer evenings I watched and listened long after I had supposedly gone to bed. I must have cut a distinctive figure, a small child in a pale nightdress, there at the open window like an unquiet soul in a Victorian novel. I loved the flittings of the pink-grey dusk: the belated martins and the wide-awake bats that circled the house with mysterious squeaks, the sound of evening under way. Sometimes an owl trailed its call through the treetops. Once I was spellbound by a nightingale. Teenagers gathered too, from time to time, where the lanes intersected at the wood.

Though decades have passed since I haunted that Sussex wood, I have an inner map of its parts and ways. From the graffitied beech tree to the striated slope of birches where fly agarics mushroomed in autumn to the depression where the temperature dropped and the air always stirred. Reverberations of the ground in certain places at certain times of year. The labyrinthine streams, beyond my usual territory, where I once lost my way and was afraid. The wide, straight, beech-lined path and the overgrown rhododendrons, darkly anomalous amongst the broad-leaved trees. I hated those rhododendrons because they sucked up the wood's light and gave nothing back, and their flowers were the colour of queasiness. I had no idea then that someone had planted them a century earlier, maybe two, nor that the banks and hollows and ditches and tracks and streams were also the work of men – a defunct ironworking topography that the wood blurred quietly, incrementally, with each year's growth and fall.

Oak: a mud-coloured layer of scalloped leaves, flat and impacted. You could lift it like a piece of handmade paper to reveal deep-smelling leaf forms in shades of chestnut through mahogany, and on down through formlessness to humus. Beech leaves bed down with a lighter touch in tones of patinated copper. They settle delicately over time, and they almost chime when disturbed with a foot. Their rot is dark and velvety, as irresistible to fingertips as greasy dust on a horse's neck. Hornbeam leaves are different: they return themselves uneasily to the earth. They are khaki like sloughed snakeskin, and they curl and writhe as the season drains them of chlorophyll, hanging on to the end of winter. Once fallen, they are unsettled by the slightest movement of air.

I was drawn to a clearing where young hornbeams reached for the sparse canopy. At bluebell time, when indigo spread to infinity, you could barely believe that this enchanted place lay just a few hundred yards from home. To my eye, bluebells are their truest colour in light filtered by the first hornbeam leaves; beech light is different. Hornbeam fascinated me even in winter. A hedge of hornbeam bounded one side of our garden, and I loved the contortions of the trunks and branches, their air of suspended animation that was not, I fancied, entirely of the plant world. Their fluted limbs were the colour of Cornish slate, and leathery like slow worms. As a young child, watching the wood after bedtime, I knew without thinking about it that hornbeam was my favourite tree. Hornbeam captured my imagination. It was a tree of this place, and it had to do with home.

PART ONE

Growing

I left home on a late afternoon in early January. A dark day that kept darkening and, around four-thirty, swallowed itself. I closed the front door and walked down the drive past dim, winter-bare shrubs. Out through the gateway.

Outside, in the lane, the hedges and sky had merged. I saw the house's empty form when it was no longer visible: if you've known a place inside out for more than forty years you can see, hear, smell, feel your way around without looking, or moving an inch.

A flurry of impressions. Frost in the air on my face and in my sinuses, sharp as this day was dull. The first evening stars. Light snug behind closed curtains. The front door shutting with a faint boom. The smell of baking potatoes and, on Wednesdays, baking bread. The languid double-click of the kitchen door. Home, safe, warm. Winter memories stored up in the senses: I used to come home from school around this time, up the steep lane from the station with a torch through trees. Nostalgia, you may say, and maybe you'd be right – but just as these things are warm with hindsight they were warm too at the time, in my teens: out of my element at school, waiting for the bell, I looked forward to them. 'Nostalgia', if you dig down to the word's

Greek roots, strip away its rosy layers, means something like 'a painful longing to return home'. I could identify with that.

Sometimes, to spook myself as I walked up the hill, I would zigzag the torch's beam through the bare branches, afraid of what I might see, or conjure. Then I'd quicken my step a little, hurry home, glad to hear the brick-hard echo of the drive beneath my feet, know that I was safely back inside the high hedges.

But on this dark January afternoon-evening, for the first time, the hedges shut me out. My parents were dead, the house was sold, it was lonely out there at the end of the drive. From now on I would have to remember my way back in.

A train stopped down in the valley then crescendoed away, and after the usual interval four cars chased each other up the lane, cornering fast as locals do. Next door but one, a woman I did not recognise drew curtains in a bright bedroom and a wall mirror reflected her back like the café mirror in that Manet painting. There were no stars. A man walked past with a flash-light, a shadowy dog and a guarded hello, and all at once I was self-conscious, lurking in the dark outside a darkened house, to all intents and purposes a stranger.

As I drove away the headlights made a tunnel of the trees. Something pale skimmed my field of vision – an owl, perhaps, or weariness. Left at the blind junction at the end of the lane, left again onto the main road, on through the accident black spot and past the entrance to the forest where, when I was little, they found a corpse in a black-and-yellow dress; the figure on the police poster had blonde hair but no face, and I used to think about that. Onto the motorway with its lanes of purpose-ful lights, bland pop on the stereo, on back to London, steering through what was left of that day towards the flashing light of Canary Wharf like a person at sea. I was suddenly, absolutely tired.

Back in, through the five-bar gate – it is a long time ago, for I was very young when the gate disappeared for a lost reason and was not replaced – up the drive and along the front of the house, where the sun's angle means it is afternoon and the hydrangeas are papery tones of blue through mauve. I love their blueness for its own sake, an impression of azure or a deepening to cobalt in their great clustered inflorescences. They get their colour from the clay soil, which is acidic: plant the same varieties over chalk or limestone and their range will be pink to Bordeaux. I remember my way on around the corner, scratching my finger-tips lightly across the warm rough bricks of local clay, earthen shading to purple. Along the side through a dark glitter of camellia foliage, over the back lawn that is shrunk and fissured by summer, hollow to the eye and foot and ear. Maybe it is 1976, the year of the drought.

An energetic sound, rhythmic as birdsong but blunt on the finish: my mother's trowel in dry ground close at hand. She only ever had one trowel, with a deep blade that she scooped into the soil and a wooden handle that she would wear to a shine and eventually loose. My father made new handles from time to time and I loved the way that one, finished with two encircling grooves, fitted to my own right hand. My father used this trowel for many years after my mother's death; when he too died I searched high and low, but I never saw it again.

Another sunny day – these early garden memories are almost always bright, contained and safe, like paradise – but today

5

the light is softer, promising, and the air fresh on my skin. I'm breathing in a spring morning, and a blackbird's alarm call is merging with the thud and chink of garden tools, complicating their rhythm. Maybe my parents are digging the vegetable plot and planting potatoes. If so, it is Good Friday, a feast day in the gardening calendar when root crops are traditionally planted, and hot cross buns without crosses will be proving in the kitchen. As the warm dough rises it will tinge the day with nutmeg and cinnamon.

I am over by the hornbeam hedge, inspecting the wild rose in the brief, absolute hope – a child's hope – of a deep-pink bud. I do this often, for weeks maybe, on my way to check on the animals: I have suddenly remembered that the rose is there, and it has captured my imagination. I'm unaware that it is far too early in the season: there is no suggestion of flowers, but globules of moisture pick out the serrated leaves exquisitely and strands of damp gossamer, half-spun cobweb, drift into my face then evanesce.

My mother planted many roses – shrubby, rambling, low-bred types that you did not prune into compliance but set loose where they could be themselves, within reason. The moyesii, with its lovely-sounding name and sea-green foliage, its crimson blooms like enamel; the bush that erupted in gold and vibrated with bees; the blush climber that scrambled about with a purple-blue clematis, carefully selected because they bloomed around the same time. The late-flowering one from which, decades later, I would cut small pink roses for my mother on the last day of her life.

There was something simple and original about the wild or dog rose. Nobody knew how long it had been there, and its briars threaded through the hornbeam hedge as though reaching for the sun or for something to grasp. The buds, when they appeared at last, were shell-pink, archetypal rosebuds. Each opened into a single-formed flower with a pollen-fuzzy halo at its centre, and the petals deepened outwards from whitishness through dog-rose pink to a trace, at the edges, of the bud's intensity. You had to seek out its faint scent, inhaling and concentrating, maybe imagining. I could not resist picking a bloom, pricking my fingers lightly as I bent the green stem back, even though I knew the petals would scatter before I could find a jar and water.

Much later I chose to leave the wild rose be, perfect and untouchable, rooting my parents' garden in the fields and hedgerows from which it was formed.

The garden was enclosed from a field that in turn was carved from the woods. A great tract of woodland, in fact, that once stretched through south-east England and earned the region its delicious descriptive name, the Weald – 'forest' in Old English. The exposed contours of hills, the broadleaf woods, the reticulating hedgerows that thicken into copses and thin to earthwork traces and dottings of trees: the topography of my home dates back to the Neolithic, when early farmers cleared wildwood to create field systems. It ebbed and grew and reverted and morphed with millennia of use: settlement and farming, fortification, iron-smelting, transhumance – a word that sounds metaphysical but has to do with grazing – and EU-sponsored set-aside. Its place names are built from Anglo-Saxon words for things of the woods, monosyllables that paint landscapes in my mind's eye. *Shaw*, copse; *den*, a pannage settlement for grazing pigs. *Hurst*, a wooded hill, like the one on which my parents made the garden.

Paradise too is a garden on a wooded hill, an 'enclosure green' crowning a 'steep wilderness' in the eastern part of Eden. The lower flanks of the hill are 'overgrown' with 'thicket' that gives way, as your eye ascends, to ranks of high trees, '[s]hade above shade', and then to a 'verdurous wall' – a plant-covered wall, or a solid hedge, or some kind of wall-hedge. This is our first glimpse of the garden in *Paradise Lost*, John Milton's great poetic meditation on the story of the fall of man. It's little surprise that when we first see paradise it is from the outside, for that is where we have been, the whole human lot of us, since Adam and Eve were expelled at the end of the third chapter of Genesis for eating the forbidden fruit. Whether the green hilltop enclosure has been cleared from the wood, or whether the thickets and trees have been planted around it, is not for us mere mortals to ask.

My parents had always walked the lanes and woods and fields together. In a photograph taken just after they met – my mother sixteen, my father seventeen, but so grown up in their overcoats and polished shoes – they are walking away from the camera along a wooded track or unmetalled lane. I loved that picture when I was small because I thought they were setting off to find their home, which in a way they were. In those early years of grafting, saving for a deposit, they often stopped at a hilltop field where two steep lanes emerged from the woods and met in a 'T'; I can see my parents now, knee-deep in buttercup and mauve-dusty cocksfoot, pacing out, building and planting in their shared imagination. Eventually, and against considerable odds, they bought the plot, enclosed it first with pig wire and then with hedges, and built a house. They worked the field into a garden: I wish I had asked them at what point the one became the other.

The garden never forgot where it came from. Our lawn consisted of species that lawn-proud people consider weeds, but it was green and that was all that mattered. What is a lawn without clover for bees or daisies for daisy chains? The garden backed on to the field from which it was enclosed, and in high summer, low lit by the day's last sun, the field shimmered with ripe grasses – couch, cocksfoot, rye grass, quaking grass – hundreds of thousands of seeds for dispersal by birds and wind and animals. Dandelion seeds drifted in on air currents that you could not feel. They hung in shafts of sun like celestial parachutes, and spun in slowest motion to the ground.

Any rural child will tell you that dandelions do not have seed heads, they have clocks. Pick a pinkish milky stem and blow on the soft star-faceted globe: the number of puffs required to strip the clock bare will tell you the time (dandelion time is always on the hour). For goodness sake, my mother said when I demonstrated this in the vegetable garden, sowing the seeds of yet more weeding – but she shook her head over the Tanners, who moved in further down the lane and took weed control to a phobic extreme. Whenever I think of them, Mr and Mrs Tanner are bent double. Their lawn was a fine-bladed thoroughbred and they weeded it doggedly and perpetually, their labour renewed by spinning, winging, dropping seeds and the underground stealth of couch and bindweed. They might just as well have rolled rocks up the hill, like Sisyphus. Their just-so house with its daisyless lawn looked ill at ease amongst the woods and fields, and its doors and windows were closed, blank-eyed, against flies and dust and children like me. Their twins sometimes came to play, and this was encouraged at first – I think we were considered a respectable family – but when I called for Susanna and Mark I had to wait outside while they were dressed and briefed for the world. I was a free-roaming child, and who knows what was on my clothes and under my fingernails. The twins were pale and flawless – starved of fresh air, my mother said – and there was something literal about Susanna's hair, of which, though she wore a single tiny clip, not one was ever out of place. I often needed tidying up. The twins needed a walk in the woods.

I haven't thought about Susanna and Mark for decades. They annoyed me back then, when we were all eight. They had been to an international school and their reading standard was, they let it be known too often, Very High (I'm Very Happy for you, my father said the first time Mark informed him of this). They wore their overprotection with tremendous confidence, as though they also knew their own minds. No, we can't go in the woods. But I go in the woods all the time – we'll only go as far as the beech tree. No. OK, we can pick bluebells on the bank. No. But it's right across from my house. No. You can't pick bluebells??? No.

There was to be no sitting on grass of any kind. No, not even on my parents' field-lawn/lawn-field, even if it had just been mown. Certainly no touching the solitary cow that waited at a gate to have its dear wide face rubbed until its eyes dozed shut. But it's a lovely cow – it will lick your hand if you're patient. We are not to go near animals. Oh come on. No. Even so, Mr Tanner would follow us up the lane in case we failed to go straight to my parents' house: I'd never felt distrusted before, and it was a relief for everyone when the twins' visits ceased as suddenly as they had begun. By the time I had started to tidy myself up, in my teens, Mark was into Billy Idol and Susanna owned a pair of Dr Martens. On balance, I think they were rather cool.

The Tanners had moved from Switzerland, and Mrs Tanner was the first person I had ever met who barely spoke English: I felt I should address her in a special way but had no idea what that way might be. She disconcerted me not just because she never really spoke to me, nor because she made me stand outside in the rain, nor because she always wore the same grey skirt and sensible shoes, but above all because I never saw her smile – ever. I thought everyone smiled at you if you smiled at them unless they were angry or sad, and nobody could be angry or sad all the time (could they?). To my eight-year-old self she was forbidding and sour, her home besieged by its own surroundings. Today, I wonder whether she also felt out of place as a foreigner in England. I could not have imagined then that I might one day have something in common with her – that I would find myself living a stranger's life in her country, as she then was in mine.

I could not imagine not being at home amongst those fields and woods, amongst the hedgerows that shared secrets with me and led me back to the garden.

I am not entirely sure what the word 'home' means, though I know what I mean when I use it. Home is where you come from – your native soil, where your roots are for better or worse, a vital coordinate in your map of who you are. It is also something that you make, like the homes in which I have lived with my husband Shaun or the patch of field where my parents marked out a plot, built a house, raised three children and, when they were not working, gardened together for the rest of their shared life. Other people moved house; my parents put down intertwined roots that only death would dislodge: their home, our home. Even so, decades after leaving the cramped rented cottage in which she grew up, my mother still called that place emphatically Home. The rest of us went down to Granny's, my mother went Home. Then we all came home. If we were out or away and she mentioned home, an inflection told everybody which one she meant.

You can be at home to take delivery of a washing machine, and you can be at home by being comfortable, happy, in a place or a situation, as I was in the garden from an age that pre-dates memory. 'Beth is in her element with plenty of mud & large spaces, quite self-sufficient', my mother noted in a rare diary entry when I was not yet two. It's an unremarkable observation to make of a toddler, even in early March with snow on the way. Yet when I came across this entry for the first time, in middle age, I felt a thrill of recognition because they are words that might describe my adult self, someone whose well-being is bound up with having a green space to tend. The garden is where I was at home – in my element – where I became a gardener, one who 'gardens'. I cannot quite define that word either. There is something special about gardening, for we do not make verbs of other enclosed spaces such as fields and yards.

It was *Paradise Lost* that set me thinking about what gardening is. I was seventeen years old and off school because it had snowed and there were no trains. I luxuriated in the crystalline garden, and threw snowballs that baffled the dog because they disappeared where they fell. I lit the fire at midday and began to read *Paradise Lost* in its twelve-book entirety: we were doing the first two books, the 'Hell' books, for A level, and I wanted to find out what happened next. In the course of Book III Satan, exiled from Heaven, winged his way towards Eden bent on destroying God's new creation, man – and early in Book IV Satan and I had our first glimpse of paradise. Paradise, I discovered to my delight, was not perfect, static, sanctimonious as you might expect it to be in a seventeenth-century poem about man's unfitness to stay there. The plants in Milton's paradise grew as vigorously as the trees and vegetation beyond its bounds: its bowers were 'with branches overgrown', just as the wilderness outside was '[w]ith thicket overgrown'. Its paths were strewn with spent blossoms. Adam and Eve, I read, must clear and 'lop' incessantly, sweep and rake, if they were to 'tread with ease', keep the garden from running or reverting to the natural world that surrounded it and with which it was of a kind. The garden must be gardened if it were to remain a garden. To garden was to deal with things that lived and grew and would, left to their own devices, be more or less wild. That was exciting. It made sense.

Until that point, gardening for me involved mud, space, fascinations and seemingly random obsessions. I loved the borders and shrubs that made my parents' garden what it was, but with one or two exceptions – the corner of the herbaceous border where the Japanese anemones grew; a crimson peony in a sea of green alchemilla – my appreciation was general. Organised planting was for adults; visits to nurseries bored me stiff, apart from the rainy day when my parents were discussing shrubs with a specialist and I wandered into a greenhouse and found a passion flower in full bloom. Its intricate geometry, its colours and its textures were unreal, unlike anything I had ever seen. My parents found me there transfixed, and the kind nurseryman picked the flower and gave it to me. I wanted it to last forever.

I don't know why I was drawn to the wild edges, to the things of the fields and hedgerows and woods that made their way into the garden. The dog rose. The hornbeam. A single bindweed flower in the vegetable plot: it was candy-striped with pink and had a bewitching scent, somewhere between almonds and those violet-flavoured sweets that cost a halfpenny for a small roll and neither tasted nor smelled of violets. I was thrilled one spring to find four or five bluebells that had made their way across the lane from the wood to the front garden. There were hundreds on the bank opposite, but those few inside the hedge were special. One of my first plants was a germinated acorn that I found in the lawn when I was six or seven: it had a tiny pair of scalloped leaves. I potted it up and watched it grow, on and off, and eventually it sold for ten pence at a school fête. I like to think that whoever bought it planted it out, and that my acorn is now a Sussex oak. The years accumulated in its woody growth rings, forty and counting.

The acorn started something: growing things. I remember the after-school afternoon when our greengrocer gave me a clementine with its pair of leaves intact. I was enchanted, for I had only ever seen satsumas half-packed in blue tissue paper; this was, remember, rural England in the seventies. The clementine was smaller than a satsuma, and more spherical. Its juicy flesh crunched when I bit it, whereas satsumas squeaked and generally delivered less than they promised. I kept the clementine's aromatic leaves and planted the pips. None of my parents' gardening books dealt with citrus fruits, but I picked up an excellent tip about creating a humid growing environment by sealing the pots in plastic bags. The pips' germination was a miracle, and they grew into little plants with leaves that were bright and fragrant, like the leaves that I had saved from the fruit and now were curled and dried in a drawer. If you pressed one gently it released a citrus-floral freshness, something that you drank and inhaled. The clementines flourished for many months, and then they died off one by one.

Someone gave us a melon: I sowed some of its seeds too and, inspired by something I had read about growing cucumbers, improvised a protective cold frame from bricks and a clear plastic sack: my parents offered me space in the greenhouse, but I wanted to go it alone. By the time the seedlings succumbed to mildew I had moved on to cacti, an obsession that appeared, full-fledged, from nowhere. I borrowed, bought with pocket money, requested for Christmas and studied every book about cacti on which I could lay my hands. I demanded to be driven to garden centres, which suited my mother because she could look at perennials and shrubs in peace while I was occupied in a greenhouse. My bedroom became cluttered with abstract spiny forms. One day I came home from school to find a pink flower, rigid yet satin to the touch, its colour intense and saturated as though it bloomed in Kodachrome, the like of which I'd only ever seen in books. It was unbelievable.

I do not recall what happened to the cacti, but I remember the texture of the compost in which I grew them: it was very fine – John Innes, probably – with added grit. It's funny how your fingers develop a memory for soil. How a place can make a gardener of you without your knowledge.

Decades later, on the night of my father's death, my mother too long gone, everything grew unfamiliar. My brother and I left the hospice late, and returned to our parents' empty house. When I woke up the following day, as recollection rose in waves and I began to swim, there was something odd about the light: it had a kind of viscosity. Distant traffic, a tapestry of birdsong, a car door slamming, the idle conversation of sheep, morning sounds were drifting in through the open window, but a special silence pounded in my head. The mindless business of starting a day atomised into actions of which I was acutely conscious, careful, as though undertaking them for the very first time. Picking up a dropped sock, running a tap with a ceramic handle, unlocking the back door. And it was the first time, for I had woken up in a new reality.

The garden too had dispersed into details that the thickened light intensified. A yellow rose was buttery, and a bee that worked it hummed in bursts of three. Another shrub rose was dotted with red. There was an empty bird bath, and the seed heads of an aquilegia were dry and buff and shaped like vases; some contained glossy black seeds. The garden had been so much more than the sum of its parts, and today those parts did not begin to add up. The garden was dispersing, receding, and I did not know how to keep hold of it.

In those first new days I picked flowers one by one. A rose-coloured anisodontea: I noticed as if through a magnifying glass the emerald star at the centre of each small flower. A bright-purple viola, and a cream one tinged with lavender. A yellow rose. A pink argyranthemum, its petals defined so cleanly that they might have been cut from plastic. Rosemary for remembrance, as if you would forget. Small bunches of flowers for ashes and flowers to hold on to.

The petals of an argyranthemum are not petals at all, but individual flowers: flowers within a flower.

Outside the garden, too, everything had changed – and once

or twice, when I was out and about, I found myself thinking it
odd that no one else appeared to notice. A special distance had
opened up between me and the world: I experienced things in
lurid, objective detail. One strange evening before the funeral,
Shaun and I drove to a place of which my father had recently
spoken. We followed the river's meander in great loops to the sea
and we were walking through sky, for pinkish cumulus and light
blues and yellows were suspended in marsh water, and printed
into wet sand unrolled by the receding tide. Sea and sky merged
where the horizon ought to be, and above us an abandoned
house balanced on the cliff's eroded edge: when I tipped my
head back to look up at it I became dizzy and felt, momentarily,
that the house might fall on us. The chunks of chalk at the base
of the cliff were oily to the touch, surprising my fingertips. We
watched the sun go down in strata of haze and cloud and turned
back along the valley towards the car. A wading bird materialised
in a marsh pool, colourless in the incremental dusk, and yarrow
flowers, off-white by day, were luminous along the edges of the
path.

Then the sun came back. It slid out of the grey in which it
had appeared to set and grew bigger, redder, duller, eating up
the dusk. It glided in geometric formations with a band of cloud
and showed itself in sectors, arcs and one perfect semicircle,
and then it gathered itself into the atmosphere. For moments
a bleached globe hung in the haze, like the sun ghosts that you
see if you close your eyes tight after staring at the real thing, and
the time when it was still visible overlapped with the time when
it was no longer there. As darkness spread out from the horizon
a single pile of cumulus was backlit from somewhere else, for
the sun never really sets and it all depends on where you are. A

chalk-pale horse might have been carved from the hill on which it grazed.

Back at the empty house, it was dark. Out in the garden some clustered euonymus bushes were strangely visible, their shiny leaves picking up light from a source I could not identify. I had never seen them in the dark before.

I found myself, as though dreaming, in a vivid distortion of the world, a place that no one else could know though our surroundings were the same. I'd been somewhere similar once before. I knew that I would have to find my way back, and incorporate that special way of being into my everyday life. And I knew that it would be OK, in the end, because of Shaun.

After my father's funeral I went into the garden that now grew for no one in particular, my parents both gone. Some geraniums had shed their petals: they needed deadheading, an odd term for the removal of flower heads when they are arguably most potent with life. When flowers are to all intents and purposes dead, seeds develop in their spent heads and the plant's reproductive cycle is complete. As the fruits or seed heads mature, hormonal changes restrict the production of further flowers. But if you remove these 'dead heads' before they can ripen, arrest the plant's attempts to set seed and reproduce, it will reward your deceit with new flushes of flowers, maybe for weeks to come.

I fetched the clippers that my father had kept on the window sill. They were tiny, like topiary shears made for a large doll: they snipped crisply and sprang back between finger and thumb, and the rhythmic work absorbed me instantly. The geraniums that my parents grew were not what many people call geraniums, the red- and pink-flowered staples of window boxes and paintings by

Matisse: those are pelargoniums, a genus that originates in South Africa and cannot cope with the idea of frost. The geranium or cranesbill is a hardy genus that includes British natives, and its flowers are as open and simple as those of the pelargonium are involved. Once, as I drove across Yorkshire with my father and Shaun on a cheerful holiday afternoon, meadow cranesbills rippled through the broad verges. The wind and light silvered their bluebell-blue petals, and I marvelled to see running wild and in masses something that I knew only as a garden plant.

A few years earlier, some time after my mother's death, my father had come across a shopping list of geraniums that she had scribbled on the back of a mailshot. My mother never made that trip to the specialist nursery on Starvecrow Lane, for the mailshot was dated less than a month before she fell catastrophically ill. The nursery had closed down by the time the list came to light; I still have no idea how the lane came by its intriguing name. We trawled garden centres and nurseries, and bagged *Geranium himalayense* 'Irish Blue' near Cambridge and *Geranium* 'Spinners', or maybe it was 'Brookside', west of Tunbridge Wells before our search stalled. Today I can Google all six instantly, but then we had only the phone and serendipity. I rang businesses that no longer existed and people who recommended other people, and then a lady in Littlehampton said yes, no problem, she could supply all of the remaining plants and would drop them off next time she was driving east. It sounded too good to be true. Three of the delivered plants were exactly what my mother wanted, but the fourth was a pink-flowered variety called *Geranium sanguineum* var. *striatum*. My mother wanted *Geranium pratense* 'Striatum', the off-white flowers of which splashed and striated with indigo. Nurseries tended not to stock this cultivar, I eventually learned, because it was unpredictable. Its flamboyant markings were caused by an unstable gene that could produce an opposite result, bleached-out disappointment, and you could not tell which it was going to be until the thing bloomed. *Pratense* 'Striatum' is a maverick in a botanical world of symmetries, for no two plants, nor flowers, nor even petals are alike. A plant with individual petal prints: what a thought. No wonder my mother wanted one.

After lunch one hot July day I drove my father to a field near Maidstone, where a lady lived in a caravan. A retired nurseryman had put me in touch with her. The field was neither a nursery, nor yet a garden, but a place filled with geraniums of which some were for sale and some were not, and each was dignified with a personal pronoun, a 'she' or a 'he'. A single *pratense* 'Striatum' waved particoloured in the scorching wind. We talked about this and that, and about my mother's list, and my father and I collected together some impulse purchases. Quite suddenly the forceful, golden-hearted lady dug up the Striatum and gave 'him' to my father, refusing payment because the plant was not for sale. We drove back to my father's house through blistering road systems and green chestnut tunnels. We sat in the garden late that evening, drinking wine. My mother's list was fulfilled, the bats were hurrying over our heads as they orbited the house, and we wondered what kind of planting scheme my mother had had in mind.

Hardy geraniums are called cranesbills because, like pelargoniums, their carpels or seed heads taper to points that are said to resemble the bill of a fishing bird: *geranos* is the Greek word for crane, *pelargos* for stork. But as I clipped away at the geraniums in the now-bereft garden I paused to look closely at a ripening seed head and saw that it did not form a point after all, or not yet, but opened out at the tip, the style, to a minute star.

And so, with the deadheading of a geranium called Irish Blue, a leave-taking began that connected me with the garden as the house ceased to be a home. In the following weeks and months, whenever I returned to check on the property, I clipped off some spent flower heads or dragged bindweed from its stranglehold on a clump of penstemons. I tied in a briar of the blush climbing rose that sagged with its own floriferous weight.

The thing about plants, those planted purposely and those considered weeds, is that they grow and perpetuate themselves regardless of what is going on in human lives. What Dylan Thomas calls the 'force that through the green fuse drives the flower' is vital and impersonal, explicable by science yet profoundly mysterious. It involves you in itself, draws you into the shaping of and caring for something that is more than field or wood: it makes a gardener of you. Like Adam and Eve, you must '[l]op . . ., or prune, or prop, or bind' the plants and flowers; you must 'direct/The clasping ivy where to climb'. And once you have your hands in the soil, there is no going back.

Even if the garden echoes with absence you will be impelled to cut back a seedy viola in order that it might bloom once more before winter, or tug out some goosegrass that is stifling the dynamic forms of euphorbias, or lop unproductive water shoots from a young apple tree of which you will never now taste the fruit. The doing and the plants absorbed me in spite of myself, in their own here and now. Rummaging amongst foliage, grubbing in soil, I found myself back in the garden, on the garden's terms.

I imagined the plants growing there long after the garden

had forgotten us, bulking up and pushing their roots deeper with the years – the spindle tree in the far corner with its delicate flowers and flamboyant berries; the purple geranium that had been there for as long as the house and whose name everyone forgot.

Every time I left the empty house a piece of the garden went with me. I would take cuttings as soon as the season permitted; in the meantime I cut flowers – that pink argyranthemum, those roses. Back in London, at the kitchen table, I studied their forms and parts. I photographed the roses massed as someone else might have painted them, and then I switched to a macro lens and captured them in close-up fragments. When I look at these photographs now I see the wavy edge of an outer rose petal just past full bloom, or four stamens like horseshoe nails coated with pollen, one of them in focus. We take photographs when we want to preserve something ephemeral, a flower or a scene or a moment, or a person in a moment. I had many reasons for framing and zooming in on and out from those flowers with lenses that my father had passed on to me – but I wonder now what I saw then, or was trying to see.

Two weeks or so before my father died, he and Shaun took their last outing together. Shaun pushed my father in a wheel-chair out through the hospice grounds, the sea ahead, the sea light and the seagulls, down to the rose garden. They made their way slowly around the garden, stopping now and then to study or smell a rose, and then they sat in the quiet companionable-ness of people who have been great friends for many years.

One day, when I went back, the house soon to be marketed, the Japanese anemones were out. The light was brighter and deeper and the air had the newness of a morning after dew. Something had shifted, expecting autumn. I love this phase between summer stasis and high autumn, a darkening at the edges of the days. A bead of moisture sits for longer on an alchemilla leaf, poised and perfect as though encapsulating everything before the day evaporates it. The flowers that appear when summer has burned out are robust and transient by turns: brick-toned sedums deepening to winter; colchicums raising frail pink wine-glass forms for little more than a day. Michaelmas daisies on the way. It's a time when, one terrible year, though we knew what was shortly to happen, my mother was still with us. I remember how she came out into the garden when we thought she was asleep, and sat with us in shade near the violas that she loved, and how I willed that moment to last.

My parents planted the anemones (*Anemone* x *hybrida*) when the house was completed in 1960 and the garden was still substantially field: someone in the village, a Mr Burton I think, knowing they were starting out and short of cash, gave them some bits of perennials from his garden. The anemones were a single-flowered kind, surpassed these days by double and bolder-coloured hybrids. I think of their unfussy shape as the quintessence of flower, by which I mean that if you were to say to a seven-year-old 'draw me a flower', you may well get something resembling a Japanese anemone. They are statuesque plants, strapping when happy but unsettled by change: they put down roots slowly, warily. By the time that I was old enough to draw its flowers, the anemone was well and truly at home. Its soft jagged foliage mounded up quietly before nut-like buds appeared on tall, wiry stems. They filled out and coloured up and then, when no one was looking, they opened: one day there were full-bodied buds, the next there were flower-shaped flowers, their faces turned to the sun. Their petals were chalky pink, at the blue end of pink's tonal range, and their greenish centres were haloed with gold.

The anemones were blooming when I sat with my mother at the old garden table one September afternoon; the silvered wood of the table top looked smooth, but I knew that it splintered viciously. The deep sun and high hedges made parallelograms that inched eastwards across the lawn, and my mother was showing me how to take cuttings. She propagated plants in this way every year, maintaining her precious stock through the vagaries of weather and disease, and it was an art – a science, too – that I needed to learn. She stripped the stems of their lower leaves and sliced them to a clean slant with my great-grandfather's cut-throat razor. Then she pinched out the growing tips, firmed the cuttings into pots of moistened compost and grit, and labelled them as she always did. On this occasion, unusually, she added the date. The fourth of September. Her last cuttings.

We talked about how I hoped, one day, when I had a garden of my own, to grow gentians for the utterness of their blue.

Earlier that summer, before everything changed, I had a long phone conversation with my mother. I was sitting at the table in the ramshackle flat that I rented near Cambridge, university finals were coming up, and from my window I could see the anisodontea: my mother had grown the shrub from a cutting, and planted it for me in a grooved earthenware pot that was lovely to touch. My mother was telling me in unusual detail about another shrub she was trying to source, and as she spoke something clicked. I was enthralled, just as I had once been captivated by a passion flower, the leaves of a clementine, yet in a new way. Later that week I spent more money than I could afford on a landmark encyclopaedia of plants and flowers published by the Royal Horticultural Society. My mother had a copy that lived on her kitchen table except at mealtimes. Its thousands and thousands of entries drew me into a new world – or a new dimension of the world in which I had grown up. I pored over the photographs and descriptions and cultivation notes. Today the encyclopaedia is shelved with my many gardening books, but in my mind's eye its dust jacket – dark green, vivid with plants – belongs with *King Lear* (blue), an olive-green collection of plays by Yeats that left me cold with one exception, and a cream-coloured paperback titled, in dramatic brown font, *Must We Mean What We Say?*, which was a very good question. I was revising for an exam on Tragedy.

Once you start looking for plants, you don't stop. That summer, when my mother was ill, I hunted for green things on her never-ending lists. I read up on them, and time disappeared whenever I stopped at a nursery: I was absorbed and very happy amongst the pot-crammed benches. I could not find a thalictrum in time, but I substituted a perovskia that caught my eye and my mother approved heartily of its violet flowers and branching whitewashed stems.

One afternoon in October, in Sussex, my mother suddenly got out of bed. We stood together at the window and looked out at the hydrangeas. Their fading mauves were still veined with pure blue, and my mother said they were the most beautiful flowers that she had ever seen. That evening she fell into a coma from which she never woke.

It is uncanny that my mother's passion for shrubs and perennials was ignited in me just weeks before we learned that she was dying. My mother had passed something on to me; I had picked something up from my mother. The timing was providential – or maybe I had just grown up. After her death, my father and I began our own conversation about gardens – one that continued for thirteen years. We learned together, shared plants and information and egged each other on. We set off for nurseries in a spirit of complicity, often on flimsy pretexts. We talked endlessly on the phone about our gardens, our lives.

The house became emptier still when the sale board went up. It was inevitable. Things that made my parents' home their home were dispersed: pottery; hag stones collected over many years from Winchelsea Beach. A driftwood root – sea art – on the dining-room wall. A ragged tennis ball that had once belonged to a dog called Alice. They meant much to me, less to others; that happens when you are gone. I have my own treasures that someone will throw out one day. Here, within reach of my keyboard, a spherical pebble, scored with rings, found on a Cornish beach, and a soft ovoid one that fitted to my hand at the Atlantic's opposite edge. A piece of driftwood shaped by waves into the shape of a wave. Those hag stones. A damasked sea-urchin shell, the colour of porcelain and far more fragile, that Shaun brought back from a seabed. Stones and flotsam, precious things.

Each time I returned the house seemed more impersonal, as though it were adapting to my father's absence; I suppose it had no choice. It was getting harder to walk through the front door, and it wasn't that I half expected or hoped to meet my father in the kitchen, or find him potting up cuttings in the greenhouse – it was that I did not. I was becoming a stranger, unsure how to behave, though I always pulled some weeds, filled the bird bath, deadheaded, did the things that gardeners do.

Sometimes alone, sometimes with Shaun, I walked the lanes that twisted and plunged through the fields and woods and had brought my parents to their garden. Steeply down amongst high banks and overarching trees, around the cambered bend where cars could spin out of control and glow worms used to brighten at dusk. On between hedgerows of hazel and blackthorn, ragged from mechanical cutting and strung with honeysuckle, past a clump of spindle trees that I had not noticed before, past the farm, now derelict, where a Border Collie once bit my sister and brother and me in turn: our GP opened his surgery on a Saturday afternoon to patch us up and give us tetanus jabs. There was the drainage ditch where I collected pebbles when I was very small, a memory so early that it may have been sharpened by family narrative. On past the place where white violets still grew and where my grandmother once lifted out a slow worm, stiff as a flexible curve, to show me its blinking eyes. Through the churchyard that I avoided when I was young because people we knew were buried there and you didn't talk about death. Past the station, up the hill through the trees where I used to scare myself by torchlight. The garden was still there when I got back, but these days the lanes did not quite bring me home.

Late April, the afternoon rush hour somewhere west of Brighton. Double lanes of traffic starting and stopping amongst concrete that glared in the sea-bright light. Normally I'd be getting impatient; a few years earlier I would have reached for a cigarette. But today I wanted the snarl-up to last because it saved me from making a decision. I wanted my movements to be dictated by someone or something else.

I was on a work assignment in Sussex, and it made sense for me to spend the night at my parents' house as I had done from time to time in recent months. But as I headed east and the traffic slowed, I discovered that I did not want to go there. It had nothing to do with being alone in the emptying house, for I was used to that. Something had changed since my last visit: I no longer belonged under that roof. I'd go back, of course, because there were things to sort out – but quite suddenly I did not want to spend the night there. I thought I might go home to London and Shaun and drive back the following day, an extra round trip of several hours.

I rode the clutch, stayed in lane, gave myself up to the flow of traffic as it picked up speed, and then, somehow, I had passed the junction for the M23 and London. I was going to the house, to the garden, after all.

I skirted Brighton. The park, the gatehouse in which my maternal grandmother or great-grandmother was born, the white-railed racecourse up on the hill. Down out of sight on the other side was a sink estate, once the slum where my father survived a brutal childhood. He would climb up onto the Downs, as high and as far away as possible, the land and sea pushing away, and lie in the grass and watch the larks ascend, listen for as long as he could to their liquid song that knew no bounds.

The Downs gave way to the Weald. The straight, broad road – nudging the accelerator, an old reflex – then hedgerows airy with hawthorn blossom, woods in young leaf. I noticed these things in passing, stopped at a Co-op to buy a flabby quiche, stopped again for a coffee because a café was still open and I was playing for time. My head throbbed and my eyes hurt.

A sinking feeling as I pulled onto the drive, in through the gateway. I wonder what I was dreading. The house was just as I had left it. I lit a candle and set it on the mantelpiece. Out through the back door.

The garden was in shadow, but a slant of sun skimmed the top of a tall conifer in the far corner. A male chaffinch swayed, illuminated, on the bending tip. His head was thrown back and his rust-pink throat rippled with song, riffs that unwound extravagantly and were answered less melodically from somewhere in the field beyond. I sat down on the old pew beneath the kitchen window, and my eye was drawn to the group of euonymus bushes that my father had shaped into rounded forms – almost organic, not quite geometric – and on to a glossy evergreen pieris beyond. Its reddish new leaf growth spread out and up, the scarlet tips rhyming with a late camellia that flowered in the background. Further down and a little to the left, an arch coaxed from a magnolia was soft with spring leaves; it led to a side garden where a young apple tree was in blossom. And I realised how my parents – together at first and then my father alone – had looked and planned and planted, and planted more, and kept looking, decade after decade, to shape this place that captured your eye and led you from one depth to the next. Their evolving genius, their labour of love.

That evening the garden was enchanted. Everything was poised, the forms vigorous with spring, the synchronicity of things as fleeting as a leaf shoot and a perfect camellia bloom and a chaffinch singing in a single fragment of sun. It was as though the garden had come together in benediction. A moment that I almost missed, and afterwards I caught myself wondering whether it would have happened at all had I not been there, had I taken that turning for London. Later the sky was deep turquoise, radiant at one edge. A crescent moon hung low and sharp, Venus brightened and wavered in the atmosphere. A bat circumnavigated the house and squeaked.

Why are people scared of bats? All those years ago, a child at the window in my nightdress, I thought them marvellous. They were elusive: they appeared out of nowhere, flew hell for leather across the garden or around the house, and disappeared into thin air. They navigated the dark by the echo of their own call. Birds seemed workaday by comparison because they were feathered: they looked as though they were designed for flying. Bats had wings that grew from their hands, just as you yourself might if you dreamed that you were flying. My mother had that dream so often that she looked forward to going to sleep. She could never explain precisely how she became airborne, but she said it was exhilarating, soaring over the fields and woods towards the distant sea.

I slept soundly that night. In the morning everything was in its place. The boiler firing like some clapped-out rocket, the muted click-click of the kitchen door, the way a wooden chair supported the wrong part of my back. The magnolia's big leaves were luminous with early sun and the moyesii, its thorns glowing red, was draped with damp gossamer. A beaded cobweb strung amongst the rose's stems was anchored at five points, as if a spider had been trying to spin a star.

The garden had brought itself into focus for the first time since my father's death, and did so when I least expected it. It would not last: a half-turn and everything would separate and reconfigure like fragments in a kaleidoscope. The red pieris shoots would turn rosy then green. The magnolia and the euonymus would grow out of shape, and someone else would have to clip them.

I took cuttings at every opportunity. Later, as perennials began to go to ground for the colder months, I dug them up and pulled them apart into individual plants, or sliced off rooted pieces with an old carving knife. I replanted some and wrapped the rest in damp newspaper. They had roots in this garden and I wanted them to put down roots in our London garden too. They had my stories.

A penstemon that my father had grown triumphantly from seed: its leaves were between maroon and green, its flowers ghostly bells. You could slice up a clump and grow a plant from every last bit. An acid-flowered euphorbia, and a rusty one that collected the sun and ignited in shades of saffron and chartreuse as the clocks went back. A Japanese anemone, transplanted from the place where it had grown for half a century. I hoped that it would find its feet.

There was the aquilegia or columbine, a plant that I knew to be native but had only seen in gardens. The shape of its flowers was unlike anything else, their colour a deep kind of indigo-violet. I loved hearing my mother say its name, which she did with relish, long before I could put a flower to it. Aquilegia. My father had given me an envelope of seeds that he collected and labelled before he fell ill, but I picked up a miniature clod on which two aquilegias had germinated, tiny plants with roots that had not yet found their element and clung still to the surface. I set the morsel of clay in the smallest pot that I could find, and covered the roots with finely sieved compost.

There was the hellebore that blooms between winter and

spring, its green-tinged flower heads turned to the ground: if you lifted one you would find an exquisite interior, paper-green and patterned with burgundy like the skin of a fantastic snake. Every year, on my father's birthday, I floated those heads face-up on water in a bowl thrown by a potter in the heart of Bodmin Moor. I took a whole plant back to London now, for you should not divide hellebores in autumn.

I love green in flowers; I love green. *Alchemilla mollis* or lady's mantle, a common and magical plant. Its soft scalloped leaves have a special texture that holds and rolls moisture in perfect drops, turns rain and dew by optical alchemy to beads like mercury. And spilling amongst those transmutative leaves its tiny yellowish flowers fizz with green. Alchemilla flourished in my garden already – but I sliced out a small root from under the moyesii, and although it would soon merge with my own established plants I'd know that it was there.

The house was under offer.

Autumn was more brilliant that year. Everything was richer and deeper than I could recall. I might have been imagining it, of course, for there had been times since my father's death when I saw and felt things with strange intensity. Chestnuts, hornbeams and field maples were clichés of gold and butteriness, the beeches one of copper, and their trunks and branches were charcoal strokes amongst the gold and copper and butter in sun.

One day, when I drove through the lanes to my parents' house, the spindles were exotic and loud, very 1960s. Their deep-pink berries displayed orange seeds, a chromatic juxtaposition found in dolly mixtures, and their russet foliage flamed against the falling afternoon sun. It was almost too much for the eye to bear. The verges were sodden green and buff, collapsed by frost, and nightshade berries shone temptingly. In the garden the leaves of the magnolia were shading to primrose, the colour of spring.

Most of those leaves had fallen when I returned in late November. The house was sold, there would be more clearing and looking for hidden spare keys. In the new year I would close the front door and walk for the last time out through the gateway. The kitchen's silence pressed in my ears and made them ring, and I was glad when the boiler resumed its ancient rumble.

Outside, the morning steamed with frost drawn up by early sun. The garden was almost monochrome – pale-sun and dark tones. It was bare boned and lovely, ready for winter. It was gathered into itself. That, I now see, is when I took my leave of the garden. Leave-taking is about connectedness: if you have no bond with a place or a person, you can close a door and walk away. Connections are indefinite forces. And I knew then, without articulating it as such, that I would take the garden with me wherever I went because it had shaped me, made a gardener of me. It was more than a place in Sussex. It was soil and light and plants, a way of being at home. Native soil in every sense.

The leafless arching magnolia framed a space of light and mist that, in the one photograph I took, was overexposed. That happens when there is too much light for the aperture of your lens.

Uprooted

London, mid-February, evening closing in, but there was brightness at the rooftops to the west and the garden showed itself in dim forms. This happens every year, the sudden revelation that the days have lengthened. It catches me unawares, an altered light that promises spring yet unsettles me in a way that I cannot define.

I was sitting at the kitchen table, in my place, drinking tea. I took this to be my place because it faced a window onto the garden. My mother always had the garden view too, the middle of the dining table aligned with the middle of the window – and she sat there with folded hands as someone else might in prayer, looking, assessing, reflecting. At mealtimes she moved along and I sat next to her, my own view obscured by my brother and the japonica, an ill-favoured shrub that became a thing of wonder when it bloomed in spring. Its lurking thorns scored the thin skin of the back of your hand when you reached in to cut a flowering twig, but that twig became something else when set in a tapering vase. The rosy blossom had a poise and delicacy that, when I was older, I would recognise in a Japanese watercolour: life and art imitating one another.

Gardeners assume certain things as their right; my mother

did, and so do I. A place from which to look and think, look and not think, is one of those things; digging up lawns without consultation is another. Only now did it occur to me, back in our London kitchen, that I had never asked Shaun if he minded his own view of the cookery books.

Outside, a rose had jolted awake with a flame-tinged bloom that was beautiful and wrong in the leftover winter. The squirrel arrived as I knew it would, barrelling in short bursts along the top of the fence, pausing as it went to look and listen and feel and smell for danger – the furtiveness, to my human mind, of a criminal bent on picking a lock. Up the trunk of the lilac tree and along the branch from which the nut feeder hung. It reached down, its fat pale belly sagging to one side, and its hand-like paws worked quickly and dextrously at the catch that I had wired shut following a spate of raids: three or four twists, though two would have sufficed.

I was edging my way around a new fact, feeling for a hold on its unyielding surface. We were going to move abroad. I had known this for a while, but the knowledge that something is going to happen does not prepare you – even when, the evening before, at a half-cleared dinner table, you have watched your husband sign a job contract – for the point at which that thing becomes fact. When Shaun texted to say that he had posted the contract, everything started pulsing at a four-time gallop. I had put the kettle on because it was the only thing to do.

The squirrel began to shake the feeder with both paws, un-fazed by its abrupt illumination when it tripped the security light. I noticed in the halogen glare that, for a so-called grey squirrel, its fur was very brown.

It was just an idea. A job's come up in Switzerland. What

do you think? Why not? (It was just an idea.) No harm in applying. It won't come to anything. You can always pull out if it does. Flights, interviews, more interviews, what if they offer me the job? Let's just see what happens. (It was just an idea.) I've barely started my new career; it's as good a time as any. A great opportunity. A life experience. We have French and German between us. No children to uproot. Nobody left who needs us here. We're the team: so long as the team is the team it can make itself at home anywhere. Like a Tudor court. If you say so. Of course we'll integrate if we make the effort. You just have to be open. People are people. I'll find a garden. Yes, you'll find a garden.

Until Shaun went to the post office that afternoon, I had thought of Switzerland as a rather abstract place: it was quadrilingual, at the heart of Europe yet outside the European Union, and a long way from the sea. That we might leave the home and life we had made together for a country about which I knew so little was still just an idea. There were no difficult conversations, no weighing up of pros and cons, because I had no way of imagining that idea into a plausible picture of my life. They've offered me the job. OK. Why not?

I was leaving home, again. Too many ways of leaving home, so many kinds of home to leave. Our home on the edge of London where the trains emerged from underground with their instant crescendo and hurtling of red and grey. The soil that I had got to know unawares, its textures read by my hands when my mind was on other things. The mineral smell and taste of earth that rained in my face as I wrenched loose the roots of a dead conifer; the soggy smack when, digging deep, my spade hit clay; the infernal sulphur stink of a seam gone bad and black, starved of oxygen. My plants. My parents' plants, so recently transplanted. My country. Our language. The people in our life. And a thousand ways of being at home that would not be known until they were missed.

The garden's shapes had expanded into darkness. The sky was bright and dark like labradorite. The squirrel had given up and moved on, foraging its way into the evening. It struck me, running my hands over the table's smooth solidity, its tight joints, that this would not be my place for much longer. I would still have my side of the table, where the beech grain was more pronounced, but the table would be elsewhere. Maybe it had ceased to be my place already, with my new knowledge. I didn't know what to think: we had not yet left and there was no going back.

The garden. What about the garden?

May was upon us, the medlar in bloom, fruit already taking shape in the spent blossoms of the quince. The air washed and early, cold shade and pale light, a gardening day in the making. There was something odd about the yellow German removal lorry that inched along our road, and as it came to a halt outside our house it occurred to me that the vehicle was driverless. Then the doors of the outsized cab opened and two boyish men emerged, one very witty, the other gentle and disconcertingly pierced. A small car delivered a second team, and the men took charge. That was a relief: an interval of suspended responsibility, like the sudden whooshing peace that you feel when your plane reaches altitude and for now you can do nothing about things that have run you ragged on the ground. We stayed in the garden, out of the way, while our home was packed up.

Alchemilla leaves piling up, soft plant geometry. Aquilegias: their purple-blue flowers had the texture of butterfly wings and reflected the morning like metal. The euphorbias flowering at full blast. The bronze shoots of Japanese anemones. And all over the garden were gaps of which no one but I was aware. I'd uprooted some of my parents' plants again – a brutal and ungardenerly thing to do – and distributed them amongst friends, gifts freighted with responsibility. I wanted bits of the Sussex garden to grow in the gardens of those close to me, but I also wanted to preserve my parents' stock: there was no question of finding a home with a garden to rent in Zurich, and who knew when I would have a garden of my own again. Our friends were accepting in more senses than one, but I spared Fran, the recipient of my father's hellebore, the knowledge that it was my only specimen.

Indoors, the emptied house had rediscovered its own acoustics. It echoed brightly and impersonally as it had on another afternoon – early spring, later in the day – when we moved in and believed that we would live there forever. The removal men had not yet arrived with our things, and from an upstairs window we watched a green woodpecker working the lawn: there was something theatrical about its scarlet cap, the yellowish eyes in its bandit-black face as it hopped back and forth through a shaft of sun, pecking for ants. Now, just four years later, our house was becoming unfamiliar again, and I wished it might have allowed us to leave first. What I thought and felt then is a mere bright echo; what lay ahead was so unknown as to seem inconsequential.

But I certainly could not imagine, at that in-between time, that we would not one day come home again. Shaun, I learned later, thought we would not – but then he had already left his own country, Canada, eighteen years before, on a one-year scholarship that grew into a life. Circumstances played a role, of course, but Shaun tends to seize so-called life experiences as though they are to be lived and not merely experienced, and that is a lovely way of being in the world. I am not quite so brave by nature, nor quite so optimistic.

In the evening we walked along our road, past the wood that cooled the air, a fragment of Epping Forest adrift in suburbia. The Central line rushing on the other side. Up the High Street to the curry house, the Bengal, where an enormous china leopard sat on the bar. Its front feet were splayed as though it had skidded on its bottom to a jarring halt, and its face was pulled back in an un-feline rictus. Shaun wondered aloud, as he always did, about the thing's provenance. Our usual order: chicken dopiaza, chicken pathia, saag paneer, brinjal bhaji, a Peshwari naan, that unwholesome greasy salt-sweet taste for which I would come to long. A last pint of Kingfisher. I asked the waiter how they removed the turmeric stains from their table linen. No idea: they used a laundry service. It was now or never for Shaun. What was that leopard doing on the bar? It was so . . . striking. We wanted to get a Bengal tiger, the waiter explained: a Bengal restaurant needs a Bengal tiger. But the leopard was so much cheaper.

The air was green and stirring as we walked home – still, just – past the wood. I knew that a group of service trees, an ancient species, kept its own counsel a stone's throw from the busy road. And in the wood beyond our garden were beds of gravel carried, it is said, from the Weald by a north-flowing prehistoric river. I loved the thought that a river had somehow brought me here. That, tens or hundreds of thousands of years deep below the suburbs and the city and the Thames and the rising strata of human pasts, a trail of gravel led like petrified breadcrumbs from the topography of my childhood to my home in London suburbia.

The last I saw of it, the garden was darkening and barely there.

The furniture and all the things of our life were in the yellow lorry somewhere, we presumed, in France. We inflated an air mattress in the hollow bedroom and lay down not so much to sleep as to wait. Into the smallest hours of the following day, too many thoughts and none at all. I slept once, deeply, for a split second or many minutes, and then it was three o'clock, the alarm ringing, and the get-up-and-go that overrides your body clock when you're heading off on holiday. We deflated the mattress, stowed it into our old blue Peugeot, and drove away.

I didn't look back at the house in the rear-view mirror. In my imagination I look back because I am sure this is what I would do – but in my memory I do not. I have never asked Shaun whether he turned for one last look.

The Dartford toll bridge was deserted when we crossed the Thames. The darkness thinning, the river oily black. Dim lights through estuary mist. The bridge's emptiness was too odd, too lonely, as if something had happened to the world. I might have continued south to Sussex, a route mapped into my being, but on this strange new day we angled south-east towards a new life.

Dover at first light, the white cliffs dissolved in grey. Nothing marked our departure from England.

A long day driving in unseasonable heat, the air conditioning unrepaired. That special fatigue that displaces you a little from your body. The great expanses of eastern France soaked up time, and I wished we could suspend our adventure there and then, between leaving and arriving. But we continued to cover ground and in early evening found ourselves on the outskirts of Zurich, heading for the centre. Nearly there – and then the cliché-surpassing helplessness of the couple in a car in a foreign city: the multiple lanes, the one-way systems, the trams, the assertiveness of those who know where they are going, the weariness, the bloody trams again, the conundrum of printed directions that you can only follow if you know where you are. The flurries of recrimination, because it is easier to blame one another than to accept that you are both helpless. When we found our street later, and by accident, there was a 'No Entry' sign. We had arrived at the wrong end of a one-way street; I hoped that was not significant.

Up square-spiralling stairs to the third floor and the flat in which we were to make our home. The kitchen was flushed blood-orange by late sun that bounced from the wall of a neighbouring block. The rooms handled our footsteps and voices strangely. We inflated the air mattress in the empty bedroom and went out to get some dinner.

There was a small restaurant at the end of the street, and I followed Shaun in with the happy anticipation of that first meal on a trip abroad. The proprietor was less happy to see us: it was nearly eight o'clock, he supposed he could serve us if we ordered immediately (the Swiss eat early, Shaun had forgotten). Light-headed with exhaustion and the unloosing of our life, a beer downed too thirstily, I mustered my best German and set about engaging with our reluctant host: I was, remember, going to integrate. We were new to the neighbourhood, I rattled as he dumped some bread on the table; we were from England, we'd arrived barely an hour ago, it had been a long day, we'd be living just around the corner, we were very pleased to be here. We were so happy to have found a nice neighbourhood restaurant, I added weakly. The proprietor shrugged and Shaun ordered two more beers. The bread was stale.

Someone's playing table tennis downstairs, I told Shaun before I was properly awake, not that I had been properly asleep. My heart was beating that animal four-time and I tried to sit up, forgetting that we were not in our bed; the air mattress wobbled and tipped me onto a hard wood floor that reeked of solvent. It was unusually dark – there were no faint margins around bedroom curtains – and I sensed, before I remembered, that the room was big and empty. The windows were shuttered tight.

The pure, instant rage of a sound sleeper rudely awoken; an imprecation that I do not need to record. You are the limit, Shaun then said, it's raining. It was raining. Our flat was on the top floor of a fin-de-siècle building with a lead-flashed roof on which raindrops percussed like ping-pong balls: some fell with a downward inflection, others like questions. A church clock weighed in close by with the long, loud strokes of my grand-mother's mantel clock – a gong-like chime that coursed around her tiny living room as though it sought a way out. When I was small, that loud reverberation meant kindness and warmth, the Peek Freans biscuit tin and *Doctor Who* on Saturdays. Later, it seemed to me that the clock was built to strike in bigger rooms, like the ones in which my grandmother had lived before her marriage to a man who got into scrapes. Two o'clock.

The relief. I'd dreaded learning the sounds of our neighbours through walls and floors, as inevitably we would. But if you are

safe and dry indoors, especially under a duvet, the unfolding of a
thunder storm, the slams and vibrations of a gale, the dropping
of heavy rain are deeply, primally absorbing. At the approach
of thunder on those summer nights of my childhood, I would
get up and open the windows, and jump back into bed before
the next flash – I was ambivalent about lightning – and settle
down to listen to the storm's symphonic playing out. I waited
for the rushing downpour that the thunder released, or so it
always seemed to me: the raindrops smacking on the brick drive
or drumming on the roof of the car. I thought I could hear them
falling on the layered canopy of the wood beyond, dropping
heavy through the hornbeams to the damp leaf mould beneath.
Maybe I could. I slept.

It is unthinkable to me that you might move home and not
introduce yourself to your new neighbours – especially if you
are sharing a wall, or have a floor that is someone else's ceiling,
or a ceiling that is someone else's floor. Of course you should
make yourself known to those with whom you'll be living in
unsolicited intimacy a wall's thinness apart. Show your face.
Start, as you hope to go on, with goodwill. Shouldn't you?

The next morning we rang the doorbell to the flat below. I
could not read the expression of the woman who answered, but
it was not welcoming. We spoke to her across an invisible yet
palpable barricade. We were moving in upstairs, we told her our
names, we were pleased to make her acquaintance. She looked
at Shaun's extended right hand and clamped her own to her
side. Three children filled in the gaps between their mother and
the door jambs. Sorry, what were their names? The four of them
stared back impassively. We wanted to apologise for the noise

that our removal men would be making that day. We really were very sorry, they'd be finished by early afternoon, we hoped she would understand. The door slammed shut and we looked at each other. Maybe we'd caught her at a bad time.

Then everything was unloaded, and the cheerful boyish men headed home in the yellow lorry with their wit and gentleness and facial hardware, back to Germany, back (an unexpected pang) to the European Union. They had intervened briefly and intensely in our life, and now there was no one in charge. This was it. We left the boxes unopened and headed out into the dusty-hot streets to get our bearings and buy a vacuum cleaner. When I say dusty-hot I mean that the air seemed thick with heat particles: the pavements themselves were swept clean. We drank coffee at a café under lime trees and it was almost, one of us said, like being on holiday in a European city. But the tables were squeezed onto the corner of a busy junction, and you don't shop for vacuum cleaners when you are on holiday.

The house rules were printed in dense columns on two and a half sides of A4. No showers nor baths were to be taken, nor appliances operated, before six in the morning and after ten in the evening. There was to be silence between midday and one-thirty in the afternoon. No laundering, vacuuming, mowing (a theoretical risk in our gardenless block), nor other signs of work, audible or otherwise, on Sundays. Gentlemen were kindly requested to sit down when using the toilet at night. There were two exceptions: noise was to be tolerated at all times if it was generated by families with children or by sex (*Liebesschreie* or 'cries of love', it was coyly put). The rules were the rules, clear and detailed, yet they did not apply to everyone. They could make you afraid to run a bath at nine-fifty, afraid almost to breathe, yet powerless to complain should you suffer unremitting noise from a flat in which children lived.

We presented ourselves for registration at the civic hall, up and up an austere staircase with a sheaf of papers that accounted for our life. A stifling room, hotter than the hot day against which its windows were shut. Flimsy chairs and hardboard partitions, at odds with the building's grand façade and civic purposefulness, the setting for a scene in which our role was supplicatory and, until pronounced otherwise, vaguely suspect. Practised frowns, a great deal of scrutinising and stamping of papers, sudden extended hiatuses and whispered conferrals into which unease seeped. I'm sure this was a standard bureaucratic performance. But I was also aware that a national referendum had recently been held on the subject of minarets, that the people of Switzerland had voted to ban their further construction, and that this expressed rather more than a collective dislike of tall pointed buildings. It had to do with cultural difference, otherness, and I wondered how deeply that sentiment ran.

As we sat in that hot, severe office it dawned on me that I was not a foreign traveller but a foreigner in the place where I was to live, and that was an uncomfortable thought. Until that moment I had not asked myself whether we would be welcome here.

A lime tree green against a window, its young leaves as soft to the touch, if you could only reach one, as they were to the eye. The heart-shaped leaves of *Tilia platyphyllos* are asymmetrical. So is the human heart, but the lime leaf's lopsidedness is perfect – as though it began with a symmetrical leaf, and a double-sided mirror were placed edge-on along the midrib to magnify one side or scale down the other, just a little, and one half of the original leaf were then fused, with a little bending and stretching, to its bigger or smaller mirror image. Lime leaves are fragile, and the slightest pressure will crush their vascular walls to dark, wet bruises. But if you were to swivel round from your work station and open that window, there would be an infinitesimal breathing of green and you might lean out to touch a weightless leaf – gently – and maybe, then, you would forget to frown.

We received our residence permits. *Ausländerausweis*, the plastic covers proclaimed: foreigner permit. I had no idea whether I was coming or going, but I now had a formal identity. I was an *Ausländerin*: a foreigner, a female foreigner to be precise.

The English words 'foreign' and 'forest' are of the same Latin rootstock: *foras*, which means 'outside'. In the Middle Ages forests were not defined specifically by trees, but by the jurisdiction of Forest Law: they were uncultivated woodland and 'waste', a word that lives outside bounds and stops just short of wilderness.

Foreigner: of the forest.

Shaun started work and I got on with setting up our life. A strange turn of phrase, that, when you think about it, as if you can root yourself out of your home, the life you have been leading, and plant yourself at will in a place with which you have no connection whatsoever, in which it would not occur to you to choose to live. As if, give or take a missing bolt, you can pitch up anywhere and assemble a new home from a flat-pack and some inchoate diagrams. IKEA bookcases are the same the world over; I put seven together during our second week.

There was much to set up besides the bookshelves: the cable connection, our trusty archaic stereo, the administrative apparatus of our life. My flabby German was exercised by paperwork and by phone calls that put me in mind of Piranesi's *Carceri*, for like the corridors and stairs in those nightmarish etchings they went up and down and around, and often ended nowhere. Disembodied words – words that are neither joined up by expression and gesture, nor written in black and white – make special demands of the non-native speaker, and I dreaded picking up the phone. Nor had I anticipated the otherness of Swiss German to a mind trained in standard or High German, the language of Germany and Austria that I studied for A level in Tunbridge Wells. Switzerland is a confederation of twenty-six cantons, each with a high degree of legislative and fiscal autonomy, but the country is also divided along linguistic lines: French in the west, Italian in the south, a smattering of Romansh in the south-east, and German, the linguistic majority, in central and eastern parts. Swiss German, unlike its French and Italian counterparts, is a dialect – a multitude of dialects in fact, each unique to its canton and not always wholly intelligible across cantonal borders. A dialect – from the Greek *dialektos,* 'way of speaking' – is just that, a way of speaking. It is neither written, nor standardised, nor taught, but acquired by the verbal osmosis of family and community. Swiss Germans learn High German as a second language, for that is the language of their written life; Swiss German, on the other hand, is understood by just a fraction of the world's German-speaking population, and spoken by fewer still.

The thing about dialects is that they are exclusive in the fullest sense of the word. They are the preserve of select groups, and they shut others out. Dialects are not just about language per se.

That an anglophone couple like us could become fluent in Zurich dialect was all but impossible. Perhaps because our efforts were sincere, most people showed willing and met us halfway in High German: we could get by. But only getting by in a language has consequences if you do it for too long, for conversations with people will always be at one or two removes. And while this is all well and good if you are getting the car inspected, or pleading with the cable provider on your mobile phone, you might find in due course that you have been conversing proficiently with many people, but you cannot remember when you last communicated with someone other than your husband. Because there's much more to understanding than linguistic comprehension.

I got into trouble. In Switzerland, most plastic is not recyclable: it goes into the garbage, for which you buy special pre-taxed bags. You can, however, take plastic bottles and milk containers to recycling points at supermarkets, as I did on the morning in question. I pushed things through holes that were set into a wall and, to avoid ambiguity, were both labelled and illustrated. It was like an educational game, and it was going well. A hole labelled *Milchflaschen*, a picture of a milk container: in went a milk carton.

Out burst an employee from an adjacent door. He was holding my milk carton and had the air of a traffic warden whose day has been made by an illegally parked car. He had been waiting on the other side of the wall, inspecting the containers as I pushed them through, and had fished the carton out of the bin. I wished I hadn't rinsed it. You cannot put this carton in that hole, he said. But the hole is labelled milk cartons, I protested; that (pointing) is a milk carton. He switched (foreigner!) from dialect to High German. The hole is not labelled *MilchKAR-TONE*, it is labelled *MilchFLASCHEN* (Milk BOTTLES), he replied with a rising inflection. It is the wrong kind of container, he continued, it is made partially of cardboard. It is also, I said boldly, made partially of plastic. I was a woman, a foreigner, and I was talking back! You must put it in the garbage, his voice rose to a new level, *Sie MÜSSEN . . . OK*, I thought, *whatever*. OK, I said, I'm sorry, it won't happen again. I walked away. He followed me: *Sie können NICHT . . .* (you CANNOT), he screamed as men generally don't. *Chill, buddy. Put it in a bin and move on. Sie dürfen NICHT. . .* (you may NOT). I was no longer sorry.

We continued around the corner, past the processed meats, the milk carton held aloft; as we went, I grabbed what I had come shopping for – a carton, as it happened, of milk. Other shoppers, who were mostly from the old people's home, had ground to a standstill and were rapt. The uniformed man was very short and I am fairly tall – a tall foreign woman – and he was telling me what was what. The air was thick with self-righteousness. *Sie MÜSSEN . . .* (you MUST). He chased me to the checkout, pelting me with modal verbs, *Sie MÜSSEN . . . Oh fuck off you ludicrous little man.* The cashier was smirking. *You too*, I thought, as I paid for my milk and wished her a lovely day.

Sitting in my place at our old kitchen table, my view through the window now was of a white wall. When I think of that rented flat, I think of white walls upon white walls, inside and out. On two sides our windows gave on to the rendered white walls of adjacent buildings inside which, I knew, were living spaces side by side and end to end, stacked high. All those people behind those blank walls. In evening and early morning the sun might strike an angle deep into our living room. Otherwise the light was reflected, borrowed – not our own. Up there on the third floor, a mere external wall between us and I don't know what. Air and nothing. The city and everything. No soil in which to ground myself.

I recalled a green place, and went out through the streets to find it again. Back in March, the contract signed, London still home, the garden still ours, we had flown to Zurich to look for a flat. A strange weekend that now and then resembled a city break, and was not. We were walking around a rather bleak quarter not far from where we would come to live, and my insides rose in panic as I tried to place myself there, to picture a life in one of those introverted, traffic-hemmed buildings. At a junction from which every way led uphill, an old house stood amongst the relentless concrete and accelerating cars. It had high gables and a whitewashed façade, wine-red timbers and bottle-green shutters. Once, before the city claimed this land, the house had belonged where it was built. Now it looked out of place – as lost there, on its centuries-old foundations, as a Kansas farmhouse transported by a dreamed tornado.

We followed a footpath up behind the house and came to a short, steep-sided gully where beeches reached high for the far-above light and the pitched ground was green with wild garlic – ramsons, as they are also known. A stream poured clean over chalky silt or silty chalk before a concrete pipe drank it down to the lake. A morsel of woodland in the city's grey agglomeration, there because its gradients defied architectural ingenuity. It might have been an excerpt from the woods of my childhood.

On that airless day in June, when I found my way back through the fumes and noise to the tiny urban valley, the ramsons were over with. Their flowers had been and gone and the plants were withdrawing underground to multiply their clusters of translucent bulbs. The leaves had grown tough and bitter, and what now remained of them was slimy and thick-veined like caul. But their onion smell, the wooded light, took me to yet another place and time.

The riverbank green and unpredictable. A loose tumble of soil and moss – not the cushiony kind, but a micro-forest of soft spiky stems – as I inch down to the water, hanging on to a sapling that is surprisingly strong. It may well be hornbeam, which is horn-hard when mature and tough as old boots when young; the Romans used it to make chariot wheels. The sapling is bent double, but the roots appear to be holding. You never know with riverbanks.

I'm not particularly old, nine at most, but I have an instinctive preference for supple young branches over older and more brittle wood: I have done since the day on which I climbed down to the pool where the river bulged and eddied darkly. No one knew its exact depth, for the bottom was soft with mud and leaf-black, and a long stick would sink through thickening resistance that never quite pushed back. I was forbidden to go near the pool, though I always threw in sticks for my grandmother's dog, an overweight mongrel that waddled on land and swam like a seal.

I don't recall what I was trying to reach or see that afternoon, only the cracking of a branch and the water at my throat – I can feel it now, hard and sharp like a paper edge – and the dragging in my wellingtons and the current pushing against me, tipping me backwards, into the water. I do not recall how I got out, but there were soft bright clumps of sedge that I took at the time to be grass, and stitchwort blooming frail and white. The unheroic dog was nowhere to be seen, off sniffing for something to eat. My squelching feet, the cold. I know that the ramsons were in bloom as I made my way along the riverbank and up through the wood, the wild-garlic smell, until the trees dispersed and there were yellowing daffodil leaves in grass, and a leggy hornbeam hedge, and at last my grandmother's house. A scolding was in order, but everyone was oddly nice about what had happened to me: I must have been more frightened than my memory allows. I cannot bear to feel things at my throat: a roll-neck sweater, those plastic bibs that dental nurses yank around your neck.

I have steered clear of the pool since that day, but I still go down to the river, let myself carefully down its banks to rummage at the edges. The water dark reflecting light. Accumulated twigs. A scalloped leaf, oak, half-dissolved to filigree: when it has dried out I'll put it in my drawer with the clementine leaves and who knows what else. In some places, unless it has rained, the river runs shallow over stones, and you can stand in the middle and feel the current pressing cold against your wellingtons. The water's weight. The floor of the wood green with ramsons, every last inch of it, each plant an upward outward reaching of leaves. They are soft and broad, and they ripple like theatrical silk in the wood's permutations of light. Their onion smell – I can't avoid brushing and crushing them as I make my way up amongst the trees, back into my grandmother's garden. Later there will be flowers, a thousand thousand hemispheres starry white on green.

The leaves were there for the picking, colonising the garden with subterranean verve, cropping up amongst the daffodils.

I'd bite on a leaf from time to time: a grassy sharpness (I have never eaten grass, but its green smell is a kind of taste), and then a pungent allium hit at the back of the throat. Ramsons are supremely edible, but we never ate them at home. Not sautéed in butter, as Shaun and I first cooked them in Cornwall decades later, nor shredded into an omelette, nor a bagful steamed to a small delicious heap. I began to wonder why that had not occurred to anyone in my family, when my mother was a stickler for fresh food and ramsons were rich in flavour and vitamins, organic, free. There is no one left to ask now, but I think I know the answer, and I think it did occur to people that you could eat ramsons. Like many whose childhoods spanned the Second World War, my mother recalled boiled nettles with a felt shudder. Foraging then was not, for many, an elective activity. For people who were not there, the Ministry of Food's wartime poster, 'How to Make Use of the Hedgerow Harvest', is packed with nostalgia – a 'sweetie of a leaflet', as I've seen it described on Pinterest. It was different for my grandmother, who had already lived through one world war. At the outbreak of the Second World War scarcity and rationing and austerity were to come – not to mention the Doodlebugs and dog fights that shadowed the Rother Valley, the garden cratered by a bomb, the machine-gun bullet that pierced a wall and came to rest on a child's bed – and she was already raising two small children in rural poverty. Of course, later, if you could, you would file those things at the back of your mind and buy your vegetables in shops.

In Switzerland the heatwave pressed on. Landlocked. The sun steadily there, the sky hot and blue and closed, a life away from air-brightening sea. Walking around the neighbourhood I could not shake my feeling that everything, even in the sun, was grey. It wasn't just the architecture, the jumble of stark functionality and period grandeur that was white and cream and beige as well as grey. It was a sense that I could not pin down, but which persisted, of closedness, blankness, as if the buildings, or people, or both, kept the world at arm's length. Maybe it was just that my smile would drift unreturned when I caught a stranger's eye. And everyone here was a stranger to me, as I was to them.

Almost everyone. One day, after passing him once or twice, I slowed and spoke to an elderly man who walked carefully along our street several times a day. After that I often fell into step with him and he would tell me, even if we'd spoken the day before, that my German had improved and that he was lonely in his room in the old people's home. I was always glad, too, to cross the paths of the friendly, overworked Austrian couple who lived in our block. Their children were small and feisty: they slid down the polished banister that wound around the stairwell, and they had hearty laughs. I liked them immensely. Often, though, when I encountered other neighbours, my attempts to introduce myself fell flat. Some people nodded tightly at my hello and kept on walking. One pushed past me as if he had not heard me, or I were an obstacle on the stairs, which I suppose I was. Once, going down to collect the post, I said hello, I'm . . . to a man who was collecting his, and he looked at me with distaste and hurried off. There was something wrong with me: I was doing what came naturally, but people reflected me back to myself as odd, unseemly. Like the Ancient Mariner, or the frail lonely soul who waited at the tram stop not for trams but for people: she buttonholed anyone and every-one and conversed with air as people swerved away, or busied themselves with smartphones and wished the tram would come. I did not know how to behave. But I didn't knock on any more doors.

Like many insomniacs, I am not a morning person. But there's an in-between time that is special however much the night has worn you out and wherever you may be. Its hour is imprecise, a while after dawn and before you are located by the day. It is when the world in those childhood memories, as Dylan Thomas knew, is 'like a wanderer white/With the dew, come back', when the wild rose in the hornbeam hedge is strung with fleeting filaments and drenched with revelation. When you go down to feed the animals and the frosted grass is blue as lichen and spangled like nothing else, the air dense with breath and the just-risen sun, and the moment encloses you in sheer possibility, safe from the school day ahead and the organised malice of teenage girls. When, walking to work through cool Cambridge streets, you drop out of the morning that you've barely begun and head to the market, still setting up, to see what is new at the plant stall: a geranium, perhaps, or a blue-flowered salvia. When you let yourself out of a sleeping house and wander the Atlantic's edge, the seagulls – 'sea-mews', Milton called them by ear – awake and yes, mewing, and you drink the gravelly echo of the waves, the scrubbing air and the pinkish light, the thought of a rinsed pebble that will shortly catch your eye.

It is a time of visceral optimism, sometimes in spite of yourself, for returning light is the stuff of life for people as for plants, and a new day looks forward. Sometimes, first thing, I walked with Shaun through Zurich's grey unsmiling streets, the sun striking eastward façades, the cold invigorating my arms and face, the extra moment snatched together from the day. That's when, sitting on our favourite bench and breakfasting on still-warm poppy-seed pastries, we looked at the lake made infinite by haze and smelled its fresh organic drifts, and heard its unhurried lapping stirred to urgency by a far-out boat, and I almost forgot the stench and roar of the city at my back. On days of special clarity the mountains would be there beyond the lake: a cliché, or a revelation.

Then Shaun headed to the office and I crossed the lanes of traffic to the market square. The market oozed cash and belonged to coiffed Swiss women of advancing years. They drank Prosecco for breakfast, propped at the coffee bar like men in a pub, and they spat venom if, when they manoeuvred in front as you waited at a stall for your turn that never came, you said excuse me, I believe I was next. There was no queue-jumping, for there were no queues.

But the market belonged to the plane trees too, their merging crowns fresh with early sun, the dappled light a counterpoint to their jigsaw-dappled bark – their scars incurred, it might be said, on our behalf. The bark of plane trees absorbs pollutants from the air, and then it falls away – in order, perhaps, that the tree might breathe – leaving those intricate mottlings of khaki through cream, that wounded beauty.

I'm not sure that I have seen a plane tree with unblemished bark. There must be one somewhere, in a place of pure air I don't know where, or in the past, in as clean a time and place as there has been since man discovered fire and created smoke. I know there is a plane tree in paradise, the 'platan' (*Platanus*, the plane's botanical name) under which Eve and Adam first set eyes on one another. Eve newly created from the sleeping Adam's rib,

Adam newly woken, his left side wonderfully healed. To 'give thee being', he tells her here:

> *I lent*
> *Out of my side to thee, nearest my heart*
> *Substantial life, to have thee by my side . . .*

An absolute poetic imagining of love.

I appreciated those trees in the market place: their light-filtering, air-filtering, air-stirring green, their dignity, their quiet, scarred, lovely endurance in the noise and the fumes and the pushing and shoving. They absorbed unpleasantness. They were greenness itself.

I sought out plant stalls compulsively, though they made me sad. There would be a shrub or perennial that belonged to the garden in Sussex or something I had grown in London, a thrill of recognition knotting into something else. A mauve hydrangea tinted infinitely blue: those last days, my mother's hand in mine. And who knew when I'd have soil in which to plant that sedum or *Geranium* Rozanne? There was another thing: the plants themselves seemed coiffed, contrived, presented rather than grown. None of the massed sprawl and spillage from the market stall in Cambridge or my father's greenhouse staging, the growing green that makes you want to reach for your trowel. Here they stood in isolated pots, their shoots clipped into order-liness, as though they were not to be trusted as themselves.

I caught my breath before I knew why. Textures like a corner of a Klimt painting, flickering shades of sun-brightened green and dottings of mellow pink that moved to the eye though the day was still. I knew that the greens resolved into small, toothed leaves on woody stems. That the rose colour of each tiny flower deepened around a pale centre and that, if you removed your glasses and looked very closely, you would see that the calyx formed a green five-pointed star in the spaces between the petals. I knew that a bee or two would be occupied amongst the flowers despite the traffic and the cigarette smoke, the market's single-minded crush. The fountainous shrub had been clipped and schooled to the shape of a lollipop, and a plastic butterfly, mounted on wire, injected the pot with lifelessness. Nevertheless it was an anisodontea, the precious plant that my mother had potted up for me before she went to the doctor and our world turned upside down.

Anisodontea capensis. This shrubby member of the mallow family was precious because my mother loved it and because it was temperamental. You could hardly blame it, a South-African native transplanted to northern Europe – yet one plant might brazen out a long harsh winter while another that had known only mild conditions would suddenly drop its leaves and die. My mother took cuttings every September as a safeguard, and of these a few would take root, even fewer survive to maturity.

My anisodontea lived on the coal bunker outside my student flat. The bunker lid was as minimal as a garden could be, but the plant thrived there and I could see it from the table where I worked – where Shaun and I, in due course, worked together. As I was fetching in coal one freezing day, months after my mother's death, I knocked off a leafless woody stem and could not throw it away. Counter-intuitively, for it seemed dead, I stuck the twig in a pot of soil and the pot in a corner of the window sill. It was no place for any plant, blasted by draughts and, when you least expected it, for my landlady felt the cold at unusual times, a radiator jammed on maximum. Outside, the shrub soldiered on through the Fenland winter and died in spring as everything else was coming back to life. Inexplicably, around the same time, the anisodonteas died in Sussex too, mature plants and my mother's last cuttings alike. I cannot quite explain what we felt had been lost. My mother's anisodontea. It was a sentimental matter, of course, but it was more than that, a visceral connection through lignin and cambium, chlorophyll, living substances. We could buy new plants, but that was not the point. It was time to throw out the broken piece – but when I tried to pull it from the soil I met with resistance. The small dead twig had developed roots, and the stem was bumpy with the promise of leaf buds. It was pure happenstance – it had to be – but it felt like an intervention. I gave the pot to my father.

My memory is still curating the details of the September afternoon when my mother took those last cuttings – the forms of the shadows, the crunch of the razor blade through a penstemon stem; the sprig print of my mother's skirt, her instructions about the compost mix – but I was slow to assume the responsibility she was handing over that day. There was too much else to navigate. My mother's death – a silence on which I cannot dwell – and, just two weeks before, Shaun's arrival in my life: we moved in together instantly, in the Fenland flat, because it was right. We were both studying for further degrees, working in pubs to make ends meet. It was my grieving father who tended the young plants through that first bleak winter and who, self-taught, his hands crippled with rheumatic disease, took cuttings every year thereafter on the fourth of September. Most of them he planted out in spring when the last frost had passed – fulfilling my mother's plans, making his own way in their garden. The rest he delivered to us, when Shaun and I at last had a garden of our own, every spring until his own final illness, his car crammed with green. Plants grown from those cuttings that my mother set into life as her own was ending. Felicia, its daisy flowers almost blue. Penstemons. The pink argyranthemum. Anisodontea: a name that slipped from my mother's tongue like poetry, a plant that you could not take for granted. A shared desire to keep something alive. To garden.

In Zurich, towards midsummer, the weather switched from blazing to grey as though something somewhere had blown a fuse. The cold, the sheer absence of light. The Peugeot stood under our window in uninsured limbo until I could arrange a Swiss policy. We had other priorities, I said, we were in the city, there was public transport. I was putting it off. The smallest administrative issue was an ordeal in a system that I didn't understand and a mutual second language in which I was not yet fluent. Every day was a montage of challenges, but one day (surely) our new life would be in place. I don't know exactly what I meant by the latter phrase, except that I felt lonely and out of place.

More than once I leaned out of the bedroom window and looked down on the head of a neighbour as he or she walked around the car and peered inside. We often felt watched, scrutinised as we came and went by people who did not talk to us. The car's interior was a mess, and I left it that way.

No problem, said the man at the insurance company when I made the call at last, you can do the application over the phone. I'll put you through to my colleague, he speaks English. That's all? Are you sure? Even though we've brought the car from Britain? No problem. The helpful man's colleague spoke excellent English. No problem, he said, call me back as soon as you get Swiss licence plates and we'll go through the application. *Oh.* Oh. How do I get Swiss licence plates? You have to contact the *Verkehrsamt*, the vehicle office.

I called the *Verkehrsamt*, and after a brief exchange of misunderstandings was offered an appointment. I took the tram and arrived in good time with my documents. The counter assistant laughed when I said I'd come to register the car. The car had to be tested first of course, she said. No one told me that when I made this appointment. Shrug. No, not at a garage (exasperated sigh), I had to bring the car to be tested at the *Verkehrsamt*. But the car wasn't insured, that was the point: I couldn't drive it to the *Verkehrsamt* until I had Swiss licence plates. Shrug. I made an appointment for the test anyway.

And make sure the car is washed, she added as I was leaving.

I cleared out the empty water bottles and service-station receipts, the scattered sheets of directions, the detritus of the journey from our old life. I discovered that it was illegal to wash your car on the street. Then I learned that this was irrelevant because, for the *Verkehrsamt*'s purposes, washing the car did not mean merely cleaning the chassis and interior, as some British people did on Sundays. It meant pressure-washing the undercarriage and steam-cleaning the engine: washing the car in every sense imaginable.

I was at the helpless end of an unfathomable logic. It was Kafkaesque, a word that rolls off the tongue in absurd situations but also comes to mind when you are feeling far from glib. When you find yourself on trial without ever learning why, or wake one morning to find that you have turned into an unspecified kind of insect.

I set about looking for a friendly mechanic. The manager of the first garage walked away while I was trying to outline my problem. I went back to the flat and put the kettle on. Then I headed up to a garage that I'd passed once or twice when exploring the neighbourhood. It was a tiny outfit with vintage signs and a cheerful air of the seventies, and I begged the proprietor for help. Herr Correlli offered me a seat in his office and spoke at length about his garden and orchard in the countryside, his weekend experiments in jam-making. The old apple varieties – Goldparmäne (a pippin) and Ananas Reinette, the pineapple russet, an unassuming yellow fruit that, when you crunch into it as I have done in a Sussex orchard, fizzes mildly with citrus or pineapple. The quince that cropped abundantly every other year. It sounded like paradise, I said, and I wondered what species of tree bore the forbidden fruit. Certainly not a quince, for its paradisiacal taste is only divulged by the alchemy of cooking, and were you to bite into a quince offered fresh from the tree it would break your teeth and scour your tongue with tartness itself. I missed my garden and my quince tree, I told Herr Correlli. He got up and went into his immaculate work-shop, making his way around an elevated car to a fridge that was nestled between a tool chest and a stack of tyres. He returned with a jar of russet-glowing jelly. Quince, he said, handing it to me, but keep it refrigerated: I've reduced the sugar proportion. He would collect the car – he was insured for that – and sort everything out.

The car was blasted and steamed and scrubbed and checked, and Herr Correlli helped me arrange dispensational insurance for the journey from his garage to the *Verkehrsamt*. He sent me on my way with a jar of white-currant jelly. It was a little cloudy, he said, because he'd squeezed the fruit when straining the juice: it extracted more flavour. He had unclipped the old British licence plates to save me the trouble, and displayed them inside the front and rear windscreens.

Off across the city, alone at my right-hand wheel with a map that I could only consult at red lights. I didn't know where I was going, and other drivers showed no mercy. At a five-way inter-section where trams entered the fray, a police car pulled me over. My licence plates were displayed incorrectly: that was an offence. We held up traffic in two directions, and the officer's reprimand was endorsed by an outpouring of fury, of horns and gestures and revving and yelling. I burned with self-consciousness – and when I pulled away at last, pursued by a still-honking SUV, I felt more foreign than ever.

The vehicle-testing officer informed me that my German was not perfect, but at least I was trying. He was, he said, SICK of foreigners turning up in Switzerland and not ATTEMPTING to speak German. He himself (like many Swiss Germans) would rather speak English than High German, but he'd wanted to test my attitude. I wanted him to get on with testing the car. There were forms to complete. My date of birth, my marital status. My occupation? I told him that I was taking a career break, that I planned to start working again as soon as I could, and for the time being he should enter 'none'. He seemed to find this provocative. You do not have no work, he enunciated, you are a *HAUSFRAU*. That is a VERY important job. You WOMEN! he spat, jabbing the air in my direction. You have your babies and then you go back to WORK. That is WRONG. It is bad for the family and bad for SWITZERLAND. You are a *HAUSFRAU*. *Oh*. Oh.

And there you have it. *Ausländer[in]*, said my residency permit. *Hausfrau*, said the car documentation. *Hausfrau, konfessionslos*, the tax papers further specified. I had become a foreign housewife of no specific religion: *Ausländerin. Hausfrau. Konfessionslos.* That's who I was on paper. I did not recognise myself.

Sometimes, at night, I visited the garden. It was not a geographic but an inward place, and its boundaries were not fixed though I knew when I was inside. It grew from the gardens that shaped me: my parents' garden – my first garden – in Sussex; the gardens in Cambridge and London that Shaun and I had left; the garden that I longed to have again one day, wherever that might be. And the garden was more than these. It was a way of being, a way of being at home.

My thoughts did not take a spatial route when they visited the garden, they navigated by plants. The Japanese anemones, rooted deep in Sussex since 1960, mapped onto London and transposed again to the gardens of our friends. Their unassuming, child-drawn sunniness, the suede-like texture of their petals. How they defined September. A geranium called 'Mrs Kendall Clark', bought for a song at a market early one morning: its foliage was green-grey, its flowers grey-lavender and marbled with white. It was spectral at dusk and just after dawn. How my mother would have noticed these things, loved this geranium. Her shopping list not fulfilled after all, but further fulfilled. The penstemon that my father grew from seed, *Penstemon digitalis* 'Mystica', its flowers otherworldly. I worried about the plants. Whether they were thriving in the places in which I had left them. Whether and when I would grow them again – have a garden, have roots. Be at home. What I had left behind and what was ahead. The small hours, their elastic length.

The hellebore. Fran, my well-meaning friend in Cambridge, mentioned that she had planted it in a pot in a lovely sunny place: I knew it would be dying for partial shade and cool soil in which to spread its tangling roots. I'd dropped a hint or two, but it was not my plant any more – not in that sense, at least – and there were feelings to consider. I thought about hellebores blooming beneath a Sussex magnolia, cool light striking their bowed greenish heads, their snaky insides undisclosed. I hoped they grew there still.

> *O flowers,*
> *That never will in other climate grow,*
> *My early visitation, and my last*
> *At even, which I bred up with tender hand*
> *From the first opening bud, and gave ye names,*
> *Who now shall rear ye to the sun, or rank*
> *Your tribes, and water . . .?*

Thus Eve upon learning that she must leave paradise, her 'native soil'. The archangel Michael has come to expel the couple for their disobedience, their tasting of the forbidden fruit, and Adam sends Eve away while he and the angel, who has assumed a human form for the occasion, speak man (as it were) to man. But Eve doesn't go far, just withdraws amongst her plants – I think – and listens in on the conversation. She hears that the angel is to send them 'from the garden forth', forth into the world.

Adam and Eve have gardened paradise together, but Eve is a born gardener in a way that Adam is not: she has a special affinity for plants. It's Eve who has given the plants their names, just as Adam has named the birds and the beasts and the fish. Eve who, in her 'nursery', has 'bred up' those plants 'with tender hand', maybe from seed she has collected, and cuttings; 'rank[ed]' or planted them in rows, 'water[ed]' them. Her 'tender' hand is infinitely so: it tends or looks after, and is tender or loving, and tends or inclines towards things that grow. It's green-fingered Eve who visits her plants first thing in the morning and last thing at night, as you do in the margins of the day, when the garden absorbs you into itself and the world is far away. Watering can in hand – for you do not water plants in the heat of the day – you inspect and notice without quite thinking, marvel almost unawares, as though the garden is conscious on your behalf. A seedling fleshed out overnight, another damped off, its stem shrivelled where leaves should be. A wild rose, yesterday's bud unfolded by new light. Dewdrops threaded on a strand of gossamer. Slugs out and about in shaded moisture, ravenous. Lilac and tobacco plants, potent fragrance stored up by day and set adrift at dusk, stopping your senses in their tracks. Pale flowers in near-dark. Bats sudden and wonderful. The idea of a nightingale. The garden self-contained, growing into night.

Who, Eve laments to herself, will tend the plants when she is gone? It's a rhetorical question, an impassioned exclamation: it has to be if it is not to trespass further on forbidden territory. What happens in paradise now that they have forfeited their right to live there is not mankind's business – and Eve's curiosity has already got her and Adam, and us, into the present fix. But maybe that is the problem – maybe Eve can't help wondering about things, asking awkward questions, her questions multiplying the more she lives and learns. She is only human after all, and the 'wanton ringlets' of her hair grow like the garden's 'wanton growth' that taxes the couple's efforts to lop and prune and prop and bind, keep it all in check. Eve is a gardener by dint of her sheer visceral bond with what grows in paradise. Facing exile from her native soil, she fixes in her grief on the plants that she has grown and that now must grow without her. The garden. Roots. What she must leave behind.

Who will garden paradise when Adam and Eve are gone? That is a very good question.

You cannot set out to make friends: like happiness, friendship materialises on its own terms. With the exception of Lars and Sandra, a Swiss couple whom we'd known for years, we were starting from scratch. But we believed that if we were open towards the people of our new country, tried hard enough to do things their way, we might with time find a place amongst them, connect with some of them.

I enrolled on an advanced German course. I had coffee with anyone who cared to have coffee with me. Shaun met people at work. We tried to reach out, invited people over, and at first many took tremendous interest in us. What were our tax arrangements, given that we were not Swiss? What was our immigration status? Did we have B or C permits? We'd find it very difficult to get a Swiss passport – very difficult indeed, not that either of us had any intention of applying for one. The coffee was very good. We bought the machine in Switzerland? How much did it cost?

I used to teach English? At a UNIVERSITY? Offers followed. I could coach someone's daughter for her English exams, set and mark some extra essays, make sure she'd covered the syllabus, that sort of thing: it would help me integrate. It would be more convenient if I went to their place – it wasn't that long a drive from Zurich – they would serve coffee, of course. I could write copy for someone else's husband's business – the website, flyers – he wanted to break into the English-language market, and it would be excellent experience for me. Why did we not have children, by the way?

People demanded personal information about us, but shared little in return. You could persuade yourself that you were getting to know someone because you'd met them on many occasions, and then you would reflect on the things they told you about themselves – the specification of a new car, how they felt about a federal tax initiative, their concern about immigrant numbers, the name of the Egyptian hotel where they had spent their holi-day, the hotel's distance from the airport – and you'd realise that you had no idea who that person was, how they experienced their life. They stored up facts about you but avoided getting to know you. Some lost interest as abruptly as they had taken it. That can happen to anyone, anywhere. It is also true that I had no useful connections and that I failed to take up those offers of unpaid employment.

Things worked differently here. It was neither a good thing nor a bad thing, just a thing, and I happened to be on the out-side. A foreigner, remember – of the forest. You were conscious of social rules and taxonomies that were rigid yet inscrutable: you felt them, you fell foul of them and sometimes were hurt by them, but you couldn't find a way inside them for they were as closed as a dialect. I'd crash into a façade that I had not seen, or graze myself on an outer edge. I wandered around exteriors, looking for ways in.

There was occasional lunching, a structured and neutral activity. Dates were set with businesslike efficiency at long but precise intervals and inconveniently far ahead – you could find yourself pinned down, your diary constrained, when you had no idea of your middle-term plans – but the same arrangements might also be downgraded unilaterally and at short notice. One acquaintance, who had scheduled lunch six or seven weeks in advance, emailed the evening before to say that her friends had just invited her to play bridge instead, and would I call the restaurant to cancel? Another informed me that she'd cancelled the reservation I had made at her request and rebooked at a restaurant closer to her home. Are you inviting me, she asked when the waitress brought the bill. I beg your pardon? Do you want to pay for my lunch? Er, no thank you, that hadn't occurred to me. Oh, I thought you might like to: I didn't want to offend you by offering to split the bill. *But I didn't 'invite' you.* Thank you, but I'm happy to split the bill.

The walls of the flat were thin, the wooden floor a sounding board. I could not bear to hear the lives of people who blanked me on the stairs or at the mailboxes. Someone setting a table, unseen and inches from where I sat. The family downstairs as loud inside their flat as they were silent at its threshold, children fighting and thudding into the small hours.

One night I jolted awake because the bed was moving. Not the heave of a husband turning in his sleep, but a subtle vibration. No sound, for once. Maybe it was blood coursing through my feet or the twitching of muscles in my leg; I didn't know. Something like this happened years ago, when I was alone in a shared house and woke to find the mattress shifting just palpably, as though something were pressing at its foot or I were on a boat. I don't know why I did not feel fear or turn on the light: I noticed the bobbing sensation, and went back to sleep. Maybe it was just me. But I can still sense something today, there in the recollected darkness.

That vibration again, high up in our Zurich flat, a night or two later, and the next. Rolling silent through the metal bed frame, felt in the mattress springs. As though furniture were being dragged across our floor, juddering soundlessly. It wasn't me – or was it? I was living on full alert. I began to think I understood how a person could go crazy. Don't be crazy, Shaun said when I mentioned it again. Then he woke up one night and said, I think I felt it too.

Anniversaries came and went and there were no violas to pick, no sprigs of rosemary or anisodontea. Argyranthemums for my father. Penstemons for my mother, later in the season.

I was not earthed, so to speak.

How do you garden without a garden? You can only go so far in your head when your hands crave soil and something to grow. In the end you buy window boxes, unlovely things of moulded off-white fibreglass that turn grey almost overnight. I went back and forth to the supermarket on a grey summer afternoon, two troughs or a small sack of compost at a time, along the street and up the spiralling stairs. There were bedding plants for sale too, begonias in scarlet and salmon-pink, lobelia an underrated violet-blue. Plants in full bloom, instant and disposable, for people without gardens – people like me. They were obvious and sensible.

Instead, the troughs filled, compost between the floorboards despite my best efforts, I sowed seeds that stood no chance. It was a stupid thing to do, but I did it anyway. I wanted to grow something from the garden we had left. In my grandmother's wooden sewing box, along with my father's deadheading clippers and the razor that my mother and then my father used for cuttings, were some envelopes of seeds. Aquilegia, labelled in my father's vigorous scrawl, just a few left now: I put that envelope back in the box, hoping that the last black gritty seeds might remain viable for a little longer, how long I didn't know. The nasturtiums, on the other hand, were two a penny: you put in a few seeds and off they went. I loved the lily-pad forms of the leaves and the way their green blued in certain lights. The red-to-gold flowers, fire tones. Their repertoire of flavours – the leaves' green spice, the warm peppery flowers, the hot astringency of the unripe seeds or, as they are aptly known, poor man's capers. And however many flowers you picked for your salad bowl there would be more seeds than you needed for the following year, ripening crinkly on the dying-down plants and camouflaged where they dropped to the earth. There's something satisfying about pushing a fat nasturtium seed into fine compost, feeling it give under the pressure of your finger, knowing that it has come from your own garden and that, all other things being equal, it will germinate fast.

Then there was the marvellous blue grass pea. I was crunching along the gravelled paths of the Chelsea Physic Garden – once an apothecary's garden, a botanical oasis still. I don't remember how I came to be there that day, but I know that it was June and my father did not have long to live, and I liked the sound of London distanced but there beyond the garden's secluding walls. It would have been easy to overlook the small flowers in the afternoon shade, but for their preternatural blue. They had the sweet pea's voluptuous form and a scaled-down precision that was all their own, finely picked out in strokes of pink. A straggly stem led me back to a label at the plant's base: *Lathyrus sativus* var. *azureus*. That evening I rang my father at the hospice and told him about my find, and then I tracked down some seeds online. The plant was so otherworldly, yet it grows so readily that in some parts of the world it is cultivated as livestock fodder. Each azure flower ripened to a pod of pea-like seeds: I collected them by the score and sowed them with abandon. I sowed some now, in Zurich, kneeling on the living-room floor.

I think I sowed those seeds to orientate myself.

I was meeting people and getting to know nobody, learning more and understanding less. A couple would not be coming to dinner after all because their plans had evolved since they accepted our invitation: they now proposed to stop by for drinks at six before going on to dinner with their friends. I'm not sure, went a response to another invitation, we like to keep Fridays free for seeing our friends. There was chronic slippage between our social norms, a lack of compatibility that was nobody's fault. I wondered when the business of integrating was going to begin. I'd been naive, or presumptuous: what did I know, back there at my kitchen table in London?

I went along to an expatriate function, hoping to find something in common with someone, if only that we were outsiders. It turned out not to be my scene, but I got chatting to a woman called Heidi, who was born and educated and had worked and married and built a house in Zurich, and had recently returned with her husband from a three-year assignment abroad. I wondered what on earth she was doing at an expatriate event: she was a *Zürcherin*, from Zurich, the rest of us were foreigners. Heidi said that she felt like an outsider too: she was finding it hard to meet people, integrate. *Integrate?* But it's your culture, your city, your dialect! You've spent most of your life here: you have a house and extended family here. It's your home. You've only been away for three years. You must still have friends. It's not easy, she said.

Heidi and I stayed in touch, and one day, over coffee, I mentioned my own difficulties: time had passed and I was not connecting with people. Was it me or was it them? Why was everyone so, well, closed, apart from kind, green-fingered Herr Correlli and the lonely old man with whom I sometimes ambled along the street? Heidi laughed. What do you expect, she said: in Switzerland we find it hard enough to make friends with each other.

I watered and watched the nasturtiums and the azure peas, tended them morning and evening, like Eve. They germinated in no time. But a third-floor window ledge is not the happiest place for plants: I knew that from the outset. The compost dried out fast, especially when the *Föhn* blew up from the lee of the Alps – the wind that gives German its word for hairdryer and is blamed for all kinds of ills, from headaches and circulatory disorders to crime spikes and psychosis. High and dry, confined to their boxes, exposed to the parching winds, the seedlings tensed into themselves. They didn't die, but they barely grew. The fibreglass troughs turned the colour of despondency. I felt confined and exposed as well. The thin walls closed in, but did not protect. I longed for soil that belonged to a place, for plants that belonged to the soil.

If you were crossing the bridge at the foot of the lake on a clear day when the *Föhn* was blowing, and you glanced across the water south into the wind, you would stop dead in wonder – unless you were on a tram, in which case, time permitting, you'd get off at the next stop and walk to your favourite bench that faces up the lake. For the *Föhn* plays atmospheric tricks, and on its warm breath the Alps that yesterday were their own distance away will be right there, magnified as if through powerful binoculars. Instinct might make you step back before the mountains' seeming advance, or crane your neck backwards to get a proper look. That's something: a wind that moves mountains. A wind that conjures Alps within touching distance of the eye, right there in the press and throng and greyness of the city.

It was time to upgrade our hiking boots, Shaun announced one morning as we ate our pastries by the lake, a sparrow waiting patiently. The water still, the mountains vague again. I should meet him after work: we would get kitted out at the sports shop, and then we'd go for a beer or two.

It was not enough for the mountains to come to us. We had to go and find them for ourselves.

PART TWO

Flora Helvetica

Grey is a bad colour for a place.

A pale-grey day followed five or six pale-grey days: no light, no dark, no colour, no nuance. No rain, which does all kinds of things – nor fog, which closes in and rolls back and distorts and disorientates and is dangerous. No isobars on the weather map, Switzerland a blank. Non-weather, flat and flattening: it affected me heavily. I'd heard of seasonal affective disorder, a biochemical affliction of the darker months, but we were two days from the summer solstice. Grey wreaks havoc with me. Dark is regenerative – our hormones need it – and it brings out things that conceal themselves by day: a haunting owl, the night song of crickets and, if you're lucky, of midwife toads. A rustling in leaves; planetary lights. Grey, on the other hand, neutralises, and when it has been grey for the briefest while I notice a dull dread. What, my body asks before I am aware, if nothing were to brighten or darken again, if colour and light and all their modulations were gone for good?

Grey spells happen in Britain too, but there is often some subtle variation – a lightening towards an edge, a texturing with deeper cloud – to reassure your faculties that the weather has not stopped. Nothing stays the same for long when you are surrounded by sea. Eastern Switzerland is different: its landlocked topography of lake and plateau, the great wall of mountains to the south, can set up periods of sheer grey stasis. It had been like this for too many days now, blunting and deadening, merging with my inner weather. The mountains blanked from view beyond the lake: I hoped they were still there.

On that pale-grey Saturday, some weeks after our arrival in Zurich, Shaun and I took a train east to the town of St Gallen. St Gallen grew up around a Benedictine abbey, today a UNESCO World Heritage Site crowned by a Baroque cathedral. I had also learned that the St Gall manuscript, a ninth-century scale plan for an ideal monastery, was displayed in the cathedral library. Copied between 820 and 830 from a lost original, this document had long fascinated me because it included some detailed garden designs. I knew my way from reproductions around the geometry of the cloister, the physic garden, the orchard-cemetery with its labelled trees, but I'd never seen the manuscript as its ancient, material self. The textures and discolourations of the parchment sheets, the stitches that held them together, the scars and repairs of the plan's 1,200-year afterlife, the aged shades of its black and red inks, the stories that facsimiles cannot tell. We'd take a look around, check out the manuscript, go for a pizza, stay in a guest house, and on Sunday we would hike up into the hills.

It was grey in St Gallen too. Grey absorbed the edges of the cathedral. Gilded crosses and clock faces glimmered oddly on the twin stone towers, and the building's curving bulk was painted grey. I wondered why you would do that – paint a cathedral grey in a part of the world that, it was beginning to appear, is prone to endless sapping spells of grey. It was dispiriting.

A side door admitted us to a contrasting world of techni-colour Baroque: Cambridge-blue plasterwork and rose marble, gilded for good measure. Epic ceiling frescoes, cloud-borne saints, too many overweight cherubs. A place like this could make a puritan of you. A society wedding was under way before the intricate altar screen, compressed by the pastel grandeur to a Lilliputian knot and incantatory murmurings. Sugary arches receded in cardinal directions to reliquaries and status tombs. I knew that it was very impressive. I wanted to be impressed, but found myself heading for the door in need of air. Outside it was still grey.

I wondered what St Gall, who died around AD 646, would have made of the confection that stands in his name today. Gall's story is a tangle of legend and history, but he seems to have been an Irish monk who accompanied St Columban on a mission to the Continent. Taken ill in the forested region that is now eastern Switzerland, Gall stayed behind to build a hermit's cell and begin a life of contemplation. He would not have been quite the loner that we expect in a hermit today: Gall was a missionary, a converter of people. He was involved with local communities, and he acquired disciples – an apostolic twelve, some sources would have it – who built cells near his. Fourteen centuries or so before the Monty Python sketch, a community of hermits was not a contradiction in terms but the monastic origin of St Gallen, the great Benedictine abbey that was built a century later. Forest clearance, construction, expansion: the landscape and the economy transformed.

Gall lives for me in an early, fragmentary story that is rich in apocryphal colour. He goes into the forest – the wilderness, for our purposes – to look for a site for his hermit's cell, and while he is walking around absorbed in prayer he trips and falls in a thicket of thorns. He takes this as a sign from God, not that he ought to have watched where he was going but that he has found his place. He marks the spot with a cross fashioned from a hazel branch, and builds his cell – the site of the future monastery in spirit if not in precise geography. In true hagiographic tradition, every detail of this story is a sign of divine providence, the hermit's holiness – Gall even awes a marauding bear into fetching firewood for him – but at its heart is the simple, compelling idea of a man finding and demarcating his place in the woods of a foreign country. The forest is wild, yet it provides: there's water, fish too, and wood for building and warmth. It is green. Maybe there are ramsons on the banks of the river where the expatriate monk settles. I'm sure he notices the plants that grow around his cell, attends to them and tends them – makes them, somehow, his own. Begins to garden his space.

Today there is no forest, only grey.

Something was wrong with the beds of roses and box that edged the cathedral square. I knew them to be a strong elaboration of complementary colours, blood-red and deep green, but what I saw was dull puce against something bluish. I've seen this sickly combination before, when I was ten years old and turned my camera on a crimson peony in my parents' garden: the camera was loaded with cheap print film that dealt weakly with reds and greens, and in any case the peony was too perfect. Colour eludes capture at the best of times. As I waited for Shaun outside the grey cathedral I shivered in the drained atmosphere, the midsummer cold, and grappled with the zip of my anorak. I was in a bad frame of mind – in a bad place, as they say.

We made our way to the imposing Rococo library. At the far

end people were gathered around a flat display case and I forgot the grey in my sudden excitement: the manuscript, at last! The stretched and dried and stitched skin of ninth-century calves, the monastery and its gardens inked in pigments corroded by time. Red mercuric sulphate, expensive and poisonous. Black iron gall brewed from oak apples, parasitic fruits of the forest. For some reason – maybe to do with the words 'iron gall' – I expected the black to be more glossy than the red. I quickened my step.

But I'd never find out about the iron gall, for the display case contained a facsimile.

Outside it was still grey.

The next day we climbed away from the grey town, up into the hills, heading west. A brisk wind caught at my hair, and the world resolved into cloud forms and sun slants and fast-moving depths. Something lifted.

Leaving the last village, our path took us around a hornbeam hedge. I could trace the twist of its limbs inside the clipped green volume but I couldn't see beyond, into the space that the hedge enclosed. I wondered what it was like – how the light fell, what grew there. Up again through a fir wood, blinded by dark and bright, tripping over roots. The dark needles almost aromatic. The special sound of wind in pines or pines in wind, an innate and happening sound, a sough. We left the wood suddenly and found ourselves in a meadow. Behind us the hills sloped down to the plateau, St Gallen still grey for all I knew. Lake Constance at the horizon, blue, holding the sky.

Fast light, the kind that makes you want to take photographs. Flowers a shimmer of their usual colours. Tall grasses with

grass-green blades and ripening flower heads hazy like heat. But-
tercups, scabious, ox-eye daisies, sorrel, grass flowers myriad and
delicate. Flowers I couldn't identify: 'deep-bronze hawksbeard-
like flowers', I noted unscientifically when we stopped to eat
some bread and cheese, and flowers with 'bell shapes; corn-
cockle colouring'. My eye was drawn to a form from a garden in
Sussex or London, the broad-toothed leaves and simple flowers
of a hardy geranium. One or two plants near the path: I was
enchanted. The flowers were metallic in the bright light, mauve
upon closer inspection, and their throats were white. The leaves
were soft emerald. Another geranium for my mother's list: I'd
identify it later, when we got back to Zurich. We spotted another, and another, and geraniums were pushing in great drifts
through the grass, pink to mauve to metal; in the shade of a tree
they were almost blue. A whole meadow of geraniums. Shaun
said something, and I straightened up from the flower I was
examining and looked. In a gap between trees to the south were
two snow-capped peaks. Not, this time, the optical illusion of
a trouble-making wind: we were finding our own way to the
mountains. It was almost too much for one meadow.

The meadow had not quite finished with me. At its far end,
on the margin of a wood where the grass was lax and damp,
my father's aquilegia flowered a shady purple-blue. I knew that
Aquilegia vulgaris grew wild in Britain and continental Europe
– but I'd never been in the right place at the right time, and for
me it was a cherished garden plant, far superior to the multi-
coloured hybrids and frilly cultivars. I loved the quilled forms of
its flowers, the rich blue-violet textures in which your eye could
lose itself.

Those few seeds that remained in the envelope in the sewing

box, the same plant here in sodden grass at the meadow's edge, wild and suddenly new.

I cannot describe what unfolded as we walked on over hills that stepped up to the Alps: when I try to remember it all into focus I see a mass of luminous particles. Unfeasible green. Air pure as the just-created firmament, '[t]ransparent, elemental air'. Mountains at eye level: choppy, textured. Rock colours. Cow bells. A whitewashed church on a promontory. A small oval lake of unfathomable colour. The musky barn scent of livestock kept well. Alpine peaks detached by haze, floating and remote and white, a child's picture of heaven (or was that just me?). Silage delicious on the air: molasses, grass. Shimmering meadows. Green meadows. A meadow's arc, ample and geometrically precise. The idea of the earth's curvature. Another frame: snow-capped peaks, a dog rose in the foreground, rosy flowers open to the sun. Mountains to vanishing point. Leaden clouds bright above sunlit green. There with Shaun in the hills and the light and the air and the moment. Being alive. The path and where the path might lead us.

Geraniums and aquilegias, familiar plants running wild in a strange and awesome landscape, a landscape that inspired awe. Undefined by garden boundaries, outside that hornbeam hedge, they were different: I didn't know them as well as I thought I did, and that was exciting. I found myself wondering whether a wild plant and a garden plant were really such different things. I wanted to walk on the path in that day forever, with Shaun.

I did not want to go back to the flat, but something was there for me now. When we went shopping for a vacuum cleaner on that first afternoon, the boxes unopened, the streets swept and unfamiliar, Shaun bought me a book: *Flora Helvetica*, the definitive encyclopedia of Swiss flora. On the fly-leaf he wrote: 'Wishing you many happy years of gardening in Switzerland.'

My copy of *Flora Helvetica* is amongst my most treasured possessions, a gift from the person who understands what makes me tick. In buying and inscribing this book for me, Shaun acknowledged what I had given up – my home, my garden, the plants with which my life was entwined. It was an expression of optimism for our future in Switzerland, for the new life and land and flora that we had to discover together. It was the promise of a life amongst plants again. A wish for my happiness.

The book itself is a magisterial work, a labour of love offered, as good science is, in a spirit of wonder and humility: '*Zum Erstaunen bin ich da*', the foreword closes in the words of Goethe, Wordsworth's German contemporary, I am here to be astonished. It is complete, the compilers caution, as far as possible ('*möglichst*') – for who knows what nature might be up to under the radar, in some small undiscovered habitat? The volume is weighty yet compact, nearly as thick as it is wide, built to fit into the backpack of a serious botanist or to be held in both hands while seated, as women often read in paintings by Vanessa Bell. On a desk – Henri Matisse's women tend to read at tables and desks – the book opens flat, whether you're near the middle (nightshades and bittersweet) or on page 1474 (ramsons and other alliums) of its 1,600-odd pages. Its spine never creases, and the sturdy cover could undoubtedly be wiped clean should the need arise. Most of the two-page spreads feature four species, each identified by a colour photograph on the recto and a corresponding description and map on the verso. Every plant is named in up to five languages – botanical Latin and the vernacular by which it is known in the country's linguistic regions. These days an app will lighten your backpack by two kilograms, but the beauty of *Flora Helvetica* is in the book: in thoughtful details such as the metric ruler, printed inside the back cover to aid identification, and in the way it demands to be handled. Its jewelled pages, their satisfying fall.

I turned those pages during our first weeks in Switzerland. Familiar plants had new names that told their own stories. Take hornbeam, *Carpinus betulus*. The Swiss-German name *Hagebuche*, or hedge beech, identified the tree as a rather functional beech, a genus to which hornbeam is unrelated (it belongs to the birch family, the Betulaceae). The francophones held hornbeam in rather different esteem: *charme*, charm, is the word that I too might choose were I invited to name this lovely spellbinding tree. The Italian speakers settled neutrally for a form of the botanical name, *carpino comune*, and the absence of a Romansh name was explained by the near-blankness of Engadine on the distribution map.

Flowers from the hedgerows of my childhood cropped up like old friends. So did species that I knew as garden plants, wild here. The delicate *Rosa glauca* with its bluish, red-tinged foliage. *Geranium sanguineum,* blood-red by name and magenta in colour. A delphinium flagged with three crosses, the highest level of deadliness, because the seeds of those impossibly lovely flowers, that cobalt-purple iridescence, are '*sehr stark giftig*', very strongly poisonous. Hundreds of plants were unfamiliar to me, some exotically so.

At the same time though, in those early days, I felt the book had little to do with me. It had to do with a world of green growing things that I'd left behind with the garden: I knew it was there but it was out of my reach, a life away from the thin-walled flat and the joyless grey city. There are as many kinds of gardener as there are people who garden – but I do not believe there is such a being as an 'armchair gardener', as the non-practising reader of books about plants and gardens is commonly called. That is a contradiction in terms – for all kinds of people may read such books, but gardeners need soil and living, respiring, photosynthesising plants as well. Even as I was enchanted by *Flora Helvetica*, it represented something lost.

But in the course of that June day – in full colour and full bloom – the book became relevant to me. Shaun and I had walked amongst the flowers on its pages. I had lifted their heads to examine their forms and markings, touched their leaves, and I wanted to get to know them better. Suddenly I could put *Flora Helvetica* to positive use, leaf through those colourful rectos until a picture made sense of my haphazard notes. The bronze hawksbeard-like flower, as it happened, was a different species altogether, orange hawkweed or, the German name specifies, 'orange-red hawkweed'. The corncockle-pink flowers were harder to identify: they turned out to belong to a rampion bellflower, but I had seen pinker petals than the 'light-blue-lilac' description and photograph suggested. *Campanula rapunculus* is a cousin of the harebell, that blue flower of the South Downs, of skylarks and expansive sea. Maybe it was my eyes, or a quirk of light that afternoon – or maybe the flower was indeed unusually pink, nature up to something beyond the book. Maybe the book was wrong.

The geranium was the wood cranesbill or mayflower, a quintilingual feast of words for woods: *sylvaticum, Wald, bois, silvano, guaud*. 'Weald', I added for my own purposes.

For the first time since pulling up at the flat on that muggy spring evening, I felt connected with something. There were topographies and soil, and above all plants with which to acquaint myself. We would rejoin the path that led broadly west, up there in the foothills and the light, the grey plateau, its grey towns and cities almost insignificant, and we'd find out what grew along the next stretch as the path rose to skim a mountain flank. Another aquilegia, perhaps, from the garden that I tended in my heart, or something new and unexpected.

Back in the city, on the other hand, I was out of my element. The adrenaline of those first weeks had consumed itself: the novelty had worn off and left me with the everyday. And what I felt beneath my feet shifted and gave, like the bottom of that pool into which I once fell. Just as I was confused by rebuffs and rages and what I experienced as selfishness, so I seemed to cause offence as I went about my business. I became convinced that people were watching me with disapproval, and though this was undoubtedly a consequence of how I felt – out of place, uncomfortable, on the back foot – it was not always unjustified.

I stopped at the supermarket one morning to pick up coffee beans: I remember the yellow packet. There was no one at the checkout, apart from the cashier, though I noticed that a basket of groceries had been placed under the empty conveyor belt. As I was digging out my purse, I had that feeling of being watched; you just know. When I was young I had an aunt who eavesdropped on our family. She would let herself into our house with the key entrusted to her, and though she crept around with the stealth of Madame Beck I always knew when she was there: it drove me mad. And once, on my London allotment, sheltering from a storm beneath a lightning-scarred oak, something made me swing round to meet the assertive amber eyes of a dog fox, his coat dripping heavily, and we held one another's gaze for long seconds, each daring the other to look away first.

This time, when I turned, I met a weighty glare. A sixty-something woman had arranged the contents of the abandoned basket on the conveyor belt. She was wearing checked trousers, the not-quite-cropped kind that look as though their wearer is growing out of them, and her eyes bulged at me furiously; I wondered why she was so hostile. *Guten Morgen*, I said, good morning. *MACHEN SIE WAS SIE WOLLEN,* she bellowed, slamming the 'm' to its maximum range, DO WHAT YOU LIKE. She had evidently reserved her place at the checkout, rather as people have been known to bag sun loungers with beach towels, and while she was off fetching something I had rocked up and paid for my coffee beans.

Another day, lunchtime, I was in the café of a department store, working my way through a pyramid of food that I had assembled from the fixed-price salad bar (it's surprising how much you can fit onto a medium-sized plate if you start with leaves and weigh them down with more interesting things). Beyond the windows the lime trees were in bloom on Bahnhofstrasse: I'd caught their heady sweetness amongst the pavement smells and the trams' mild acridity.

At the next table an older couple were eating in silence with an air of glum routine. A knife clattered at my feet. The woman looked down at it, her fork in one hand. I picked up the knife and set it back quietly on her table. I caught her eye and smiled briefly. The woman put her fork down and glared back. Her husband turned slowly, and they stared at me in outraged concord. I looked away. People at other tables had turned from their plates and were watching me too. I looked back to meet the couple's continuing glare. I was at the centre of a staring censorious silence that I didn't understand, and a cherry tomato rolled from my overfilled plate.

Later, I began to wonder whether I had exaggerated the episode in my mind, for I had come to expect collisions and slippages, displeasure and occasional wrath, as I tried to go about living in Switzerland. Then I told Sandra, our Swiss friend, what had happened. You should never have done that, she said. What? Pick up the knife. I don't understand. The woman would have thought you were interfering. But I couldn't leave it on the floor. I would never have done that. You mean you'd have left the knife on the floor, right by your foot? Yes, of course. *I don't understand.*

I still have no idea whether that trivial, mortifying incident had to do with Swissness, or Britishness, or a general faux pas: it could surely have happened to a different person amongst other people elsewhere. Whatever the case, such episodes fed my feeling that the people amongst whom I was trying to live did not get me any more than I got them. I felt that I did not know how to behave, and it made me self-conscious. Maybe I was growing hypersensitive, too used to being an alien.

When I stopped for lunch at the department store some months later, the cashier weighed my plate. I asked her why. They had discontinued the fixed-price system, she explained, and were now pricing by weight. Oh. My plate was piled densely, and as salad lunches go it cost a fortune. It's your fault, Shaun teased me later, they changed the system because of greedy people like you.

*

Then something happened that shook me up. I had a pair of boots reheeled, and the next day one of the new heels fell off. No problem, said the man when I took the boot back, I'll do it within the hour. All sorted, he said, holding out the boot, when I returned. I reached to take the boot. Oh no, he said, whipping it away, that will be twenty francs. No way, I said, you know I paid you forty francs yesterday; I still have the receipt. He lapsed into dialect and his voice began to rise. Please just give me the boot, I said, the original repair was defective. He was shouting now, incomprehensibly, though I heard the word *Weib*, a disparaging term for woman. No, I said, I'm not paying for it twice: you know that's not right. He came out from behind the counter, still holding the boot, and stepped very close to me, the rage in his face, and then he pushed my chest hard with his free hand, forcing me back a step or two. I was breathless, speechless. I'd been shoved and elbowed and jostled and bumped many times since we came to Switzerland – but no one had actively laid hands on me since my primary schooldays, some playground spat or other. I had no witnesses and no recourse. I needed the boot, so I handed over a twenty-franc note.

I did not know how to think about what had happened. The physical impact wore off soon enough, but I carried the fact around with me, wondering what to do with it. Sandra was shocked when I told her: he'd never, she said, have done that to a Swiss woman. I did not know how to think about that, either.

Home. My mother had always gone home or Home, but these days I went back to the flat or back to Zurich or back to Switzerland. 'Home' was a word that had fallen out of use. We'd sold our house in London, Shaun's job was for the long haul, and I began to entertain the possibility that I might never be at home here.

But it depends on what you mean by home.

> *Thy going is not lonely, with thee goes*
> *Thy husband, him to follow thou art bound;*
> *Where he abides, think there thy native soil.*

Thus the archangel Michael, briefing Adam and Eve for their exile into the world, reassuring the distressed Eve with words that might be calculated to offend a feminist reader. Or not – not if you hear in 'bound' not subjugation, but visceral and emotional bonds, the stuff of mutual belonging. Not if you enjoy the great good fortune of 'meet and happy conversation' that, Milton had written in a controversial prose work, 'is the chiefest and the noblest end of marriage' and the lack of which justified divorce. Back then, the adjective 'meet' – fitting or suitable – had residual connotations of equality, while 'conversation' could still mean not just talking, but the whole business of living amongst people. It was a raw subject, for in 1643, when Milton published his first treatise on divorce, he was smarting from the failure of his first marriage: the previous year, after just a few weeks of mutual incompatibility, his unhappy teenaged bride had gone to visit her parents and neglected to return.

You should not underestimate what Milton described as meet and happy conversation and we called the team. Shaun and I rubbed along pretty well. We had made homes and decisions together, and pulled through our share of adversity. We hiked at the same brisk pace. We had a common need for books and greenery, liked to laugh, and occasionally infuriated each other. A friend once observed that we completed one another's sentences, though some might consider 'hijacked' a more accurate verb. We were quiet together: when I am with Shaun, I am most myself. The team could make itself at home anywhere, as we said back then in London when speculative process became sheer fact, a contract signed and posted.

'Native soil' is a way of talking about human belonging: the myth of Eve created from Adam created from the earth. The word 'native' stems from the Latin for birth: it's concerned with geographic origin, with having roots in a place. Native people, native plants, native soil. But the angel suggests that this is not entirely the case. 'Must I thus leave thee Paradise? Thus leave/ Thee native soil . . . ?', Eve laments. No, the angel tells her, you're being too literal. Home, native soil, is more than a place. It's an abstract, emotional thing. It's not just this garden-home, but the stuff of a portable bond. If you are with your soulmate you will be at home wherever you may find yourself.

Shaun and I had always believed that too, before we moved to Switzerland.

But the world into which Adam and Eve are about to be sent is not yet populated. What Milton calls 'conversation' and the dictionary 'having one's being in a place or amongst persons' is also a way of talking about home: a human need that telescopes between a team of two and a broader community or society. Home is about belonging amongst people – a people. No man, nor couple, is an island.

At weekends we packed our rucksacks and followed our path on through the foothills, the Alps to the south: the 'whole upheaval of Switzerland', Patrick Leigh Fermor put it with casual precision. That dynamic solidness, that sense of something caught in the business of coming into being:

> *the mountains huge appear*
> *Emergent, and their broad bare backs upheave*
> *Into the clouds, their tops ascend the sky: . . .*

That's blind Milton again, conjuring the third day of creation, making it happen before our eyes. His mountains appear emergent and upheave into the clouds, ranging over the line breaks of the verse itself.

A path trodden over the brow of a hill. Beyond was a high plateau from which a steep slope unfolded to the angle of an opened laptop. Its lower reaches were storybook-green, the uncleared fir wood dark towards its craggy ridge. The haze implied mountains beyond. A piece of meadow framed by the viewfinder: grasses, orchids, hawksbeard, buttercup.

The cornflower should not have been there. It was not the common cornflower, *Centaurea cyanus,* a wiry-stemmed annual that graced the fields of pre-glyphosate Britain with wind-silvered blue, but a larger perennial that belonged in a garden like the one I'd left behind in London. *Centaurea montana,* the mountain cornflower or great blue-bottle, though I knew it as 'montana'.

A few weeks after we moved into our London home, in early spring, clumps of tapered ovate leaves had begun to appear in the garden. They were a muted blue-green, the colour of heritage paint, with a whitish aura that made me think of magnesium. One substantial group must have been planted in the border, but as the weeks went by smaller plants turned up everywhere and anywhere. In May their scaly buds opened on thick stems to flower heads that resembled airy blue thistles. Something about their deep-cut florets suggested movement: they appeared to whirl around the reddish-pink centres, reminding me of a handheld windmill that I had as a child one spring holiday in Cornwall. The windmill had six or seven individual florets, and I held it in the slipstream, thrilled, as we drove through the deep lanes on a morning rinsed by rain. When a gust of wind snatched the windmill over a plant-encrusted drystone wall – a Cornish hedge – my father turned the car, and drove back, and climbed the hedge-wall, and searched the field beyond. I was briefly inconsolable when he returned empty-handed, but I think I knew that not every parent would go to such lengths: my father was a kind man. He reported that the field was enormous and, like a field in a storybook, grazed by Friesians. I can see them now, black and white and burnished by the salt air. If you sat still in that field for long enough you might feel the robust prod of a nose at your back, or the rasp of a bovine tongue on your neck, and you would turn around to find that you were being investigated by a herd of curious cows.

The montana was a beautiful, generous plant: it had striking flowers in a colour that I love, and it bloomed for months with occasional deadheading. It also exasperated me. It grew like a weed, but I could not bear to dispose of the surplus plants as if they were dock or ground elder. I dug up pieces over and again and offered them to my father, neighbours, friends. My father thought it a handsome space filler, but before long the montana was oppressing his less assertive plants and he too began to root it out. The 'Greater Blue Bottle', the botanist William Curtis wrote in 1790, 'will grow in any soil or situation, some will think too readily'. With the persistence of a persistent fly, it's tempting to add, though the plant is called 'blue-bottle' for more anodyne reasons: the bases of its blue flowers are bulbous, as most wine bottles were until the end of the eighteenth century. I thought of the montana as common in the modern sense of vulgar because it was common in the sense of frequent or familiar: its weed-like ubiquity detracted from its loveliness, as if a plant could be too easy to grow. And that, I'd not yet learned, is no way to think about a plant.

Paradoxically, while I was trying to curb the montana in the garden, I was growing its wild relative – that delicate agricultural weed – on my allotment. You can buy *Centaurea cyanus* seeds in all kinds of hybridised pinks and reds and mauves, but that makes no sense to me: *cyanus* comes from a Greek word for dark blue. *Centaurea cyanus* is a blue flower by definition. I filled small vases with that simple blue that faded slowly through lavender to nothing: cutting the flowers only encouraged further blooming, though I always let a few plants run to seed that sowed itself. Pesticide Pete, the allotment busybody and a heavy organophosphate user, complained that I was growing wild flowers instead of productive crops (they are productive, I told him, they bring me joy).

Now, years later in Switzerland, I wondered what the montana was doing there in the Alpine foothills, far from the gardens and garden centres of south-east England. It was clearly at home, for when I looked around there were scores of the things: they spun motionless in the glancing sun, richly blue and free, unchecked by gardeners who thought they grew too readily. Left to their own devices in their native soil they were far from common: they were lovely, new. I looked for the first time at a tiny floret that radiated from a flower head: it was pinned to the glowing centre like a ragged starry dart, and its fine petals spread about as seaweed does in water.

Some things are too obvious to notice – the names of plants, for example. *Montana*: of the mountains. Of course. *Flora Helvetica* confirmed it with a single graphic. The distribution map for *Centaurea montana* shows two dense parallel bands across Switzerland: a thick swathe through the Alps and their foothills and a thinner one through the Jurassic arc, the older, smaller mountains at the country's north-western edge. I wondered what the Jura was like: everyone talked about the Alps, but I liked the idea of little old mountains in the back of beyond. Where the montana was also in its element, at home.

That was a new thought for a gardener. Maybe the montana had been out of place in our suburban London garden. It had been purchased and planted, and as it grew and spread, behaved like itself, it was arrested and hacked and calumniated as though it were at fault. It was a living thing with ways of its own and I had judged it, found it wanting, because I did not understand those ways.

Up in the green contours, the feeling of connection deepened. It was not just the thrill of recognition when I chanced upon something that had grown in our London garden, or my parents' garden. Familiar things can make you feel not more, but less at home should they turn up in a place where you are not at ease: a coiffed anisodontea for example, plagued by plastic insects on a too-smart market stall; the kitchen table from which you once looked out into your own green space, transposed to a place of white reverberating walls that might, at any moment, crush you.

And while familiarity does not necessarily breed contempt, it does make assumptions. You can think you know a person or a plant well, only to find that you barely know them at all.

Alchemilla. Aquilegia. Geranium. The montana or mountain cornflower. *Dianthus carthusianorum*, the Carthusian pink, pinker even than its common name suggests. Growing wild, doing what came naturally in a place to which I was alien, these plants were not so familiar after all. I'd thought of them as belonging to the garden, but they were at home here, in the mountainous upheaval of central Europe, miles and topographies away from the Sussex Weald and London. They were growing where it suited them and not where it suited a gardener like me. They resisted my assumptions. Those first encounters showed me things that years of growing and tending and reading had not: the different, vigorous beauty of plants in their element. Their habits and their magic. They were not garden plants, they were simply plants. That thought was like the path: I would pick it up from time to time, find out where it led. New perspectives had opened up on what I thought I knew. There was so much, suddenly, to learn.

Sometimes, when I looked anew at a flower running wild, I found that I too was in my element.

The sense of adventure, the gung-ho determination to engage with people, the enthusiasm for doing things the local way: these attitudes may smack of the tourist or traveller who will go home at the end of their trip, but they are essential for those whose journey is one-way. They carry you along in a spirit of optimism and novelty while you find your feet, identify the coordinates that you need to start making a life. You may be culpable of naivety, but that naivety buys you time and gives you sticking power. At some point, though, you will recognise in your being what your head has known all along – that this is not a finite adventure, it is your life.

Time passed. There were moments when I thought I was getting the hang of things, and then something would happen: a smartly dressed man pushed in front of me at a checkout and berated me when I objected, or that lunch arrangement was cancelled for a game of bridge. We'd convince ourselves and each other that we were building a social life and then find out, through trial and mainly error, that we were categorised as network. This outer circle was bounded rigorously, and once you were assigned to it you could not make your way inwards. Once or twice the word *Netz*, network, cropped up in conjunction with a verb, *pflegen,* that has a capacity to say one thing while meaning another. My German dictionary lists the definitions or uses of *pflegen* as to look after, care for, nurse, tend, groom, foster, cultivate, maintain: it sounds like an attentive and caring word, but it wanders into pragmatic and functional realms, concerns itself with the visible surfaces of things, and this is not where you want to be in a social relationship – not, at least, where I want to be. *Das Netz pflegen*: to maintain your network, groom and manage it. If you are assigned to the *Netz*, you may find yourself cultivated assiduously yet held at arm's length, and this paradox confused me. Should you blunder towards an inner boundary you will be pushed back, and only then will you learn how you are classified.

We were not often invited into people's homes, but when we were, usually by someone Shaun had met at work, I assumed that our hosts wanted to get to know us. Once or twice they did. But often these dinners for four were nothing of the kind. They were convened and adjourned like meetings, the two men seated opposite each other for serious talk, the two women for parallel feminine conversation at which, for it was both compulsory and firmly superficial, I was not adept. One host took my coat, offered me a drink, and ignored me until it was time to return my coat to me. When we reciprocated the invitation I sat down opposite him: he was at my table now, he could speak to me, the four of us could converse as equals. As if by instinct, he pivoted on a buttock and aligned himself diagonally with Shaun. I found it odd that the wives colluded in their own segregation, and expected our household to observe the same protocol. It seemed so . . . outdated. But I was in a foreign country: they did things differently there. Swiss women were not granted the right to vote in federal elections until 1971 (the women of one canton waited twenty more years to vote in local elections). Maybe there was a connection, maybe not. One thing was certain: my official classification notwithstanding, I was not going to cut it as a *Hausfrau*.

The rules by which I was required to live had intricacies beyond my frame of reference. I failed to grasp that however much you might think you had hit it off with someone – for it had never occurred to me to categorise a person whose company I enjoyed – you were expected, if you were classified as network, not to follow up in between meetings. You must come back for a day next week, one wife said to me as we were leaving her house, we can have lunch and do some baking together; I'll show you how to make *Linzertorte*. Oh that would be lovely, I said – I needed friends, after all – I think I'm free every day next week apart from Monday. What works best for you? Our hostess froze, and said she would be in touch. Subsequent meetings between our husbands took place over lunch in public venues.

Milton wrote about paradise and its loss, about native soil and human bonds, because he knew what it was like to be an exile – in his own country, as it happened. A puritan and a republican, a writer not just of poetry but of forward-thinking prose, he came of age in 1629, the year in which Charles I dissolved parliament, and his adulthood spanned uniquely turbulent times. There were eleven years of ever-more arbitrary government, and England's concomitant descent into civil war. Following the second Royalist defeat, there was the thinking of the unthinkable: the king's trial for treason and, on a January afternoon in 1649, his decapitation in front of a groaning Whitehall crowd. Oliver Cromwell's commonwealth ensued, falling apart when it was barely formed, and then the restoration of a Stuart monarch in the mood (as you would be) for revenge. The numerous treatises that Milton published in the commonwealth cause included, shortly after the king's execution, a defence of the principle of regicide – and when Charles II returned from exile in 1660 the author of *Paradise Lost* found himself a marked man, 'fallen on evil days . . . and evil tongues', alone with his ideals of liberty, in 'darkness, and with dangers compassed round,/And solitude'.

The darkness and isolation were more than political. Milton suffered from a progressive eye disease, and by 1652 – when Nicholas Culpeper's great, levelling people's herbal appeared – he was fully blind, 'from the cheerful ways of men', he put it starkly, '[c]ut off'. He depended on others to read aloud to him and to transcribe his prose and poetry – to turn works composed by tongue and ear into writings. I cannot imagine what it must be like, as it is for many, to have to absorb a book at someone else's pace. To have no power to skim back and reread a sentence or a phrase, allow a word to catch your eye, underline things as you go or, if you think it heresy to scribble in books, insert a scrap of paper or a Post-it note. Jot things down. I cannot imagine creating with words when you cannot read your words: work and rework them in private, on your own terms. Move things around, cross things out, select and delete and start again, or take yourself off for a walk.

But what, above all, if you could never again see a face that you love, a familiar face, any face? Look into someone's eyes? That must be a special banishment. 'Seasons return,' Milton reflects, 'but not to me returns/Day' – nor, he goes on, 'the sweet approach of even or morn', nor the sight of a spring flower, a summer rose, a flock of sheep, a herd of cows – nor, the list ends searingly, 'human face divine;/But cloud in stead, and ever-during dark'. 'Human face divine': man created in the image of God, God incarnated in man. And the sheer sublimity, for a man who will never see one again, of the human face.

In these manifold dimensions of loss, dictating from his bed or (an early biographer heard) '[s]at leaning Backward Oblique-ly in an Easy Chair, with his Leg flung over the Elbow of it', Milton composed *Paradise Lost*. A story of exile from a garden, from the 'native soil' that echoes wistfully throughout its twelve books (ten in the first edition). A poem that speaks feelingly, in centuries and circumstances beyond its own, of grief and up-rootedness, of human bonds, of the continuity between being human and being a gardener. If you try to compare yourself with Adam, or Eve, or Satan, or Milton himself, you are missing the point. You must listen to the words, feelingly.

The myth of the fall of man offers, if not an explanation for how we are, the so-called 'human condition', then a way of conceptualising it. Paradise – the original garden from which we imagine ourselves collectively expelled – may be our culture's oldest way of thinking about happiness and belonging, of talking about displacement and loss. But Milton's paradise is more, hundreds of lines more, than the garden in which the Genesis story of the fall is set. It is the setting for a vast theological undertaking, Milton's stated aspiration to 'justify the ways of God to men'. But it is also the garden of a gardener, one whose very being is bound up with green things. I knew this when I first read *Paradise Lost* as a teenager grounded by winter – long before I read, in another early biographical note, that Milton 'alwayes had a Garden where he lived'. Only a gardener would know, with Eve, those liminal times of day, that 'early visitation' and the 'last/At even', when for an unspecified while there is nothing but the garden. When you tend and look, as Milton would have done before blindness robbed him of dawn and dusk. As my mother is almost always doing – unless she's sitting at the table, looking out – when I see her with my mind's eye, or in the photograph on my desk.

When my mother died, someone who had never met her asked me to show them a photograph that captured something of who she was. It was a difficult request, and not because there were too many images from which to choose, or not enough. I've always taken photos – it is part and parcel of how I look at things. But faces are problematic: the more I look at a photograph of a face I know well, the less familiar it seems. It is static, stilled from the infinite and infinitesimal movements that make up an expression, a person's presence; isolated from whatever it was that prompted you to reach for your camera or iPhone. The picture must be completed by your memory or, if too much time has passed, or you were not the photographer, by your imagination. A photograph robs a face of life even as it captures it.

A corner of my parents' garden beyond the magnolia arch, the light late and syrupy. A mallow vigorous with mid-green leaves and funnelling pink flowers, a hearty northern cousin of the delicate anisodontea. My mother and her mallows. She is bent to a perfect perpendicular, hands clasped behind her back as they always arranged themselves when she examined something, on this occasion holding a pair of secateurs. Her face is obscured, but she is absorbed in the garden on that summer evening. I wonder what she was looking at in the patch of ground beyond the mallow, whether something had put on new growth or lost leaves to an undiscriminating slug. Maybe a toad was stirring in the cool half-decay beneath a fern: a shifting of the ground's loose surface as with oddly localised seismic activity, and then that indeterminate moment when a knobbled back or head takes form amongst its camouflage. If your garden is healthy there will be slugs where there is green growth and toads where there are slugs. Maybe my mother was looking as if for the first time at something she'd seen a hundred times on her morning and evening and in-between rounds. Not an aquilegia: I can hear her saying its name, but I'm certain that my father planted the aquilegias after her death – as certain as I can be. The leaf of a hellebore perhaps, dark and palm-like: a ray of low sun catches one from behind, and you notice that its bright veins form an internal pattern for which there is no analogy.

That is the photograph I chose. I'm glad I took it.

Late one afternoon, twenty years later, there were mallows in sun as our path fell steeply from the edge of a wood in eastern Switzerland. A deliberate descent that kept your eyes on the ground and, as my father would have said, sorted out your knees. Stopping to look up, the mountains dropping behind the hills though it's we who were dropping. And then the mallows, shaggy and emerald, their pink flowers filled with brightness: they might have been imagined from that bright corner of my parents' garden. I clambered across the slope to take a closer look at the divided leaves, their recessed veins, the petals' streaked shades that made up their show of solid pink. If you go and fall . . . said Shaun.

Back in the flat I compared my snapshots of the mallow with the photograph on my desk, and then I opened *Flora Helvetica*. The mallow that grew between my camera and whatever my mother was looking at was the mallow on the hillside where the Alps withdrew from view. *Malva sylvestris*, the common mallow. It is, I learned from the book and would discover for myself, widespread in Switzerland. It's native to England too, though less common. That the common mallow is a 'wild' plant did not stop my mother from growing it in her garden; why should it have done?

That mallow was more than familiar: it was a link with my inner garden that took on new life, put on new growth, when I came across a familiar plant in its native soil. And I realised that to seize on the familiar for its own sake, as an uprooted person is liable to do, is to collude in your own displacement. It is to look only for replication, for something frozen and sentimental that will keep pace neither with the world that you have left nor with the world into which you are transplanted. Newly strange in their familiarity, wild and in their element, the montanas and the columbines and the mallows deepened and nourished connections with what I thought was lost. They were the stuff of living memory. A memory is like a garden: it grows as you carry it around with you.

Flora Helvetica, the book and the plants, revealed botanical links between Britain and Switzerland, between my gardening life and my rootless present. Out in the hills with Shaun, I felt like myself. Shaun was in his element too: he told me so, though I knew in any case from the ease of his shoulders and his gait as he strode out ahead, unaware that I had stopped to look at something. As we walked west across the country, bit by bit, I discovered plants from home growing wild, and new forms of familiar plants, and new plants altogether, and I felt involved with something. With the soil. With what grew in myriad permutations of topography and geology, the earth and rock beneath my feet. In woods and meadows and damp, shadowy, in-between places; in scree that looked barren and harboured life; at altitudes that took your breath away. A native plant is by definition of its place – and if you visit a plant in its native soil, I had learned, it will tell you things about itself that you cannot glean from books and the internet.

But I'd begun to lead a double life, and the gap widened as time went on and a year became two. Plants were one thing, people another. There were those surfaces and slippages, those yawning, undefined distances (how long is an arm's length?). Sometimes it seemed that the disconnect deepened the harder I tried. Sometimes I was not so sure that I wanted to keep trying.

When I think of that flat now, the walls tilt in like vertical planes of a troubling dream, the kind that hangs about the following day. We hung pictures and filled the seven bookcases I had assembled, one shelf back-to-front, but the walls were still there, exerting their inward forces. I thought I could feel them at times; I certainly heard them. I felt that vibration too, in the small hours, shuddering silently through the metal bed frame. It was a lonely, unquiet place, even when I was not alone.

Then I went out, and small things wound me up or I got into trouble. Someone barrelled in front of me at the bread stall. I was halfway over a zebra crossing when an approaching car accelerated hard and swerved around me. It happened again. And then again. People streamed in front of an elderly woman who was trying to board a train, or rushed into a lift that other people had not yet exited. A man racing a woman for the checkout berated me when I pointed out that he'd pushed his trolley over my foot: I was wearing sandals, and it hurt. Someone shoved me sideways on an escalator when *Entschuldigung*, excuse me, would have achieved his end, and later that day someone else did the same thing on a pavement. I wondered why so many people needed to be first, to get in front of the person in front of them. Why everyday life had to be so difficult, so – negative.

Why are all these people so sad? a Middle-Eastern man wondered in our hearing, on the tram.

I knew that Swiss rules regarding zebra crossings were not black and white, and that queuing is considered an amusing Anglo-Saxon quirk in many other countries besides Switzerland. I knew that these slippages and collisions were matters of cultural difference and not grounds for criticism: the individualism, the introversion with which people went about their lives; the avoidance of interactions on which small courtesies depend; the many occasions on which someone pushed me and I felt assaulted. But they affected me.

You can't get upset every time this happens, Shaun said, for such things happened often. You need a thicker skin, he added, and although it was made lightly, to buck me up, that comment shocked me because it was true. If I were to find a modus vivendi amongst these people, I might have to change who I was. That had not occurred to me before. But I didn't want a thicker skin: I didn't want to get used to behaviour that, whether or not it was socially acceptable, I experienced as selfish or unfair, or rude, or aggressive. I wanted to be me.

London, briefly. Blue sky, fast clouds. I was walking along Aldgate High Street, the City ahead: I marvelled at its curves and edges and latent shards that I'd seen a hundred or a thousand times before. The dusty pavement, the old unmuffled throttle of buses. Sacks of refuse clustered around lamp posts. Snatches of my language. A sheer sense of being alive – and not a leaf in sight, not the faintest daub of chlorophyll. My shoulders felt oddly loose, and I was breathing freely amongst the traffic fumes. I'd grown used to being tense, I realised then: at some point since our move to Switzerland, tension had become second nature.

A man hurried past me, brushing my elbow. I'm so sorry, he said, slowing his pace. Thank you, I replied. He stopped: he looked as surprised as I felt by what I had said. It must have sounded sarcastic. I'm so sorry, I explained, I live abroad, I've only been back for a couple of hours, you were so polite – I'm not used to it. Sorry, you just took me by surprise. In a very nice way.

I stopped at a supermarket for oatcakes and a newspaper, two things for which I longed in Switzerland. It's so nice to see you, the cashier told me as I was paying. Do you know, you're the happiest person I've served all day.

I'm happy to be here, I said.

Facing our apartment building, on the other side of the street, was an imposing fin-de-siècle house with a small garden. A high privet hedge screened it from the road, but from our third-floor window I could see into the grassed space within. Every Monday morning, just before eight, a minibus delivered three gardeners to the property. They were armed with state-of-the-art machinery, and in a fuming roar they trimmed hedging that had not had time to grow, blew unseen leaves from the driveway, strimmed and mowed where they had recently strimmed and mowed, as though they were fellow sufferers of some compulsive affliction. And when I saw gardeners at work in the city and its suburbs and its endless grey dormitories they were cutting things down, clipping things back, applying herbicide or insecticide or sweeping, sweeping. Curbing and controlling the visible signs of growth and fall, battling the cycles of the natural world, its threat of untidiness or of who knows what. The forest, perhaps. The foreign.

Of course gardeners must lop and prune: if they don't, paradise will grow to wilderness and the garden will be no more. 'Tending' or inclining 'to wild' (Eve's words) is what gardens do: it is in their very nature. It is also in the nature of gardens that, apart from that first mythical garden made by God, they are made – enclosed and designed and shaped and planted – and gardened by people.

It's an imprecise relationship. Cutting things back stimulates stronger and denser growth than would happen in the
wild. Deadheading is an unnatural intervention that prolongs
flowering. I love the geometry of clipped box – a solid green
underlining, or a ball (or three, or eleven) lending structure and
depth, punctuating a space like a well-wrought text. Gardening
is human involvement with the natural world, a complex thing
that affirms life and is full of compromise. 'Involve': a word with
roots of rolling into (Latin, *involvere*) and medieval growth rings
of entanglement, enfolding, envelopment.

But the gardening that I now observed around me seemed
grimly unilateral, focused on containing or in some way con-
quering the very life of that natural world. Tidying it away, as
a good *Hausfrau* orders her home and her self. A perfectionism
that allowed nothing to flourish or be slightly untidy, as living,
growing things cannot help but be. These immaculate, functional spaces with their place for barbecuing, their place for sitting,
their well-presented patch of grass and maybe a swimming pool
were the antithesis of paradise, its 'fragrant' and 'fertile earth',
its 'odorous bushy shrub[s]' and 'beauteous' flowers of 'all hues'.
Its wanton growth and honeydew, its propensity for wildness.
Its flourishing imperfection (the word 'flourish' grows from the
root of 'flower'). If a garden were perfect it would be a lifeless
space and not, therefore, a garden at all.

Gartenpflege, I read on the side of the prepunctual minibus.
That word again: *pflegen*, a verb with a chill. To care without
necessarily caring. To show people that you care. To show someone or something to be well kept. When I was that child on her
doorstep with hair that stuck out every which way and traces of
the woods beneath my nails, Mrs Tanner doubtless thought of

me as *ungepflegt*, uncared for, which would mean not that I was neglected in any human way but that I was untidy, unpresentable. She'd say the same today of my unmanicured gardener's hands. Susanna, her every hair in place with that mysteriously small clip, was, like her parents' lawn, *gepflegt* to within an inch of her life. *Pflegen* is a long way from tending, as Eve tends her garden and my mother tended hers.

You know that you should take more care of your hands – they are not, after all, getting any younger – and sometimes you put on a pair of Marigolds before going out to do some weeding, or whatever else the garden might lead you to do while you are there. The gloves smell foul, especially when they are new, and they asphyxiate your skin. You remove them in order to inspect an unfurling bud, or to handle a delicate seedling, and your skin thrills to the cold spring light, and before you know it your hands are in the soil. Where they belong.

If you only had a garden now.

What, I wondered at the window of our flat, if a daisy should crop up in that homogenised lawn beyond the privet hedge? It would be noticed, probably, and dealt with long before it could form a bud and the bud open – but what if it did just manage to bloom? Might someone, noticing that lone wild flower, look and marvel at its crisp geometry? See a heaven in it, as Blake did? Or would they fetch a knife and gouge the weed out, or complain to one of the three gardeners? Would they ever know that each of those small white petals was in fact an individual flower?

I once dug up a lawn, so great was my need to grow plants. Shaun and I had moved to a terraced house in a part of Cambridge that estate agents describe as 'vibrant' and was intensely urban. It had a tiny walled garden that, but for a diminutive patio and a path, was laid entirely to grass. It was a garden and a paradise – for each of these words at root means nothing more than a space enclosed by a fence or a wall. 'Yard' and 'garden' grew out of Old-English and Indo-European words for 'fence'; 'paradise' appears to have begun, in Ancient Persian, with *pairi*, walling or constructing 'around'. But the roots of words are one thing and what you mean by 'garden' another. Ask twenty people what they think a garden is and you'll get eighteen different opinions and one or two don't knows. Like the word 'home', I know what I mean by 'garden' but cannot wholly articulate it. A garden involves soil and roots and green, growth and decay and growth again. It involves me in those things.

From the kitchen window I looked out at the walled grassed space, the empty little paradise, and thought aloud about shrubs and perennials. Shaun observed that there was plenty of space on the patio for pots, and I dropped the subject.

One March day, when Shaun was at work and I was working from home, I dug up the lawn. It must have been a calculated act, though I do not recall it as such. I fetched a spade and began to dig. Once I started slicing under the matted roots, shaking back the soil as I piled up sections of turf, the lawn's small area translated into a voluminous mound. Shaun rang to say hello, as he always did, and to ask how my day was going. I burned with shame. Fine, thanks, I said, I'm just taking a break, pottering outside for a bit. I resumed my digging – there was no going back – and when I'd finished I started to panic. I rifled through the Yellow Pages, and within the hour two men appeared with a flatbed truck and spirited the turf away for a sum of cash. What remained was the muddy gravelled path flanked by two areas of bare earth. The larger patch, too wide to manage from the path alone, was broken by a residual grass dog-leg. It was a mess. We'd just moved into our new home, and I had decimated the garden. I rang my father to tell him what I had done. You did what? I dug up the lawn: there was nowhere to grow anything. What does Shaun think? He doesn't know. The idea was sound, my father decided, and we both thought my mother would have agreed, but I'd gone about it in a high-handed and insensitive way. It was Shaun's garden too: what would he say when he came home?

Shaun came home. You dug up my lawn, he said.

Not entirely, I corrected him, facetiously. I had not paused to reflect that Shaun may have liked having a lawn, nor that he would undoubtedly have agreed to a border or two at its edges. We were the team and I had gone it alone. It was not a pleasant feeling.

That said, the lawn had to go.

My father rang the next morning: had I thought about putting in some dwarf box? The garden was so small, and a box edge would give the new borders some definition – not that they bordered the garden, he gathered, so much as constituted it. Three cuttings from my mother's anisodontea had pulled through the winter and were growing fast: he'd bring one of them when he next visited, and he thought he could spare a felicia. I should have a piece of Mr Burton's geranium. We ought to get around to looking up its proper name – it had been in the garden for over forty years now. Some new seedlings were doing well in the spare bedroom – another cosmos variety, and a penstemon that had intrigued him; I could have some of those too, when they were ready. And shouldn't we take a drive out to that perennial nursery on the other side of Essex? We could have a pub lunch while we were at it. We might find the viola that my mother had loved and that disappeared one night. 'Lorna Moakes', creamy-yellow petals outlined with purple: I remembered deadheading it in those last weeks when my mother could not. More recently I'd seen the label, printed in her clear hand, tucked with pens and bits and pieces into a pot on my father's kitchen window sill, awaiting a new plant to mark.

I would fill that space with more growing things than you'd believe it could possibly hold. Its tiny dimensions would become infinite with life and growth. Shaun, with his own propensity for tending green spaces, would clip the young box plants as they grew and merged to a crisp green outline. For my birthday my father would give me another encyclopaedia of garden plants, newly revised and expanded into two splendid volumes. I'd learn from it that Mr Burton's geranium was *Geranium* x *magnificum*. And the penstemon would thrive in ways of which my father could not have dreamed when he pricked out those first seedlings and grew them on in the bright greenhouse at the end of his garden.

An October afternoon, the clocks fallen back overnight. I might have dreamed this landscape. The mountains were no longer a denticulate backdrop that came and went and rose and fell, but a new world that spread around us as we walked above the treeline into the falling sun. Rock browns and greys, the grass shades of buff. An air of violet and blue. The sky was azure as the grass pea. Crags and peaks and dips and craters dusted and infilled with snow. Our path led through sodden-frozen alpine moorland, ice giving way to adhesive mud where contours caught the sun, the mud mashed with snow as we passed into deep-blue shade. Pure sound: water running around and beneath, springs and streams and thawed snow, the high lonely air like a seashell held to an ear. The snow had been softened by day and frozen by night, worked and reworked into scales that glittered like a fishmonger's floor: they rustled heavily when I dragged the tip of a walking pole through their accumulations. The snow was every colour but white. It was not autumn up here, nor early winter. These heights had a season all of their own.

Shaun saw the first gentian in wiry grass at the path's soggy edge: three stars of utter blue, a blue that my eye craves because it is seldom to be found. Maybe it does not exist at all, for what is colour but reflected light? My mother knew what I meant when I talked to her about gentians at the garden table on that precious afternoon. A bottomless blue, deeper than Odilon Redon's *Mystical Boat*, a pastel drawing that I love. I've never understood why pale, old-lady colours are referred to as pastel shades. Pastels are as rich and delicious to the eye as they are to a hand that strikes them through fibrous paper, or to a smudging, blending fingertip. They are the colours of a cobalt-blue boat with a yellow sail on a sea-green sea. Of anemone reds and poppy flames and rudbeckia golds and leaf greens and delphinium blues in vase after cobalt vase of Redon's flowers.

Once, in a garden centre, thinking about my mother, I bought two spring gentians (*Gentiana verna*) and planted them in our Cambridge garden where the lawn used to be. For weeks they did little, and then they yellowed and browned back to the earth. Gentians have a reputation for being fickle or 'difficult', but there was no horticultural reason for not trying again: after all, this alpine perennial once made itself at home in southern England, far from its elevated habitat. Britain's wild populations have long since retreated to Upper Teesdale – but in 1597 the herbalist John Gerard wrote in *The Herball or Generall Historie of Plantes* that the species grew 'plentifully' in southern England from Salisbury Plain to Hertfordshire to the Sussex Weald, and that its flowers were 'perfect blew'. '*[P]erfect blue*', echoed Culpeper in the 1653 expanded edition of his own herbal, adding Kent and Bedfordshire to the list with special mention of 'a piece of wast Chalky ground as you go out of *Dunstable way* towards *Gorhambury*'. With a little more care and some coarse grit I might well have persuaded gentians to grow in Cambridge. But I found that I no longer wanted to try.

Gardeners are only human, and every gardener has now and then, in ignorance or zeal, asked a plant to grow in a place to which it is unsuited and to which it will never adapt. In my first garden I planted lavender in partial sun, which is to say partial shade, where its silvered spikes grew green and weak. Delphiniums in fast-draining soil, because for as long as I could remember I had coveted their shimmering blue spires: I became a slave to their unquenchable thirst, watered them morning and evening, worried about them if we went away, and still they would not grow upwards; the slugs got their sorry, straggling forms in the end. Then there was the exotic, purple-flowered solanum that I could not resist on a market stall: it died, as I knew it would, at the first prickling of frost. The hydrangea that I once dosed with ferric sulphate in order that it might bloom blue when, in our soil that deep down met Cambridge chalk, it inclined naturally to pink. I only did that once, for when I thought about it later I was vaguely ashamed, as though reminded or informed of something I'd said at a dinner party the night before – and in due course the hydrangea shaded back from blue through lilac to a serviceable salmon.

I had come to feel that the gentian did not belong in low-lying Cambridge, but somewhere high and abstract. On a mountain – and mountains were unreal to me, for at the time I had only ever been to a Munro – or in an idea. A conversation with my mother.

All those years later, on the mountain path in eastern Switzerland, I understood. Shaun's first gentian led us amongst constellations of utter blue. Not the spring gentian – it was too late or too early in the mountain's own season – but the Bavarian gentian, *Gentiana bavarica*. In some places its petals were darkly iridescent, violet on something more than cobalt. Struck by sun their colour was indefinable as light reflected by water. They were at home, calibrated exquisitely to those further reaches of exposure and altitude, and it struck me then as unfair that a plant should be labelled difficult, somehow at fault, because a gardener has tried to make it grow out of its element. Gentian blue is out of place in a city garden six metres above sea level. It is an ephemeral blue. A blue of extremes.

A blue that you think you know but of which, like utterness, you can never be sure. In any case blue is the colour in which we see gentians and not the colour that they are. Colour is not intrinsic to a flower or to anything: it is the work of light and perception and variables, a wavelength bounced from the surface of an object to the retina and interpreted by the brain. A colour may be another shade for you than it is for me, though we will never know for certain. When I tell you about a scarlet pieris shoot or an indigo aquilegia, I'm telling you how I see these things and not necessarily how they are.

It is hopeless to photograph gentians, for the camera's way of seeing will homogenise that fugitive blue. If you truly want to see a gentian you must go to the frozen-running mountain moor. You must let your mind's eye look long and hard, there in the high-pitched air and falling western light, and then you must leave it be – for the gentian belongs there, and you do not.

Somebody's wife insisted on a palm tree for their Zurich terrace, so they paid an enterprising firm to collect it once a year and store it through the city's cold damp winters. Someone else carpeted their garden with AstroTurf: it required less maintenance than grass, they told us, the colour was close enough, and they didn't like plants very much. From October to May, in private and public gardens around the city, the prestigious tender forms of tree ferns and giant grasses were replaced by amorphous fleece-wrapped packages that made me think of winding sheets. Sometimes they were tied with twine in several places, like murder victims in films. It bemused me that you might choose to look at something like that for half the year when a hardy tree or shrub would sing the seasons before your eyes and grace your winter with a stark, lovely form. An amelanchier, its bare branches flowing like a charcoal sketch, or a hornbeam twisting with implicit life.

And then, to one side of a block of flats or in a tiny green garden that stopped me every time I walked down the hill, I'd glimpse grass in which primroses had spread themselves unchecked, and I would know that my world was still there, somewhere, in the cracks of the hard grey city.

*

Shaun's inscription in my *Flora Helvetica,* his wish for many happy years of gardening in Switzerland, was prescient – and not just in his conviction that I'd one day have a garden here. Indeed, as those early days in the white-walled flat became months, years, I sometimes feared that I might never have a garden again. Something else was going on, and only later would I understand what it was.

In this encyclopaedia of native or 'wild' flowers, Shaun had given me the key to my education as a gardener. It took me to a place, in the hills and in my heart, where a plant was neither a garden plant, nor a wild plant, but a plant. I'd known that deep down since those early childhood mornings when, in a garden that would be there forever, or so I then believed, I attended to a dog rose in the hornbeam hedge.

And *Flora Helvetica,* the plants in their native soil and the book of those plants, connected me with the things of life. They showed me my way out of the city: the way to my garden.

To the Wooded Hill

The path was chalky now, cool and damp through the steep forest. Beech, field maple, hazel, hornbeam: shades of green on green. Fullest greens, the weight of summer behind them, vivid with far-above sun. It was the end of August, time for Japanese anemones. For reddening sedums and fleeting colchicums. The season looking forward.

We followed the path uphill between limestone cliffs, each step slipping on the soft greasy rock. A chalk stream rushed and tripped and fell towards us, first on one side and then on the other. I'd love, I told Shaun, to live within earshot of moving water. In places where the rocks thinned and the stream deepened, I looked into the water and thought it still. The water's special clarity over chalk: an idea of blue. Springs fed the stream or branched out on their own. Trees were rooted improbably on the sheer limestone sides, firs darkening towards the top. '[A]nd over head up grew/Insuperable highth of loftiest shade': Milton's green words came into my mind, and stuck.

The air stirring cool around the stream, the smell of being amongst trees. The green light and surround sound, water and birds and something else. There were hart's tongue ferns and liverworts, mosses glowing in half-light. Inky palmate leaves that surely belonged to a hellebore – though their leaflets were finer than those of the plant I had entrusted to Fran. I walked past a cluster of tiny harebells in a shaft of mossy light, and Shaun called me back to look.

The 'high-climbing hill' – Milton again – the hill that climbs high, the hill that is high to climb, the hill that you climb high: any and all of these.

We climbed steadily with the path for some while – you do not want to know the time when you are walking in woods – and at some point I noticed that hornbeam had disappeared from the deciduous weave. Hornbeam does not like altitude. There were more firs now and, where the trees thinned in places, montanas or mountain cornflowers: *Flora Helvetica* had told me I would find them here and so I did, blue-violet on limestone in pools of light and bright, bright clearings.

Out of the forest and into a new dimension. The sun strong on my skin though the air was cool. It starkened and defined in the way of late-summer sun, the sky deep, the shadows absolute, the light clear as old amber. The soundscape changed instantly. A chirping, a ringing, an echoing, a pleasant shrill: stridulation, the immersive sound of crickets that you do not hear at once, but of which you become aware. There were chalkhill blue butterflies, far from the South Downs. And a meadow slope gently alight with colchicums or autumn crocuses, their chalk-pink goblets brimful of the day and marvellous.

I once planted colchicums in our Cambridge garden, a bare handful for the bulbs were not cheap. In September the flowers appeared on tender whitish stems that buckled within a day or two: it was easy to miss their moment and find that they had been and gone, their forms collapsed like broken butterflies. There was something incomplete about them, for unlike most flowers their stems did not emerge from foliage but pushed themselves up from bare soil, as though they had forgotten something or were not quite ready for the world. The flowers of *Colchicum autumnale* seldom appear at the same time as their leaves, which is why in Britain they are commonly known as naked ladies. I was ambivalent about them precisely because they seemed so incomplete, so, well, naked – but that was my problem, a gardener's problem, and not theirs. For I now discovered that colchicums, left to their own devices, will clothe themselves with grass and light up a meadow, fleetingly complete.

Those flowers, hundreds of them, wild, raised as though they drank the sun's health, their moment intersecting with ours: that too was a benediction.

We were deep amongst the mountains of the Jura, a region of limestone and marl that arcs around the north-west of Switzerland and shares a border and geology with France. Its fossil-rich limestone defined the Jurassic geological period that, thanks to Stephen Spielberg, lay people like me associate with the diplodocus and stegosaurus – and its crests and ranges date from the earliest phase of the upheaval that gave rise to the Alps. The Victorian art critic and writer John Ruskin put it rather more poetically when he recalled a captivating moment during a stay in the French Jura:

> *It is a spot which has all the solemnity, with none of the savageness, of the Alps; where there is a sense of a great power beginning to be manifested in the earth, and of a deep and majestic concord in the rise of the long low lines*

of piny hills; the first utterance of those mighty mountain
symphonies, soon to be more loudly lifted and wildly broken
along the battlements of the Alps. But their strength is as yet
restrained . . .

The name 'Jura' originates in a Celtic word for 'forested mountain': unlike their younger Alpine cousins that peak far above the treeline, the altitude beyond which trees will not grow, the Jura's more modest ridges are densely forested. They may not be lofty (the highest point is 1,700 metres), but their sides are steep: the Jura is settled and cultivated in the lower reaches of valleys and on high plateaus, with tree-thick gradients in between. The little old mountains, wooded hills.

The path levelled off in high pasture cleared from dense firs, the grass in sun against evergreen. *Pâturages*: we were in French-speaking Switzerland now. The clearings were nuanced artfully: specimen trees had been left to grow here and there, and heavier scatterings muted the boundaries of pasture with forest. That phasing made me think of old country estates, their contrived naturalism – but while I have never cared much for parkland there was something profoundly pleasing about these spaces shaped from the woods. Two horses approached us, bays of around fifteen hands, their heads nodding hospitably in time with their pace. One curled a velour upper lip to investigate my hand, the other rubbed its head against my arm, shoving me sideways, and settled down to chew my hair. I was nine years old again, the grain of my fingertips picked out by silty horsehair oils. The smell of horses is a friendly smell, I thought then and still do. If these animals had a stable it was green as this pasture – whinnying and green, like the one in Dylan Thomas's bittersweet paradise:

So it must have been after the birth of the simple light
In the first, spinning place, the spellbound horses walking warm
  Out of the whinnying green stable
    On to the fields of praise.

Later we descended amongst hundreds or thousands of dark firs on a narrow path from which the hill fell sheer away. The trees grew out of the precipitous slope and reached straight up for the light, roots perpendicular to their slender stretching trunks. My feet dropped down in a steady rhythm that I knew I must maintain. But my head did not keep pace, and the infinite verticals tilted, and I thought I was falling because I could not see and the resonant green chatter had risen to a high-pitched tinnitus. I stopped, my insides tumbling and ringing still, and the forest slowly pulled itself back into focus though the trees would not right themselves entirely until my feet had reached the bottom.

Fir trees clinging to rock. Birdsong all around, the birds unseen like angels. The path flanked by foliage that I knew from elsewhere. More of those hellebores, in great drifts this time, and the evergreen rosettes of wood spurge, *Euphorbia amygdaloides;* their green torch-like flower heads had burned themselves out weeks before. Late-summer notes of the Sussex garden, dark glinting leaf forms, amplified in this steep faraway forest to abundance that beggared belief.

The forest had resumed its chattering silence. Time seemed far away.

We came to the river, the trees upright and deciduous again, hornbeam brightening the canopy. Ahead a whitewashed, red-roofed church, its tower neatly gabled, sat birdlike amongst a clutch of matching houses. As we entered the village a garden bank was buoyant with anemones, their faces open to the falling sun. Japanese anemones may not take kindly to transplantation, but if they decide in due course that their soil and aspect agree with them their fibrous tangly roots will spread with permanent intent and colonise that place, make it their own. And just as they were at home in that cherished corner of Sussex clay the anemones were in their element here too, on the sloping Jura limestone. Plants with whose roots my own were entwined, flourishing here, at home.

It wasn't just the plants. It was the day, the place. The little old mountains that drew you in amongst themselves. Their ruggedness. Their unsublime greenness. The landscape's human dimensions, the spaces cleared into the woods for grazing and farming and living and growing. The horses in their tree-walled paradise. It was unlike any place that I had known. I was happy, I told Shaun, there and then.

I could live here, one of us said.

A poster appeared at our local tram stop. It stopped me dead as I went to post a letter. The crude style of the black-and-white-and-red graphics was something that I associated with history books and did not expect to see on the street where I lived: it bothered me before I had grasped its agenda. A black tree, archetypal and sinister. A few branches bore red apples, but the poster centred on a nightmarish claw of roots with the shape of Switzerland in their grip. The country, red and white-crossed like its flag, was cracking and fissuring amongst the pernicious black roots. *Masslosigkeit schadet!* the poster shrilled: Immoderation is damaging Switzerland! *Masseneinwanderung stoppen*: Stop mass immigration.

A referendum was coming up. Switzerland was to vote on a populist initiative to restrict immigration, and the black roots gripping the shattered red country were not only an abstract menace, nor a tide of displaced humanity from further afield, but also people like Shaun and me. Suddenly the poster was everywhere, in stations and on billboards and on roadside hoardings. The tree turned up on campaign flyers in our mailbox, even though we had no right to vote and the initiative was directed, inter alia, against us.

In a stock image that the populist campaigners put out from time to time, a white sheep (sometimes more than one) kicks a black sheep off the red, white-crossed flag. The kick is a multipurpose backward buck: in the act of kicking the black sheep off Swiss ground, the white sheep turns its back on the generic foreigner and slips in, for good measure, an insult of the highest order for people of Middle-Eastern origin: showing someone the sole of your foot, ungulate or otherwise. It is not a pleasant image to encounter when you are walking down your street or waiting for a tram or train, and however many times you see it you are shocked because, where you come from, such things would never make it into the public realm. I am glad I was not in the country around the time of the referendum that resulted in a ban on minaret construction. The poster for that campaign featured the red Swiss flag spiked with black minaret-shaped warheads and, looming in the foreground, a sinister black burqa-clad figure. The conflation was far from edifying.

There was something crude about the new tree image. Roots have rich figurative possibilities: they can signify origins and etymologies; connote belonging, connection, emplacement, enracination (there's a word). But if you are going to use these possibilities to make a point, your image or metaphor ought to acknowledge what roots are and what they do – and whoever was behind this publicity campaign seemed not to care. When roots break things up – pavements, foundations – they do so from underground. These root-claws, oddly, behaved like a JCB grabber. They dangled the shattered country in mid-air, a medium in which roots do not belong: they look wrong, as an uprooted plant looks wrong and an uprooted person feels wrong. It was a mixed metaphor, a scattergun offensive of visual and verbal associations. Immoderation! Foreigners! Roots! Evil! Claws! Our country in foreign claws! Our flag in pieces! Our country shattered! Our red fruit poisoned! Our country stolen! Black! Other! Root of evil! Mass immigration! The poster did not want to make sense: its mission was to scare you, whenever you encountered the idea of immigration, into reading or hearing or thinking 'mass immigration'.

It succeeded. A great many voters opposed the initiative, but a majority voted for the restrictions. The result saddened me, and gave substance to my feeling that we were not especially welcome here. It is one thing to feel out of place, a bit of a black sheep – alienated – and another to learn that there are some objective grounds for that feeling: that more than a few people really do consider you an alien. And I wondered what it must be like for those against whom the most specific graphic extremes – burqas, soles of feet – were directed.

For the first time I thought about what Shaun and I had done.

We had uprooted our life so lightly, assumed – presumed – that with time and effort we could make ourselves at home abroad, because people are people (aren't they?). A fact had placed itself in my way. I'd evaded it for a while in my fragile over-enthusiasm, my slightly manic efforts to build a life amongst new people, but now it was there, inescapable: you can want very badly to integrate, try as hard as you can, but you cannot make yourself welcome somewhere. That is up to the people in whose midst you have arrived.

Essex. A hornbeam hedge, the colour of early summer. Aquilegias. Anemones, heaping up green for August. My father's penstemon, bronzed clumps and clumps of it. Irish Blue, slaty pale against golden brick. The colours' conversation: you could almost think that the wall had been built for the geranium, or that the geranium bloomed, that day at least, solely for the wall. The sun moving on, slanting now through the hornbeam leaves. Their pure green brightness. Frida's garden.

I postulated the hornbeam hedge years ago, when our friends Tom and Frida moved house and invited my opinion about the garden. I thought it needed a hornbeam hedge and was thrilled when they planted one. I passed on pieces of perennials, and when Shaun and I left London for Zurich I filled the boot of Frida's car with plants that had grown, not so long ago, in my parents' garden. It was a sunny April afternoon, and before we loaded up the pots we had tea and Bakewell tart in the garden that would shortly cease to be mine.

Pieces of the garden. I'll do my best, Frida said.

It's one thing to give a friend a box of stuff for safekeeping, another to give that friend a carload of plants and an obligation to keep them alive. Unlike books and crockery, plants put down roots: they do not sit in someone's garage, they grow in someone's garden. They belong to your friend now, as they belonged – the tense is misleading, for in your heart you never let them go – to you and to your parents. One day, you hope, you will come back to take cuttings and divisions for another garden of your own, and when you do the plants will deepen those human connections. For the need to get bits of plants about which you care into the gardens of people about whom you care is as strong as the need to conserve and perpetuate that plant. It's a powerful need, part and parcel – for you at least – of being a gardener. Your friend may not be aware of the plant's back story – that your widowed father, himself terminally ill, grew the penstemon from seed because your mother had loved penstemons; that your parents' garden began with the Japanese anemone and *Geranium* x *magnificum*, and that these plants enchanted you when you were small, helped make a gardener of you; that the geranium came from the garden of a man called Mr Burton who had his own untold story; that the anemones were blooming on the last day that you gardened with your mother. And that is not the point, for you want your friend to appreciate the plant in his or her own new way and the story is there anyway, alive and growing in the plant's green memory.

Maybe you never really own a plant. Maybe plants do not belong to you but rather take root in your life. To what extent, I wonder, can you really own a living thing?

I did not know what to think when I walked through Frida's house after too long away, out into the garden, going in by going out. Here were plants from the garden that I visited on sleepless Zurich nights, imagined in an earthy garden of my own. They

were in their place, multiplied and vigorous – Frida was free
with the spade or carving knife, or whatever implement she used
to divide them – as if they had grown here since time immemo-
rial. It warmed my heart to see them mature and at home in her
garden, tended wonderfully, but the joy that I felt was weighted
with regret. I thought about the time that had passed since I
potted up those plants, a rootless time. I thought about how
familiar they were, how precious, and how they nevertheless had
so little, now, to do with me. It was not my garden. And I had
no soil in which to grow them myself.

It is not for me to say that the people amongst whom I now
found myself were humourless, for humour is a culturally sen-
sitive faculty, apt to be lost or worse in translation – and in
Switzerland I was not only on the wrong side of a vast cultural
hiatus, I did not understand a word of dialect. There was plenty
of laughter within our small household, but I found little in
my dealings with the world beyond – certainly not over rigid
lunches, nor at strictly configured dinner tables. Out and about
amongst people, moreover, in cafés and shops and trams, on
pavements, the stairs to our flat, I could not help feeling that
many took themselves more seriously than they needed to – and
it had nothing to do with cracking jokes. It had to do with that
single-mindedness, that avoidance of incidental interaction – of
minor courtesies and pleasantries, considerateness – as though
people would prefer other people not to exist. I felt that one of
life's dimensions had been closed down, or never opened up,
and it affected me like greyness itself.

Ahmed, who ran a small Moroccan restaurant on our street,
felt it too. You two eat up my food, he said to Shaun and me one

evening, you talk to each other, you laugh. Not many people do that around here: these people seem afraid to enjoy their lives. Ahmed himself nipped back to Morocco once a month: he'd go nuts otherwise, he said.

Then I injured a knee in an accident that ended my brief and troubled skiing career. Following surgery to reconstruct the joint, my rehabilitation programme included a course of hydro-therapy that I resented because I dislike swimming pools as deeply as I love the sea. It is not uncommon for one language to lift words and source catchphrases from another – but context is everything, and my hydrotherapy class had the dubious title of 'Wet Vest'. In practice it was a far cry from the antics of Butlins or *Hi-de-Hi!*. The garment in question was no T-shirt, but a buoyancy vest with a flap that you pulled down over your rear and fastened back over your stomach, such that you appeared to be wearing a huge nappy. Then you hopped on your crutches down a ramp, and when everyone was safely in the pool the floor was removed from beneath your feet to leave you dangling upright in the water. The dropping floor was disconcerting, for your body never quite forgets a close call in a river. Thus sus-pended you would circuit the pool, limping through the water, while a physiotherapist barked orders like a ringmaster. Clock-wise. Long strides. Anti-clockwise. Bicycle legs. *Why am I not moving?* Frau Lynch, you are not moving. I know. You must use your legs more, Frau Lynch. I am trying. You must pretend that you are pedalling, Frau Lynch. I am trying. You must try harder, Frau Lynch. *I am TRYING, for Christ's sake.* I am TRYING. *Why am I not moving?* Why am I not moving?

But I disliked the Wet Vest class above all because there was no camaraderie: far from it. There were seven or eight of us, lurching and bobbing in a way that brought Teletubbies to mind. Where I came from it would be impossible for a group of people in that collective undignified state to avoid a modicum of interaction. At the very least there would be some hellos or all rights? A nod or two, a quip. One person would enquire where another lived (had he or she travelled far?), and there might be an exchange of war stories – accidents, operations. Some cursory discussion of the weather, for talking about the weather is how you engage with people you do not know in incidental situations. Show goodwill. Acknowledge their existence. Acknowledge your shared existence.

The pool culture here was otherwise. Everyone greeted the physiotherapist, of course. One or two said good morning to each other and, when I forced the issue, to me – but most did not. It was the oddest atmosphere, a kind of stony respectiveness, as if everyone were trying to pretend either that they were not there, or that everyone else was not there. Now for the catwalk, I said as I fastened my nappy-vest for the first class, feeling smug that I knew the German word, *Laufsteg*. A young man of similar attire scowled, and my other classmates stared into one middle distance or another. I enjoyed one further interaction in that first class, with an older woman who tailgated me as I floundered around the pool. I was holding her up because she was stronger than I and my bicycle legs were not working; I could hear her muttering, and was sure I could feel her breath on my neck through the splashing water. Please just overtake me, I said to her in the end. She paused to look daggers at me, and then she thrashed and harrumphed her way past, sorely inconvenienced.

One day, when I emerged from the changing cubicle, a

woman I had not seen before was adjusting her Wet Vest. Propped on our crutches, we cast an appraising eye over each other's outfit and began to giggle and could not stop. Our class-mates were unamused. Other than with Shaun, I hadn't laughed for quite some time. I could not remember when: a few weeks back, perhaps, on the phone to Fran in England.

After the class we hobbled together to the clinic canteen, where the salad bar was not yet priced by weight and Ingrid subversively added garnishes reserved for the set menu. We continued our conversation two days later, finding our feet on the exercise bikes, and by the time we had hopped and limped and eaten and pedalled and walked our way out of the rehab programme I found that I had made a friend.

Ingrid is a spirited woman with a demanding career and a cheerful home filled with children and dogs; visitors to her house are urged to keep their shoes on in case they should dirty their feet. I warmed to her reflectiveness and her sense of absurd-ity – and back then our brief shared history was absurd enough. After sustaining a similar injury, Ingrid had been airlifted off her mountain; I had been sent down mine in a cable car with five laden refuse bins, and had hitched a lift to the village centre in a passing gas-delivery truck. I'd then driven back to Zurich and gone about my life for a fortnight, manipulating my detached kneecap into place every few steps. We both found this very funny. Even the doctor had laughed when, after Shaun had lost patience, I finally made an appointment. There's nothing wrong, I said – I'd practised for the walk from the waiting room – my husband is over-solicitous. In Ingrid's company I felt something like my old self, and that gave me pause – for only then did I realise that I'd grown accustomed to uncertainty and self-censorship when I was around Swiss people. Not being myself was about much more than being, on paper, a foreign housewife of no specific religion.

I was finding it harder, these days, to conceal from myself a feeling that I can only describe as a kind of dread. I thought I was lonely because I was often on my own, but that was not, I now see, entirely the case. Looking back, I had to do with more people than I realised at the time – but more often than not I felt lonely with or amongst them, lonelier than when I was alone. I longed to be in a place where people thrown together in a situation – a hydrotherapy class, say, or a delayed train, not that trains in Switzerland were often delayed – might exchange a look, or talk about the weather, or indulge in a spot of jocularity. Acknowledge one another's existence.

There was a spate of small incidents involving friends who visited us from home and abroad – though these days home itself was abroad, wherever that might be: England abroad from Switzerland, Switzerland simply abroad.

Frida, a woman capable of magnificent or, if you happen to be its object, terrifying assertiveness, accompanied me to the market one morning and left minutes later to join Tom, who had already disappeared. She was sorry to leave me to buy the salad things alone, she said, but she could not cope with the pushing and aggression: the way people behaved in this place was unfuckingbelievable. Tom had gone to find a bench by the lake, and they would wait for me there.

Another friend was crushed against a wall in a famous coffee house while believing herself to be queuing for the Ladies. We never established precisely what happened, but when she had collected herself Julia found that she was waiting behind two additional women, savagely lipsticked and of a certain age. I'd probably fallen foul of them myself, in the market. Julia reported that their handbags were very expensive indeed.

A sweet-natured seven-year-old burst into tears as we returned from an afternoon of sightseeing in the city: I want to go home! We are going home, said Fran, her mother, Beth is going to cook some pasta when we get in. NO! the little girl roared, I want to go HOME. TO ENGLAND. NOW. So do I, I told her from the bottom of my heart. So do I.

I no longer knew where home was – Sussex emptied of the people who had made home home, our house in London sold – but I knew it was contoured to the garden that I carried within myself. I thought it might have some kind of hornbeam hedge. A dog rose too, perhaps, or a spindle tree.

I had that dull, detached feeling that comes with an early start and too much sugar. It had snowed overnight, and when I left in darkness for the airport our drab street had become an other-worldly cliché of atmospheric lamplight and creaking powder. When I was a child I did not enjoy *The Lion, the Witch and the Wardrobe* as much as I suspected I ought, but the lamp post in the snow captured my imagination: I can see the line drawing now, embedded in the text of a fifties paperback that smelled of browning pages.

The Alps were inky forms to the south as the plane climbed out of Zurich: I only saw them because I knew where to look. I slept through the sunrise and woke over northern France, its unfenced planes of tone and texture. And then, at last, the sea: I'd missed the sea. And then an accumulating coastline, its coordinates stretching and shifting with my aerial vantage point: the harbour walls of Dover or Folkestone; the triangular beak of Dungeness; Eastbourne or Brighton glittering away as the plane dipped inland. The sea and the free sea light. The edge of home: the edge of England, and the edge of the landscape of my childhood. It made my heart sing and it made my heart heavy, for I was not going home: I was on my way to visit friends and family, and I had a return ticket.

I had never seen Dungeness from the air before, though I'd flown across the English Channel many times. Maybe the ness had always been obscured by cloud or haze, or I had just not noticed it – though I always looked out of the window as we descended into London, reassured myself that everything was still there. Maybe the flight path had changed. Whatever the case, I now saw for the first time the shore's sweep from Romney Marsh to a great shingle point – what geographers term cuspate foreland. On that sea-bright winter morning the ness was almost equilateral: it looked man-made though it was the work of waves. The tip was dun, the colour of barrenness, and I could see the hulk of the nuclear reactor, the long straight sea road, the sprawling cottages.

Winchelsea Beach, further west around Rye Bay, is where my family went for air and driftwood, hag stones and headspace. At high tide the beach is a ridge of shingle, of a piece with the ness and hatched with breakwaters washed and weathered to an age beyond their years. It is strewn with flotsam and jetsam and blotched with blue-green crambes or sea kale. When the tide turns it recedes indefinitely. The brown sand is textured by waves that leave something of themselves in scalloped runnels, and as you splatter though the surface water you will always, somewhere, hit a patch of black-grey mud that oozes repulsively between your toes. You never go home empty-handed, and some of those sea-pierced stones and pieces of wave-smoothed wood will stay with you forever. Without your odds and ends from the sea, in fact, your desk would be barren despite its books and detritus, its photographs and unexplained coffee-cup rings, and whenever you move house, as you seem to do often these days, you cannot sit down to work until you have located them and arranged them within your reach.

It was a long enough drive to Winchelsea but we went there frequently, on the spur of the moment, on weekend afternoons and especially after dinner on summer evenings. The A road, the B road, the stretch through the hornbeam wood, bluebells in spring, the long twisting lane through low sheep country. Dumb Woman's Lane. The river in which an impatient heir contrived for his senile aunt to drown. The marsh, the sky-coloured pools and busy reeds where, one year, a flamingo turned up, balanced dutifully on one leg, lurid as a fibreglass pond ornament. It looked lonely, out of place. One day it had disappeared – or maybe it was still there, faded into camouflage amongst the fawn reeds because its new diet lacked the carotenoids that make flamingo feathers flamingo-pink. Beyond the marsh was the sea wall that withheld the sea but for a faint sea-silence, and only when you had clambered up the steep unrailed steps would you know whether the tide was high or low or some-where in between. And out there, where the bay curved vast to the horizon, was the nuclear reactor at Dungeness, pale by day, blinking and flickering as the light closed to dusk, my favourite sea time. I thought of the reactor as an Emerald City, whatever that might be. It was so remote, insubstantial yet there. A place that you would never reach – that, as you approached, would recede with the horizon. Piling back into the car, home in the almost-dark, fingering something new – another hag stone, or a bright-orange sea-rusted bolt. A piece of copper, once, twisted and pocked with verdigris. If there was school the next day, it was a long way off.

We went to Winchelsea often while I was revising for my A levels. My mother would decide that I was studying too hard (you'll make yourself ill); I would object, my mother would win, and the dog, sensing a development, would be waiting by the door. I fretted in the car (I can't spare the time), and then we'd climb the steps and disappear into the light and space, the things to be discovered, oblivious to time, unaware too of what was afoot out at the Emerald City. That spring, the artist and film-maker Derek Jarman had bought a fisherman's cottage on the bleak shingle of Dungeness. Soilless, the reactor's strange hulking presence a stone's throw to the west, radiating pylons and rails, it is not an obvious place for a garden. But then you can find a garden almost anywhere.

Jarman's garden at Prospect Cottage, his partner Keith Collins wrote, started 'accidentally': like St Gall in my imagined version of his story, Jarman began attending to, and tending, what was there. He collected pieces of driftwood and rusty metal to mark self-seeded crambes, protecting them from trampling when they were dormant underground, and to support poppies and fennel against the barrelling sea winds. For Jarman the garden properly began when he planted another native, a dog rose, and staked it with a piece of driftwood, and draped the driftwood with a string of hag or 'holey' stones. Over the next seven years or so, as he fell terminally ill with AIDS, Jarman coaxed and shaped and

nurtured his space into a place of wonder. The beachcombings
– the wood, the metal, the stones – were more than functional,
collected and sorted and arranged as things that were lovely
in their own right, artefacts. The local valerian and gorse and
crambes and poppies were tended and curated, moved around,
and other plants selected for their resilience began to join them,
'plonked' into a hole filled with manure from a local farm and
'left to take their chances' in the salt winds. Gardening made
of Jarman an ecologist and a plantsman, a haunter of nurseries
including the geranium specialist on Starvecrow Lane; I love to
think that his path and my mother's might have crossed there
once. He tended his life-affirming garden as the virus destroyed
his body. He wrote about these things in his last book, enriched
with photographs by his friend and fellow gardener Howard
Sooley and published after his death.

'I can look at one plant for an hour, this brings me great
peace.'

We knew nothing of Jarman's garden until the book appeared as my mother turned sixty: I read a review somewhere.
The garden was about to become famous – a place of pilgrimage,
a must-see on the garden-touring circuit – but in this interval it
drew us in quiet and very personal ways. It beckoned from the
Emerald City of my childhood. It spoke our family language of
hag stones and driftwood and things from the sea. It expressed,
with even greater poignancy than we realised at the time, one
man's deep and deepening connection with his corner of the
natural world, its all-absorbing, healing power – something that
I recognised in my mother and soon would discover for myself.

On her birthday, of course, I gave my mother a copy of *Derek
Jarman's Garden*. Then I packed a picnic and we set off with my

father in the car down the A road, the B road, the lanes, past the turning for Winchelsea, along the sea edge of Romney Marsh, on to Dungeness. Though it was July an easterly wind buffeted the car as we turned south onto the ness, marsh now to either side. The verges in bloom. The reactor far away though we were close, wrapped in its own atmosphere. A tarmac road straight over shingle. An expanse to the left: huts and hut skeletons, beached boats, tufts of things, the sea implied beyond. To the right, gorse and simple cottages, there it is! Prospect Cottage, black-timbered with yellow window frames amidst a gathering of plants and abstract forms that, even from a distance, looked subtly organised. The work of some green-fingered Prospero, a magician washed up on a not-quite desert island. You could not tell exactly where the garden began or ended – whether, at its outer reaches, a crambe or scruff of gorse belonged to it or was beyond its bounds. The garden was at one with its surroundings, but you'd know when you were in the garden.

Another photograph. My parents are standing close to the road at what they have taken to be the garden's edge, the garden accumulating around the cottage behind them. My father is holding a champagne bottle in one hand, and my mother is laughing helplessly as they raise their glasses in the gale that is tugging at their hair and inflating my father's jacket and twisting my mother's clothes around her; we would eat our smoked-salmon sandwiches in the car. It is a picture of hilarity. A happy day. I treasure that photograph but it haunts me too, for my mother's face is gaunt despite her laughter. It would be another year before the tumour was discovered, and then it was too late: it had been too late for some time. You've lost weight, Mum. No I haven't. Are you sure? A niggling back pain put down to digging or bending or lifting or reaching: you'd think nothing of it, would you, if you were tall, and a gardener, and not the kind of person who goes on about their aches and pains? There is a shadow over that photograph that only I can see. But I can also see that my parents were happy, for I remember the moment too.

For as long as I can recall, my mother had a hag stone on her key-ring. It was brown, soft to the touch though the stone was hard, and she found it on Winchelsea Beach. After her death, my father transferred it to his key-ring. Now it hangs on mine: it catches my eye sometimes, swinging from the ignition.

It was getting harder to go back to England because I knew I could not stay. I missed the sea, the sea light at the edge of everything even when you are inland. Our friends. The font of British road signs. Caring about the politics of the country in which you live. The smell of a certain London street, and the different smell of a Cambridge one. Laughing. Vacuuming on Sundays, if you needed to. Incidental courtesies. Paper news-papers. The garden.

The home of our old friends Paul and Fran – the place in which, these days, I felt I was at home. Their endless gener-osity, welcoming us over and over again, making us at home with them for a day or two. Always the same though the girls were growing up, the rest of us growing grey or greyer, changes starkly collated by our time away. I knew the distinctive sound of their front door closing, their gas boiler firing, like the sound of my own home. Home, safe. A conversation with a seven-year-old about the shape of a flower. The young hornbeam hedge: I'd convinced Paul and Fran that they too should plant hornbeam when they ripped out an old fence. I believed it to be sound advice – I still do – but I had my own agenda. I was gardening vicariously, for I longed to plant a hornbeam hedge of my own.

My father's hellebore, exposed and dry in its patio pot, two leaves waving like desperate green hands. Have you – um – thought about putting the hellebore in the ground? In a bit of shade? Not really – ought I to? Well, I don't want to interfere – it's your plant (a half-truth) – but I think it might appreciate a bit more soil and some shade. Nothing urgent (I lied). It's no big deal (I lied). There was always a meal of smoked haddock, conjured out of kindness because, of the many foods that I could not find in Switzerland, smoked haddock is what I missed above all.

A tightening at my throat as I boarded the plane for Zurich: I felt I was gasping for air though the passenger next to me, a Londoner, gave no indication that he noticed as we chatted now and then. For many months I had ascribed my tiptoed dread to the gardenless white flat, to the thin, double-dealing walls that shut you in so you could barely breathe yet exposed you mercilessly – but it was not just the apartment, I knew now, it was everything. Switzerland. The country's fortification, unseen and palpable, against what was not of itself: the European Union that surrounded it, foreigners, people of the forest. The impenetrable circles within which people enclosed themselves, and the myriad closed circles of dialects, cantons, linguistic populations, the Swiss Confederation. The wariness with which many people within any one of those circles treated those who were outside it. The rules, and how the rules made people behave. The coldnesses, and those rages that blazed out of nowhere. The landlocked country in which I was at sea, an ugly paradox – for that I could feel so confined yet so outside did not make sense to me.

No salt air, no sea light lightening the edges of the sky.

The plane bored into cloud shortly after take-off, and I was glad not to know when we crossed the Channel. I did not want to leave the sea behind.

December can be a cruel month. We invited everyone we knew to an informal buffet party, hoping to convince ourselves and each other that we had friends in Switzerland, a life here in the making. Its success was questionable. We discovered that the Swiss idea of a buffet supper differs from the one with which we'd each grown up, for we had put out plenty of seating on which we thought our guests would perch with plates, but our guests expected to eat at tables. Our faux pas became manifest when chairs were pulled up efficiently to window sills, which fortunately were deep, and people hunched cheek by jowl over two low coffee tables. Out in the hall, two people had folded themselves onto a step and were eating from plates set on chairs upon which they might more comfortably have sat. We had failed as hosts, though we'd laugh later about the buffet that was lost in translation. Less amusing, when our guests had left, as they all did very suddenly, was the feeling that we'd hosted a networking event. People had gathered into groups and conversed assiduously in dialect. It was not their fault that Swiss German was too unstandardised, too various for us to learn – yet we all shared a second language, High German, and it saddened me, as I did the rounds, that I could not get myself included in any conversation. I felt the exclusiveness of dialect acutely then – those closed circles – and I felt self-conscious, like the child in the odd-numbered class who ends up with the single desk. In the end I'd settled for refilling glasses. I had been an outsider at my own party, the opposite of what we'd set out to prove.

We were the team, we could get through anything together, we said, make ourselves at home anywhere, party anywhere, just the two of us. We'd make the best of Christmas, do some nice things together, roast the guinea fowl that I'd ordered in plenty of time. But deep down I knew that making the best of things was not just for Christmas, it was for life, or for as much of our life as we would spend in this country. Back in the UK it had never occurred to me that a couple who pulled together and loved being together could ever be lonely – but then I took our language and culture, the proximity of our friends, for granted: it was our life, I knew nothing else. The strength of our little team was never in doubt – if anything, it was reinforced by the difficulties that we now faced in Switzerland – but we had begun to find out for ourselves what was obvious, that even the most devoted team must belong to something beyond itself. Ours was drifting and bumping off surfaces, or being pushed firmly away.

Sometimes I was aware of a stirring in the margins of things. It may have been the proverbial black dog, stretching and yawning; I did my best to ignore it. Then something else caught my eye – a yellowing sheet of A4, crumpled by humidity, that was tacked to a corner of my pinboard. It had been there long before the removal men packed the board, pinnings and all – so long that I'd ceased to notice it. Dopiaza, pathia, saag paneer, brinjal bhaji: the words now pressed themselves upon me from the takeaway menu, and I wanted more than anything else to be back in the curry house with the china leopard that would never be a Bengal tiger, and to walk home afterwards with Shaun along the edge of the wood. The trees would be bare at this time of year, apart from the hornbeams, and they would show themselves solemn and haunting in the headlights of passing cars.

I've had enough, I said to Shaun, in spite of the flowers and the hills, our paths through the green. I can't do this any more. I can't keep trying to make it work. I want to go back to England. Where we have friends. Where I can do laundry on Sundays. Where people queue, on the whole. Where you're never more than seventy miles from the sea. Where I feel alive amongst people. I want to live in days that don't have to be got through.

But Shaun's job was going well, we'd sold our house in London.

Or I need a garden, I reflected. If I have a garden I think I can be OK, I think I can be me.

For as long as I could remember, longer still according to my mother's diary, I had been at home in a garden. To nurture a corner of the natural world, grow things, was the means I knew best of making myself at home. I believed that if I had a garden now, a green space to tend, I could put down roots and belong to something, be OK.

I want you to be happy, Shaun said. Let's look for a garden, and a house.

It was as simple as that.

The previous summer, on my mother's birthday, I had driven north-east from Zurich to find a garden – or rather, a series of gardens. The Carthusian monastery at Ittingen, now a conference centre, was founded in the Middle Ages, destroyed by Protestant reformers in 1524, and rebuilt a century later. Faithful to medieval precedent, each ground-floor cell of the seventeenth-century building opened onto an individual garden. I was compelled by the idea of these walled or fenced or hedged spaces for private cultivation and meditation. St Gall had one too, in my version of his story, forty miles to the south, bounded by a wattle fence of supple young hazel and hornbeam twigs. I thought of the hermit on the imagined site of that future monastery, tending and cultivating the space around his cell in the woods. For when you slice a spade into textures of soil, or feel that connectivity as you scoop your trowel deep, loosening the earth, and ease in a lettuce that you have raised from seed, a viola from a cutting, an alchemilla lifted and divided, and the soil grains your hands as you firm the plant in; when, like Eve, you make your daily visitations, noticing, watering, absorbing and absorbed – then you are meditating, engaged in a kind of worship, whether you believe in God or not. Gardening is devotion in every sense.

It was a brute of a day, the sun full of itself, the *Föhn* – the hairdryer wind – blasting hot from the south. The car park was full when I arrived, and when at last I found my way to the monks' gardens they were packed with visitors. One or two plots were still outlined by hedges, but most had been opened up to form larger areas – and despite a wealth of roses and the finely preserved façade, each cell with its door and a tiny latticed window, these spaces did not speak to me nor invite me to linger. Inevitably, for the site had not been a monastery since 1848, the little gardens were more real in my imagination than they proved to be when I saw them for myself.

I was walking away, my thoughts on espresso and cake, when I found myself confronted by a large plant that reminded me of something. It had the green stems of a perennial but grew like a shrub, taller than I, six feet and counting. The shape of a leaf, when I opened out its shallow pleats, was almost a heart and not quite a spade. I ran a thumb lightly across its surface: it was softer than the skin of a peach. Like peach skin it was textured by tiny hairs, and they made the green soft too (there's more to texture than touch), and when I looked from another angle they cast the foliage in a silver-grey sheen. I looked around briefly, picked the well-thumbed leaf, and continued to feel it in my pocket. The flowers captivated me: I had not seen such a colour before, a purplish white, a white that could taste of violets, and their centres reddened brightly deep inside. They were pale and lovely in the shade of a wall. It was the flowers' funnelling shape that I recognised, the shape of mallows in a cherished photograph: my mother and her mallows. I rummaged at the base of the plant and found, as you often don't, a label: *Althaea officinalis*. The name was familiar, though the plant was new to me: marsh mallow, a member of the mallow family or Malvaceae. It had a long herbal history as a remedy for throat and gastric disorders: I'd used extracts myself, on occasion. Furthermore, I had read somewhere, millennia before refined sugar and corn starch and bumper bags, as far back as ancient Egypt perhaps, the sweetish slimy sap of the plant's roots was mixed with nuts and honey to a gelatinous confection: the original marsh mallow. The words 'marsh mallow' still prompt in me a childish yen for pink and white sweets, pillowy and synthetic-tasting – but the plant was something else. It was exquisite, with its 'hoary' foliage and flowers that – as one eighteenth-century writer put it, striving for precision and touching poetry – 'come out from under the wings of the leaves, . . . and are of a purplish white'. I wanted one, even though I had no soil in which to grow it.

The way to the coffee shop led past a small nursery area in which some common herbs were for sale. Sages, thymes, a single glaucous-leaved rue. A further section, labelled *Nicht zu verkaufen*, not for sale, contained more interesting things. There was nobody about, and I stepped over the repurposed railway sleeper to take a closer look, and picked up an unlabelled marsh mallow with those distinctive hoary leaves. I expected the plant to be confiscated at the till, but the cashier rang it through as a large herb and I went on my way feeling that I'd paid a fair enough price. I tucked some tourist brochures into the bag, concealing the foliage in case I bumped into a hawk-eyed employee from the garden department.

Only a gardener will understand the euphoria of bagging a plant that you simply have to have: anyone else will look at you with bemusement should you try to explain how, having succeeded in buying a perennial that was not for sale, you forgot about coffee and cake, so high were your spirits, and walked on air through the stifling heat as you headed back to the car.

But as I drove back to the city I wondered how on earth I'd keep the mallow alive until I had somewhere to plant it. Indoors is no place for a hardy perennial – there are no elements nor seasons there – but late in the autumn, almost by instinct, I cut the still-leafy stems back to within an inch or so of the compost, contriving, I suppose, the plant's seasonal return to the earth. I kept it on the bedroom window sill, the coolest place in our overheated flat, and it made me think of another mallow on another window sill long ago, the near-dead twig of my mother's anisodontea that my father tended back to life.

While *Althaea officinalis* is native to much of Europe, *Flora*

Helvetica confirmed that it does not grow wild in Switzerland. That did not surprise me, given the plant's common English name – for a country that has no interface with the sea has no salt marsh, no place for marsh mallows. I read elsewhere that while British populations are in decline, the species still thrives in Romney Marsh, and I remembered plants that fluttered with whitish flowers as we drove on that wind-blown birthday, my mother's last but one, across the marsh to Dungeness. I'm sure now that they were marsh mallows, as sure as I can be. Jarman saw whitish mallows too, and called them 'angels dancing'.

At Christmas the marsh mallow was still alive. But it needed a garden, a garden with soil. Soil for roots, soil in which to be itself. So did I.

We began searching for the garden on a grey day after Christmas. That time when a year has neither ended nor begun and the world is not quite about its business, and the dates slide into one another.

We drove as we had often walked, west. The mountains to the south, dark and light as though rendered in pen and ink. The wet black roads amongst fields of snow. A thousand shades of monochrome, wintriness itself. We drove though towns and villages gauging, imagining. What were people like out here? We stopped at bars and cafés, thirsty for clues. A thrill of anticipation when we turned off our route because a local signpost pointed down a single-track lane to a hamlet that was not marked on the map and maybe, just maybe.

The cloud lifted sometime between dusk and dark. We checked into a guest house for the night. A village centre deserted, everyone indoors or away, doing family things. Cobbles.

A fountain amplified by silence. A full moon rising behind the Moléson, the dark sky luminous, the mountain solid and darker than night.

A coin tossed into the fountain. The water pale blue in the pale stone basin, rippling in street light. Did you do that because you thought it might bring us luck? I did it because it's a nice fountain to throw a coin into.

The winter night still and sharp, as though something had clarified.

That night, I dreamed that my father was there. I don't know where, for the dream would not be summoned back – but I remember that I was happy to see him, and that all was well.

Many reasons lay behind our decision to look for a home in western Switzerland or Romandie. So long as you avoided the built-up shores of Lake Geneva there was more green space out there, and house prices were lower. We could not begin to afford a garden in the concrete erstwhile villages and village-dormitories that sprawled from Zurich – but that was a moot point, for Zurich, we believed, was the problem to which the garden would be a solution. Furthermore, Romandie was francophone. Its people spoke standard French, in which Shaun was fluent and I was keen to improve: there were no dialects, with their practical complexities and parochial baggage. Western Switzerland shared a language and a border with France – and while the Romands insisted on their difference from the French, and vice versa, they were also separated from their German-speaking compatriots by a linguistic and cultural divide known wryly as the *Röstigraben* (*Rösti* – a dish of grated, fried potatoes associated with though not exclusive to German-speaking Switzerland; *Graben* – a ditch or rift). We hoped the west might be different, more, well, open. That we'd stand a better chance of integrating there.

We had already hiked far and wide in Romandie – the Alps and pre-Alps to the south, the little old mountains of the Jura to the north, the hills that rolled up from the plateau in between – and found enchantment there. Our green path through the Jura, the hornbeam and euphorbias, the horses and hellebores. Another place that I might have dreamed, to the south where hills became mountains: meadows that were oceans of papery narcissi, spectral and pheasant-eyed and so fragrant in the mizzle of a grey June day that you thought you might drown, or wake up. Not for nothing is this flower called *Narcissus poeticus*, the poet's narcissus – but you will not understand why, despite the potted bulbs that fill your home each winter with pure headiness, until you meet a scented white narcissus in the wild. There were gentians in the west too – out of everyday reach, of course, in alpine scree on an August afternoon, a climb that took your breath away in every sense.

In the new year we registered with estate agents and trawled listings on the internet. Every weekend we headed west in search of home. We had little idea wherein that might consist, other than that the house should be small enough for two and the garden big enough for a quince tree and a few perennials. And one or two shrubs, of course, and maybe a potager. We were taken to many houses that covered the surfaces of their plots – sleek, ultra-modern boxes; seventeenth-century farmhouse-barns – for land is at a premium in this small, mountainous, densely populated country. Thank you so much, but I think I mentioned that we want a garden. The agent was incredulous. But this is a garden: there's a place to sit and a place for the barbecue. *I don't want a barbecue.* I'm sorry, but we really need a garden with soil. Space for growing things. Plants.

We explored regions, villages, houses, places, imagining ourselves there, or trying to. Sometimes, for it was a hard winter, we strapped on our snowshoes and set off across new meadows in creaking giant steps, the clean air stinging our nostrils and eyes, the snow immense, the trees their barest forms. Moonwalking by day: weightless downhill strides that made you carefree in spite of yourself.

A farmhouse at the westernmost tip of the country: the house was dark though the day was bright, and the owner had been drinking though it was early, and you could almost speculate that the gloomy house had driven the man to drink. A new build, further south, that had a prestigious view of the Alps if you chose your viewpoint with care, and an unbroken one of a motorway. Places in between, the wrong location, the wrong property, or not quite the right one whatever that might be. What about the Jura, Shaun or I said as we inched back east at the end of a fruitless day, the traffic slow and peevish at Biel, the lake dull, the plateau left grubby by winter. Why haven't we been looking there? Funny you should say that. We had each felt the Jura's quiet green force, an affinity: we just hadn't paid attention to it as we drove around western Switzerland in our undefined search. I could live here, one of us had said on that day, a while past, when we climbed with the path by the stream to the bright pasture on the wooded hill, the horses at home and gentle. The limestone cliffs that referenced Caspar David Friedrich. The vaulted trees that were not cathedral-like, but the very model for cathedrals. The meadows cleared from woods and shaped by hills. The bright grass green.

We set off for the Jura on a grey Saturday in early spring. I was credulous about the first viewing we had arranged, an old house that the vendor was selling privately: he'd emailed warmly of its peaceful village-edge location and the garden's immense potential, and he was convinced that it would suit us perfectly. We would then visit four or five houses with a local agent. There was one other property that I'd seen a few times on the internet and put to the back of my mind. The garden looked green and ample, even allowing for the wide-angle lens, but the cottage was described as very small, and the shots of the interior were dark, and we both craved daylight. But once we were on the motorway I recalled that the cottage was advertised by the agent with whom we were to spend the afternoon. It made sense to take a look, if only to benchmark prices. I texted the agent: could we see the cottage too, while we were at it? It was definitely not the property for us, he replied, the house was far too small, it would be a waste of everyone's time, but if we really insisted he supposed he could call the vendors.

When I was fairly young, eight or nine perhaps, a gut feeling that I had about someone told me to run. I ran, and many years later I learned that it had been the right thing to do. I had that feeling again when Shaun pressed a grimy doorbell to the old house at the village edge – a light-industrial area, as it happened – and the door opened too instantly. A middle-aged woman stood there, silent. Her expression unsettled me: it was as though she had spent a lifetime biting her lip. A man materialised from the darkness, as effusive in person as by email – but his eyes conflicted with that display of warmth and something else about him bothered me. *Run.* I can't go in, I muttered as the pair turned to lead us into the dark hall, we have to leave now.

We can't, Shaun said, now that we're here. It would be rude.

I could not make sense of the house's configuration. Its insides twisted and turned darkly, choked with balding velvet drapery that gave us both the creeps. Amidst the muffled décor hung a smell of mildew and the works of a prolific amateur artist. The man drew our attention to things in moist and cloying tones: the view from his desk, which contrived to exclude the surrounding industrial area; the garden with *le véritable sapin jurassien*, the genuine Jura pine that was a newly replanted Christmas tree, a Norway spruce – a species that is widespread in the Jura and, for that matter, throughout Switzerland, and in central and eastern and northern Europe. The woman followed us, silent and staring. When I caught her eye she stared back coldly and steadily, and when I looked away I felt her eyes pin me still. One room, murky and mousy with old velvet, contained a lone bathtub; another, a gleaming Harley-Davidson. The paintings, poorly executed by any standards, were almost pornographic and deeply unpleasant. The man went on and on about the genuine Jura pine whereof no species existed: the place had nothing else to recommend it.

I need to wash my hands, I said when we got back to the car, though I'd thrust them into my pockets as we entered the house, and kept them there. I could use a shower, said Shaun. We drove away from the village and stopped at a lay-by, where we rinsed our hands with bottled water – it was better than nothing – and ate petrol-station sandwiches. Then, still feeling tainted, we headed off to meet the agent. It was a wearying afternoon. The agent was very agreeable, and there was nothing creepy or sordid about the houses to which he took us: we just could not imagine living in one of them. Late in the day, as we left another house that filled its own plot (but we want a garden . . . no, a garden with SOIL, space for growing things), we'd had enough. We had made no progress, we were tired, and what we wanted more than anything right then was not a house but a shower, a beer, a pizza, and the end of the day. We both wished I hadn't insisted on seeing the cottage. So did the agent, for he knew it would be a waste of time, but the vendors were expecting us.

We followed the agent at high speed; he knew the roads and had a Saturday evening to begin. Under hills through fume-dusty tunnels, up over others, the dark-wooded slopes and the bright meadows, villages spread over west-facing flanks and tucked into angles and clustered in valley bottoms. Isolated farms in high clearings: how peaceful they must be, I thought, and how alone. Then, out of nowhere, a familiar farm: the gate to the path that climbed by the stream amongst the hornbeams to the horses' green place. We passed the farm and turned onto a smaller road that wound with a river, bend after hairpin bend, through a narrow gorge. Broad-leaved trees leaned in as we sped, shades of new bronze greening into spring, and the limestone cliffs above were pale and dark with firs. Wood anemones star-dusted the riverbanks, white in the coalescing shade, though I knew their frail petals were streaked with pink, as angels' wings must be, and that if you presumed to pick a flower it would turn instantly to a withered reproach. There were rippling suggestions of bright new green: it certainly looked like a place where wild garlic might grow.

A couple of dilapidated Jura houses, their roofs broad and sloping, their whitewash coloured and chipped away by time, the underlying stonework at one with the cliffs. A garage fore-court crammed with cars of unroadworthy aspect. Almost as soon as we entered the village we turned off again, threading our way amongst whitewashed buildings and creosote-dark barns. Forking right, and right again. A burst of acceleration, uphill past a house that was decked with junk, to an abrupt halt. The lane had ended at a neat whitewashed cottage that, to all appearances, grew out of the hill.

We were home.

PART THREE

Where the Hornbeam Grows

I should have known that I would find the garden on a wooded hill. A wooded hill is where my parents made their garden. It's where, downstream from the Weald on that ancient buried river, I made another garden in London suburbia. It is where Milton locates the 'enclosure green' of paradise.

Enclosure green: a garden of the woods.

The house looked comfortable with itself: it belonged where it was, built into an angle where the hill climbed up in two directions, north and west, from the village. I suppose the cottage had in a way grown out of the hill, for its robust bulges and deep window recesses signalled that it too was built of stone beneath the whitish render.

Above the house, to the north, trees grew out and up from a sheer limestone face, holding on by I don't know what. Their high branches were ochre-blurred, hinting at leaf. Field maples maybe, too early to tell for sure. To the west – a gentler upward slope, though it was all relative – a stone wall retained the property at a ground level above my head, the first floor of the house. Vegetation grew along the top of the wall, concealing the garden beyond: a straggle of elderly shrubs, their branches crusty with lichen, and a tall section of leylandii that looked peculiar, not a hedge so much as an excerpt from a hedge. There was a lovely amelanchier with dark fluid branches. I wondered what lay on the other side – but I was also glad to wonder for the time being. There was something self-contained about the place: it gave little away, waited to be discovered bit by bit.

From its elevated nook the house faced south out over the valley. The small village sprawled to the east, the church tower white and gathered like a bird for flight. You could read the clock from where we stood. Opposite were two dark-wooded mountains, their lower slopes overlapping, the V-shaped space in between filled by a distant crest, as a child draws imaginary mountains: the mountains were the very idea of mountains. Above them, with a special squiggle that is pleasing to have mastered when you're six or seven years old, that child would add a stylised bird or two – but the buzzard that glided above us as we made our way to a side gate was magnificently real. I could almost see its hooked beak as it scanned the valley floor for flesh.

On the eastern side a small, brick-paved garden brought us to the front door. Someone cared for the little garden very much. It was neat and cluttered – carefully cluttered, with pots of winter bedding and an ornamental menagerie that included, besides common or garden terracotta beasts, a smirking blue anthropomorphic hedgehog and a gnome. In my mind I began to fill the space with free-ranging plants. Hellebores. Dwarf *Narcissus* 'Tête-à-tête', the daffodil distilled. Aquilegias would bloom later, and geraniums of course. Alchemilla infilling, green two ways. There would be real toads too, I thought, judging from all the rocks, and who knew what else.

A horseshoe was nailed to the wooden lintel, and a well-oiled iron carillon showered bells when the agent tugged its handle. Before the door opened, before I'd set eyes on the back garden, I was sure that we were going to buy the place.

Indoors the cottage was certainly small. Like the front garden it was crammed immaculately with stuff, but it felt, if not spacious, then comfortable – an agreeable quality in a house. The uprights and beams were exposed to the high-pitching roof, and the building consisted less of rooms than of successive spaces that lived and breathed and undoubtedly creaked, the trees its very bones. It was around a century old, a two-storey workshop that had been extended and modified over the years until it was a house; the triple kitchen window, an architect told us later, was a likely sign of watchmaking. For behind the luxury brand names that line the way to baggage reclaim in Swiss airports lies their economic converse, a history of cottage industries scattered around the sparsely populated Jurassic arc. The *paysans horlogers,* farmer-watchmakers, supplemented their rural livings, especially in winter, by making components for the watch industry that spilled out of Geneva. A watchmaker's most precious resource is daylight – and just occasionally, out and about in the mountains of north-western Switzerland, you will notice a triple or quadruple window in an old farmhouse or outbuilding, and know that intricate parts of iconic timepieces have more likely than not been crafted in its unassuming light.

The extra-long window sill was a deep limestone slab, the top sawn and polished, the edge rough cut. Later I would discover that it matched the altar in the village church. Instinctively I ran a hand over the sill's smooth surface, and felt the pocks that may or may not have housed minuscule shells. Limestone: rock made from the leftovers of life, billions upon prehistoric billions of marine organisms, as great a marvel to my mind as a perfect dinosaur fossil.

Upstairs, at the level of the main garden, was a cramped sitting room. There was still no sign of the garden itself, for the roof sloped to the ground, and I thought that would drive me mad – to know that the garden was there and not be able to look out at it. But you can always raise a roof. At last, from a small side room, the back door opened. A narrow walkway edged around a deep stairwell serving a disused cellar door; one part was railed, the other an accident waiting to happen. Improvised paving led perilously across the top step to an incoherent terrace at the eaves of the roof: surplus floor tiles and bonded gravel, bits of concrete and rock, a jumble that was all the more bizarre for its extreme cleanliness. The surfaces had not been merely swept, but swept clean with authority. I wondered whether someone had used a vacuum cleaner, so dustless were the surfaces and so infinite the sources of dust and debris: the slopes and overhanging trees, the birds, the land, the world. There was a time when I'd have said that was far-fetched – until a summer evening at home in London, when an indoor sound came from outdoors through the open window of my study. I looked out, and called to Shaun. Carol's vacuuming her drive. Yeah right. No really, look – with the Henry. Oh my god: she's vacuuming the drive.

To the other side, the north, a slope of meadow grass reared at a dizzying gradient to meet the woods as they edged into the garden. A mature lime tree with a lopsided crown and ancient-looking bark grew from the foot of the slope. A lawn stretched ahead, bounded on one side by a concrete path and interrupted by jutting flowerbeds that were edged with concrete as if to keep the roses and bedding plants firmly in their place. I noticed that there were no dandelions in the lawn, though the steep meadow abounded in their lush serrated leaves – they'd be tender at this time of the year, and the right side of bitter. The grass looked odd, incongruous: what happened to those thousands of parachuting seeds once they had told their dandelion time? A flight of steps led up towards two shaggy firs that loomed in the departing light, and I assumed that the garden ended there. I paused at the foot of the steps. There were some promising shrubs, a bushy one with scrubby spindle bark – *Euonymus alatus* probably, the Asian winged species – and that sinuous amelanchier. A shed so clean and organised, inside and out, that it almost went against the nature of sheds.

Like the house, the garden was made of limestone. There were drystone retaining walls that held the many-sided space from inward collapse. Lumps of limestone that had tumbled down the meadow slope, or surfaced in beds and borders with the soil's perennial settling, the rock's perennial rising. A de facto rockery to one side of the steps – an unearthed seam of limestone with which nothing else could be done. A contrived rockery near the terrace, its stones arranged in too orderly a fashion. The topsoil through which all that limestone erupted would be both shallow and alkaline: if you mixed a sample with barium sulphate and added pH test solution, the resulting suspension would almost certainly turn litmus paper darkest green – green as a fir tree at sundown in March. That would be a new challenge: I had largely gardened in mildly acidic or neutral soil, a range in which, all other things being equal, most plants will grow. In our tiny Cambridge garden, which sat above a seam of alkaline chalk, I would never have planted a magnolia or witch hazel or other deep-rooting calcifuge, as horticulturalists call acid-loving plants (fugitives from calcium: a poignant term for a living thing that, being rooted, can run from nothing). But even there, where a hydrangea bloomed pink, I grew more or less what I wanted, so deep was the topsoil that overlay the chalky bedrock. I'd taken my freedom for granted, and bought on impulse if I happened to be where plants were for sale – a nursery, a market, a website, the hospice car park, a roadside stall. The Chiltern house, now a small museum, where Milton took refuge from the London plague and worked on *Paradise Lost*. He would have sat and walked in that garden, taking the 'airs, vernal airs' in every possible sense: moving airs, breezes on skin and in hair; scented airs; musical airs, the melodies of birdsong, stirrings, leaves, the garden's *je ne sais quoi*. Gardening with words in his blindness. A few surplus plants were for sale there too, and although Shaun counselled against the purchase of a *Geranium psilostemon*, for we were several miles on foot from the car, he carried the three-litre pot back over the hills, mostly without complaint. Milton's geranium, emerald-leaved and shocking pink in flower.

Highly alkaline conditions dictate rather more specifically what you can and cannot grow, and while that would be a constraint it excited me. I might have to think more carefully about what I planted; look around, beyond the Japanese maple in the patio pot that clearly contained ericaceous or acidic compost. I would walk and walk, with Shaun, and find out what grew here of its own accord – in the mountains and woods and meadows and marginal parts, in the wilder world that straggled and clamoured green at the boundaries. I would spend time with *Flora Helvetica*. Learn from nature, for nature was here first. If you plant something that is suited to the soil and climate of a place, especially an indigenous species, it will stand a strong chance of flourishing. Because the plant is, as it were, at home it will need fewer interventions to keep it healthy and happy – less watering, or feeding, or pest control, or worrying about than a plant that is out of place – and that is good for the environment. Your plant will look good too, rhyme or chime with the native flora, maybe converse with relatives beyond the garden's boundary. It is also the case that if you know something is wrong you will see it as such – yet the Japanese maple in its pot amidst the limestone looked as alien to its surroundings as those tree ferns in Zurich, or a lush green lawn that once offended my eye on an arid Greek island.

But plants, such is their connectivity, their emotional power, will make a hypocrite of the most principled gardener. It is a personal thing in the deepest sense of that often-used phrase. It might be a gardenia that someone gave you on a precious day in Italy. A passion for salvias, or a weakness for gentian blue. Or it might be an inner root system, a map of connections with people and places and feelings and memories, the things that make you who you are. And I knew, even as I embraced my resolution and looked forward to learning from nature, to ecological soundness and its concomitant whiff of complacency, that I would not keep it. Not entirely, at any rate: I couldn't. If we bought the property, the plants that had grown in my parents' garden would belong in this one whether they liked it or not. There were astilbes, geraniums, penstemons, aquilegias, anemones, sedums, euphorbias – even, with luck, the hellebore – to round up from the gardens of our friends in England. I hoped some at least would cope with the alkaline soil and brutal winters: I'd learned on that steep, green, exhilarating August day that Japanese anemones and native euphorbias and hellebores grew hereabouts. But I decided that I would not even read up on the others, for regardless of their own requirements my need to plant them in a garden of my own was absolute. There was the marsh mallow too, alive – just – against all odds in the stifling flat. A limestone hillside was not an obvious place for a marsh plant, but that was not the point.

I was getting ahead of myself: I'd not even seen the whole property.

The house did not connect with the garden, nor the neat, controlled garden with its wilder surroundings, yet already I felt at ease there, a long-forgotten feeling. The garden seemed to me to be holding its breath, as though it had been ordered to pretend that it was not deep amongst the woods and hills, but belonged to a clean-swept suburb. To pretend that it was something other than itself. It was *gepflegt*, like Susanna's hair, and those Zurich gardens, and those neatly drawn outer social circles: impeccably maintained, shown to be cared for. I wanted to get my hands on it, to tend it as Eve tends her garden: to let the garden breathe again, let it sing with the wildness at its edges, for I was sure that, like paradise, it was wild at heart.

The others were engrossed in conversation down by the house, so I eased my fingers into the soil there and then – it was dry despite the early season, and granular – and scooped a little into one of the food bags that I kept in a pocket of my jacket, for you never know when you might need to filch a cutting, or pick some wild garlic. I was sure I still had my soil-testing kit in a box, labelled 'Garden', that remained unopened and had made me sad. Litmus paper, I reflected, as I straightened up and cast an eye over the sapped boundary shrubs, their mottled, shaggy branches, is made from lichen.

I wandered on up the steps, the light gone now to a western sky pale umber behind the trees. The garden entered a new phase. A bank inched down to the boundary fence, dense with periwinkle of which most was variegated. There was another patch of lawn, and a reed-edged pond. A vegetable plot contained by old railway sleepers. The sheer northern slope was uncleared at this end, and the wood swept around behind the pond, beyond the firs, until a chain-link fence materialised faintly amongst the scrub and trunks.

There was hornbeam in the garden too, down near the house, at the foot of the meadow slope. Another clipped vertical slab that was neither tree nor hedge and seemed to deny the tree's very nature. That, I regretted, would have to go, along with the sloping roof and the variegated periwinkle. And the sleepers in the vegetable plot: they'd be laden with creosote, and asbestos dust from braking trains, hardly what you wanted near your vegetables. But hornbeam grew here, and that was what mattered.

We bought the house from an irritable man with a penchant for pyrethroids and glyphosate.

The Schmidts were Swiss Germans on the wrong side of the *Röstigraben*. Herr Schmidt was in his eighties, and the first thing that I noticed about him was the unfeasible crispness of his shirt. It was made of high-quality cotton, the kind that takes a great deal of ironing, and although Herr Schmidt's arms gesticulated at the slightest vexation his sleeves barely twitched at the inner elbow, where most shirts crease as soon as you begin to button them up. Perhaps they didn't dare.

The second thing that we noticed about Herr Schmidt was how demanding he appeared to be. When he wanted something – a document he had mislaid, or someone's attention – he really did snap his fingers, and on one occasion Frau Schmidt really did come running. I'd always thought that a mere figure of speech. Frau Schmidt was a good quarter-century younger than he and jolly in a nervous, exaggerated way. She was desperately keen to sell the house, which I think had belonged to the first Frau Schmidt, and when we returned for a second viewing she took us aback with hugs and kisses and befriended us with familiar pronouns that the German language does not take lightly. She offered us coffee, she'd baked a cake, and we all sat down at the dining table to talk about gardens, the Jura climate, how Shaun and I loved to hike, wildlife we'd seen along the way. Frau Schmidt ran with these themes. There was so much wildlife here, we'd just love it: there were herons and newts, and rare singing toads, and hedgehogs that hibernated under the shed – oh yes, and adders lived in the drystone walls. *Adder: my shudder word.* One had bitten the Schmidts' dog a year or two ago – the dog had nearly died – and they'd caught two more in the cellar just the previous summer. Morels grew in the garden too, every April unless the spring was very dry, but she wouldn't tell us where in case the neighbours found out. So I never used garden chemicals? Ever? Well, the Schmidts' garden was PERFECT for us because they gardened organically too. The garden was TOTALLY organic: *ALLES bio.* I wondered whether Frau Schmidt's idea of organic gardening was quite the same as mine, for there were yellow blains in the bricked front path where moss appeared to have been doused with herbicide – and, come to think of it, there was something a little too impeccable about the winter pansies and hosta shoots despite all the rocks, the crannies in which slugs and snails were sure to be at home.

The neighbours were a bit different, Frau Schmidt went on excitedly, there had been one or two problems. Ah well, we said, as Shaun had said in London, that job offer on the table, people are people. Herr Schmidt raised an arm and sent the subject flying. We moved on to more anodyne matters: the price of heating oil; who ploughed the lane when it snowed; the second-ary electrical circuit that Herr Schmidt had installed himself; whether we might care to buy the table at which we were sitting.

In the coming months, as we moved in and made the house our own, we would happen upon evidence of a thoroughgoing preoccupation with order. The tiny bathroom was fitted with an industrial soap dispenser, holders for three different types of paper product plus spares, many hooks and knobs and, besides the towel rails, hanging rails of various lengths and unclear purpose. The house bristled with hooks, in fact, and until you had got the measure of its interior you could snag clothing or imperil an eye because a hook was at a height or in a place where you did not expect to encounter one. Brushes appeared to generate themselves: two or three push brooms, a push-broom head, a snow broom, a besom, three or four straw brooms, scrubbing brushes, bottle brushes in a range of grades and sizes of which some were duplicated, wire brushes, paintbrushes, decommissioned toothbrushes, mysterious brushes. There were labelled boxes that contained, respectively, almost thirty socket spanners in six sizes, one in octuplicate, and thirteen tape meas-ures of which four were broken. Thin offcuts of plastic pipe that

Shaun, who knows a thing or two about plumbing, pronounced unusable. *Schlüssel:* a tin that rattled heavily with many keys to no doors. People talk about the archaeology of cultures and civilisations; this was the archaeology of a temperament.

Back in the Zurich apartment, the house sale agreed, I dragged out the garden box at last and rummaged amongst treasures and junk, my own archaeology. A stack of seed trays, and one of miniature pots in which my father had grown seedlings on: cosmos, nicotiana, intoxicating burgundy petunias, that ethereal penstemon. Muddy plant labels, my half-formed scribble, bundles of twine and a reel of wire, and a tangle of both that I'd planned to reuse. A splintered section of bamboo cane, its tip mildewed by underground. Plant ties, an old carving knife, a ball of scrunched-up seed packets that had spent time in rain and then in a pocket. A long-bladed weeding implement bearing a faded label, 3 for £10, which may have accounted for its buckled condition. My beloved hand tools with their blades and tines of copper – things that, as William Morris prescribed, I knew to be useful and believed to be beautiful.

The soil-testing kit was there too. It included a miniature test tube and a booklet of litmus strips that lent seriousness to the proceedings: chemistry was one of the few things I enjoyed about school. I still had the little bag of soil that I'd collected on our first visit. I set everything out on the kitchen counter, mixed up soil and powder and testing solution and shook it all vigorously, and then I dipped a page from the booklet into the murky suspension. The litmus paper, lichen paper, turned alkaline green. As I knew it would: you could hardly miss the calciferous stone with which the whole region was pale where it wasn't green, the cliffs and tracks and houses, the rock-strewn fields. The soil test was important for other reasons. It was about opening that box of garden things, connecting quite literally with soil. Getting ready to get gardening.

In addition to the scorched moss, I had noticed on our second visit that the 'wild' daffodils on the meadow slope were nothing of the kind. I wondered whether the morels would materialise. Not to mention the singing toads: have you ever heard a toad sing?

I have, as it happens, and so has Shaun, when we still lived in Cambridge. One early summer dusk, the air shifting as the still day cooled, we became aware of a new sound in our little urban paradise. It was a single note that piped purely when the neighbourhood blackbird, balancing on his uppermost branch, paused between phrases of his evening song. The note introduced a tranquil counter-rhythm to the ebb and flow of voices, traffic, the city in summer and out of doors. It invoked and defied analogy: it was electronic, like a smoke detector with a low battery, but not quite; it was sonar, redolent of a Cold War submarine film, and it was not. It had to be synthetic – yet, unlike a smartphone keypad with enabled sound, it wasn't aggravating, and the single note was far from monotonous. There was something else about it, something – whole. If water dripping from leaves after rain could splash in thin air, maybe it would sound like this. We couldn't pin it down, and if I was certain that the sound came from one place Shaun heard it elsewhere, possibly beyond the garden, it was hard to say. A neighbour questioned us thoroughly and incredulously about electronic devices.

The piping continued every evening for weeks. Occasionally it struck up before dusk, but only if I was watering: it had to be of the animal world. The hypnotic one-note music assimilated itself to our summer nights. It found its way into sleep and deepened it. Then, in August, it stopped: we missed it.

It resumed the following year, in early summer. This time a second, lower note responded to the dominant one and sometimes interjected. A minor third, I thought. I remember an evening when the walled garden felt richly dark, cloistered from the haze of street noise and light. We sat out late and the two spellbinding notes sounded, it seemed, from every direction. Something stirred at the edge of the path as I got up to go indoors: a small toad encrusted with charcoal-coloured bumps. I held it up to the light of the kitchen window where moths clamoured silently, and looked into the creature's yellow eye; its pupil was vertical, for night vision perhaps, or hunting, like the pupil of a fox's eye, and I wondered what it saw. And as it sat there in my hand, vulnerable, its tiny loose throat moved in synchronicity with the note that seemed to come from the garden next door but one. I showed the toad to Shaun, then set it gently under a fern where darkness absorbed it but for a glittering yellow eye.

Later I learned about the midwife toad, *Alytes obstetricans*. That it is so called because once the female has laid eggs the male carries and incubates them – a cue, when I shared this intriguing fact with friends, for predictable reflections upon what men might learn from the amphibian world. I found out that they sometimes secrete a foul-smelling toxin when touched, and that they are native to western Europe but not to Britain. That they were introduced accidentally in a consignment of Victorian water plants, and that their British populations are confined to isolated pockets including the part of Bedfordshire where I had bought some ferns. Maybe an egg-carrying male had stowed away beneath a hart's tongue or shuttlecock; maybe the toads had just turned up, one way or another.

One summer, after we had moved away, we went back to Cambridge to visit friends, our former neighbours two doors along. The house that had been ours gave nothing away as we passed. We sat outside with Joanna and David as we'd done many times, and it was strange to peer into the intervening garden – to see the outside of our old boundary wall, which was the inside of our next-door neighbours' wall, and to know that beyond it lay the garden that I had crammed with things of green. The afternoon cooled into evening and I listened to the city's crescendos, the pub door open, a blackbird's big competing song – but no toad sounds splashed in the air. Maybe the creatures had departed as mysteriously as they had arrived. Or, a sad but more likely hypothesis, they had failed to establish and reproduce in their accidental city home. Oh no, said Joanna, not at all. The new owner, it appeared, had asked her husband to kill the toads because she couldn't stand the sound. That preys on my mind still, ten years on. I wonder about the day the toads fell silent. I wonder whether the new owners sleep more soundly, now that it is quiet.

The singing toads had amplified our tiny garden: they had made it more ample in every sense, and held us there.

I want to do something with that shady strip by the garage, Fran announced when I next visited, do you have any ideas? *The hellebore!* We went shopping: some ferns, a euphorbia, a lovely dusky geranium, a *Pachysandra terminalis* or Japanese spurge that we did not especially like but was worth a try. Tea and Bakewell tart. It's the perfect place for the hellebore too, of course: I'll plant it myself if you like. Oh, and could I borrow an old carving knife?

I'd expected the hellebore to be pot-bound after its sojourn on the sunny patio, but it had put down few roots since I'd dug it up in London all that life ago: it must have been just holding on, and there was little to divide. In any case it was the worst time to do such things, when the plant was or ought still to be in flower. Nevertheless – it could not be helped – I sliced off a shoot that had barely broken the surface of the compost and had some tentative roots. I wrapped it in damp kitchen paper and a food bag, and tucked it into my suitcase. Then I went back outside and planted my father's hellebore, in the ground in the shade, and as I watered it in I hoped it would put down roots at last and bloom for my father's birthday, and for the birthday of Fran's little girl who drew flower-like flowers and squiggle birds and who, like me, had wanted to go home.

Our moving date was set for July, but we drove out to the village often in the course of the spring and early summer. We had a contract to sign, an architect to meet. There were necessary and unnecessary details to discuss, the price of the dining table to agree, little to keep us in Zurich at weekends, hills and valleys to explore. What surrounded the garden, what it was of. The lovely paradox that is the Jura landscape.

The word 'wild' carries so much baggage these days that I am wary of using it at all. But there is something raw about the limestone cliffs and the steep, dark-wooded hills of the Jura for which there is no other word: they look wild, and when you are walking or scrambling in the margins of those dense unscalable forests they feel wild. And there is something else altogether about the high pastures and the meadowed valleys, the grass-green human landscape carved from the forest or into it, the lanes contoured to the hills. Ruskin captured this paradox when he wrote of the Jura's 'pastoral mountain[s]', a term that has a romantic ring to it – it was the 1840s, after all – until you go there and discover for yourself what he was getting at. Almost any landscape (certainly any garden) is a dialogue between the natural world and the human one, and the Jura has its own distinctive conversation. There's a wildness to the little old mountains, but also the 'restrained' quality that makes Ruskin speak of them, in the same breath, as 'long low lines of piny hills', the mere first rumblings of the Alps. Ruskin, like me, cannot decide whether he should call the Jura's peaks and ridges hills or mountains, albeit 'pastoral' ones, and so he calls them both – as I do, depending on how I feel. Officially – in place names, in encyclopaedias – the Jura is composed of mountains, but I often think of them as wooded hills. It's a shifting relationship: sometimes they are out there, wild, implacably themselves, sometimes they are accessible, managed, inhabited.

When does a hill become a mountain? I asked my friend Ed, who is something of an authority on mountains and words. I expected to tighten my terminology in light of some firm criteria, but to my surprise Ed, when he eventually got back to me, endorsed my own imprecision.

When does a hill become a mountain? When you feel that it does, he replied.

The Jura in a nutshell.

From the house at the end of the lane, an overgrown grassed track headed uphill along the garden's long boundary at the edge of the wood. The grass was thick and soft, shady grass, the kind that looks sodden even when it is not. The shade came from a ragged line of ashes and field maples on the outermost side of the track: almost hedgerow, no longer wood. And there, to my delight, was a spindle. I recognised its branching, army-green laxness, a distinctive geometric phase in which the young rounded stems acquire planes and become 'fower square', as Gerard put it, and your fingertips feel the edges of something that they know to be edgeless – for the branches grow round again as they thicken and whiten with age. The hedgerow shrub that showered pink and orange in the Sussex lanes, that my mother loved so much she planted one in the corner by the compost heap where grass snakes were said to live. Growing here, just outside the garden that was nearly mine. *Euonymus europaeus,* common or garden and end-lessly enchanting, not to be confused with the shrub that most people know as 'euonymus': that is *Euonymus fortunei*, evergreen and often variegated, about which I have mixed feelings though it grew in my parents' garden. *Pfaffenhütchen, berretto da prete, chapitscha da prers: Euonymus europaeus* is commonly named in German, Italian and Romansh for the resemblance of its 'fower square' berries to the Catholic priest's biretta. Birettas have been less common in Protestant Britain – though before his fortunes changed with the Reformation Thomas Wolsey, chancellor to Henry VIII, had one in cardinal- or berry-red – and the English common names of spindle or prick-wood are firmly functional. The shrub's tough, sharp-splintering wood was once the stuff of spindles, laundry pegs and skewers or 'pricks' such as Wolsey's father, reputedly a butcher, might have used. Not to mention toothpicks, and watchmaker's implements. Maybe, a couple of centuries ago, some farmer paused here after checking on his cattle, one eye on the tools of his winter trade, and tested the strength of a maturing spindle branch, flexing it back and forth.

A stream rushed down beneath the trees. It ducked underground in places and surfaced again in full-flowing sound past the garden and the house. I'd love, I had said to Shaun, back on that day when we climbed through the forest by a dropping chalk stream, to live with the sound of water.

At the end of the garden the track ended too, in brightness and a red metal gate that clanged through the valley when we heaved it shut behind us, my hair snagging on hawthorn. A meadow, upward and grass-green. To the west it clambered steadily along the valley side. To the north it reared steeply to join the forested flank that rose from the village and took in the garden and culminated in a peak high above. It was a mountain undoubtedly – today at least – though lower down, on the track by the garden, it had felt like a wooded hill. And I almost wondered if where we were was real, for the northern flank rippled with darkest-sea-green hellebore leaves, clumped in their hundreds and ringing, on that early spring day, with green flower heads. A green somewhere between light and mid – fuller than lime, not quite apple, stinking-hellebore green. I'd come across such leaves in recent months, and wondered about the flowers, and now I saw, strange in its sheer wild proliferation, a plant I once bought at a Cambridgeshire nursery because I thought it exotic. *Helleborus foetidus,* the European or stinking hellebore, is a very different species from my father's hellebore, *Helleborus* x *hybridus,* which has origins further east. Allegedly, for one thing, *Helleborus foetidus* stinks: its foliage, when crushed, is said to release the foetid smell for which the plant is named – though when I picked a leaf and ripped and worked it in my hand, hoping to be disgusted, I smelled only a cold green tinged with musk, so cold that it was almost fresh. Its fleshy stems and clustered flower heads are their own shape, but bring jingle bells to mind. And while the greenish cups of my father's hellebore wear their patterned insides openly, those jingle-bell flower heads are tightly wrapped and their rims are painted lipstick-red.

What I think of as a hellebore flower is not a flower at all but a calyx, its petals not petals but sepals, which enclose and protect the tiny flowers inside. This is why the hellebore's so-called flowers are often tinted green: like true leaves, sepals contain chlorophyll, a pigment essential to photosynthesis, whereas most petals do not. Then again, chlorophyll – a green, green word – is anything but green. The wavelengths of light absorbed by chlorophyll for the synthesis of food are red and blue; what we see is the colour of wavelengths for which the leaf has no use. The leaf is green, and it is not.

A hillside daubed with green flowers is too good a thing to be true. It was then, and it blew my mind.

There was something sculptural about the lower reaches of the valley, its ample dips and rises landscaped by the elements. We scrambled up a hillock that seemed man-made and was not, and looked back down on the trees at our feet, the trees thinning where the garden was, the garden at one with the wood, and the village down beyond, the white church nesting, and from the village a road vanishing quietly east, and in the furthest east a faint high line of trees that closed the valley like an Alpine dam. Give or take a high bright pasture, the slopes and peaks and ridges were draped with forest. Inky evergreen firs and sketched deciduous trees, their bare forms blurry with budding leaf. Soon the dense striations would be blended out with green.

Heading west, up a little and along the valley, into the latening sun. The contours, the green geometry of light and shade. An isolated farm held low within a dip. A lane that ribboned with the valley's curves and ended nowhere, the valley's end.

There are valleys in heaven too, an angel tells Adam: the world's topographical 'variety', its 'pleasure situate in hill and dale', is modelled on them. You could almost believe, discovering this valley, that the converse were the case – and I wondered whether once, before his vision blurred through grey to dark, Milton too had walked in a place like this.

At close quarters those grassed lower slopes were rough with stumps and young scrub: juniper, berberis, bramble, dog rose, saplings sprung from maple seeds that had winged their way to earth. The meadows were not cleared of trees, they were perpetually being cleared, negotiated with woods that, given half a chance, would have them straight back. I thought of the garden below, bounded by woods as paradise is, '[t]ending' or inclining 'to wild': it too was going to need lopping and pruning and propping and binding if its precincts were to be kept from wilderness. A few lone mature trees punctuated the slopes with that park-like artfulness. Tall firs, isosceles and solid, sitting tight on unlikely gradients. A lightning-splintered oak. A tree of near-perfect symmetry, its crown sweeping up to roundedness and hazy with new life: a sycamore, I thought, though time would tell. An archetypal tree on a low rise, shaggy and ancient and decked with mistletoe, a crab apple beyond doubt. I knew at once that I would come to love that tree, that I'd visit it at sunset as its form intensified against a deep-colouring sky.

And I thought I glimpsed, at last, the 'hairy sides' of the

'steep wilderness' where Milton located paradise. The words 'hairy sides' had perplexed me since those precious days, three decades past, of snowballs and *Paradise Lost*: the image that they evoked, when they formed one at all, was weird, incongruous. Who knew what Milton saw with a mind's eye sensitised by loss of physical sight, 'wisdom at one entrance quite shut out'? As a student I came across the odd psychoanalytic theory about Milton and hair, but it was the kind of literary criticism that told you as much, you suspected, about the scholar as it did about his subject. Now, all those decades later, in the steep valley, the 'hairy sides' made sense and it was simple. The 'humble shrub,/ And bush with frizzled hair implicit' were plants that spilled and tangled, briars such as rose and bramble. Honeysuckle too, perhaps, and those straggling cascades of spindle stems.

Or, instead of following the valley to its westernmost end, we angled north and climbed sheer amongst the hellebores and juniper to join the uphill forest. Pausing to look back, my chest rasping though I'd thought I was fit, the village down below, diminutive, the treetops where the garden was, the green valley flowing. We did not look up at the child-drawn mountains now, but across at them – and they showed us new perspectives, slopes beyond receding slopes, the transverse gorge with the winding road that bisected the valley: the mountainous volumes of those hairpin bends.

Into the woods, beech and fir. Scrambling on the gradient. The happiest hills are those up which you cannot walk, but must scramble. They involve you with themselves, for the steeper the hill the closer you must hold to it, and you notice things in a way that you do not when your eyes and nose are your own height from the ground. The hill's sheer physicality. Your sheer physicality, your body harking back to childhood: you are hauling yourself, one folded-up step at a time, a handhold of thrift maybe, up a Cornish cliff from a cove that is not, strictly speaking, accessible – your mother had a knack for finding ways to such places, a roaming sixth sense – and your legs are thrilled by the exertion, your senses absorbed, and you feel inexpressibly alive.

Beech leaves bright underfoot, slow winter sheddings: they were damp now, settling down to decay, but they chimed mutedly as our boots kicked and slid. Hellebores bloomed here too, in the vaulted wood, their own green on fallen copper. Leaves clumped with the promise of things to come: euphorbias, aquilegias. Woodruff and Solomon's seal. Our greasy climb, beech mould slipping dark and loose on the damp limestone. The smell of humus, earth that has lived. If ever there were a high-climbing hill, this was it. And that, as it turned out, was an uncanny thought.

For the wooded hill or mountain where the garden was had something more to reveal. Precipitous landscapes confound your sense of distance, for a short way on foot or by crow flight can be many miles around by road. As we followed the agent in that Saturday dash through the villages, we had recognised a farm, a gate. And now, when we came out at the top, the forest cleared to meadow, the hills dropping away to France, we saw that we had climbed the other side of the high-climbing hill that started with hornbeam and ascended to the whinnying pasture. Where, back on a lucid August day, one of us had said, I could live here. And now we were going to: we'd a contract to prove it. Something had brought us back to that hill. A small house with a big garden happened to be for sale. A coincidence, of course, yet . . .

It was too late in the season to dig up my parents' perennials
and hack or tease them into pieces. But I'm coming over in the
autumn, I warned Frida, with the car.

On a morning in May, summer on the air, ramsons and aquilegias flanked the river road as though they led us home. The
ramsons were setting seed, the leaves darkening and past their
best, but they washed the riverbanks green still, rippled in light
borrowed, to my eye, from the wood below my grandmother's
garden. The aquilegias bloomed on the other side of the road, the
grassy slope in which our wooded hill began. *Aquilegia vulgaris*,
the commonest and loveliest form, blue-indigo-violet, though
the flowers gleamed on this brilliant day like light itself. The
plant of which a few seeds remained in the precious envelope
that bore my father's scrawl, surely unviable now – though I'd
scatter them in the garden come September, just in case. Bring
them home – an interesting thought – to where they ran wild.

Hornbeam. The trees along the road, the river, were in full
leaf now. Maple and hazel; hornbeam in abundance, luminous.
Leaves from a Sussex bluebell wood, from the hedge of a Sussex
garden. That living, connective something that is more than
recognition – that grows and morphs, and sometimes sparks in
new places and unexpected ways.

Culpeper did not dignify hornbeam with a heading of its
own. His main entry on beech mentions in passing the 'other
small rough sort, called in Sussex, the small Beech; but in Essex,
Hornbeam': it would be another century before Carl Linnaeus
laid the foundations of modern botanical classification, and
hornbeam was still widely assumed – the assumption lives on in

many of its common names – to be a kind of beech. An inferior kind, Culpeper seems to suggest here, small and rough: lesser, coarse, unrefined. But you should not be too quick to hear disparagement in those words, for whether hornbeam is intrinsically smaller than beech in stature or in leaf – I've often taken the one for the other from a distance – 'rough' is an accurate descriptor. Hornbeam is literally rough around the edges. Its leaves are serrated like the blade of a wood saw, and the crown of a hornbeam tree or the outline of a hornbeam hedge, unless it is newly clipped, is more textured to the eye – rougher, paradoxically softer – than its beech equivalent. And the rough edges of the hornbeam leaf are formed by pleats that gather individually between its ligneous veins and filter light in that incomparable way: the visceral green of coming home. Enracination.

I love that word, the whole business of rooting or putting down roots, and something more. I love the way 'en*rac*inate' takes root as you say it, that stressed second syllable rooting the word as it were in its own origins – the French *racine*, from the Latin *radix*, both of which mean root. The word's oppositeness, in meaning and on the tongue, to '*de*racinate' – an English word deriving from the French *déraciner* and meaning, the dictionary states, to 'pluck or tear up by the roots; uproot, eradicate, exterminate'. Not so long ago, though, thinking about words and roots, I opened the dictionary and discovered that there is no such word as 'enracinate'. At some point I had picked up the French verbs *enraciner*, to root, and *s'enraciner*, to put down roots or settle. If the French *déraciner* has an antonym, I had assumed, then surely our 'deracinate' had one too. It's a pity that it does not, for 'enracination' is the word that comes to me when I think of how we found our way to the garden on the wooded hill. Connecting with a place, soil. Putting down roots, taking root, rooting selves and plants – something that is always happening and happening further, for if roots end they end in atrophy, or rot. But you cannot unthink a favourite word, even if you have learned that it does not exist. You wouldn't want to.

On the first of July I put the grey city behind me. The funds had cleared, the house was ours. The Schmidts had proposed a handover time of eleven o'clock, and the removal men would follow in the afternoon. Shaun would come home after work, not back to the apartment this time: home. The marsh mallow was tucked behind my seat, feebly alive. Alongside it was a small pot of compost in which I'd buried the hellebore fragment: I had watered it from time to time, but it showed no sign of life.

The grey day, the ill-tempered motorway: I barely noticed. Off at Basel, the long road south-west, the valley twisting on and on, the road with the river with the rail tracks. Many villages and two small towns. A roadside heckling as I entered the first – *NEIN! NEIN! NEIN! NEIN!* – poster after poster, another referendum on the way (YES! I heard myself say, unconcerned with the referendum). A quince tree trained against a gable wall. It was big with leaf, and it branched up and out into a perfect tended form. The valley sides: limestone, Scots pine, Norway spruce. A whitish track curved through a steep meadow, shaping a landscape. A road sign in French – the *Röstigraben* crossed – and, in the green valley bottom, a bridge of complementary red.

The cloud lifting and splitting with light. South now, straight for the hills, their green light through rent cloud. The winding road and the hornbeam. Nearly home.

The spindle at the foot of the track by the house was spangled with green-white flowers; they'd be over with in Sussex, morphing already into those outlandish berries. The flowers of the spindle tree are widely described as 'insignificant' – but if you look at one carefully you may well disagree. It has four pale petals that radiate from a bulbous green centre like a four-bladed propeller head, and four fleshy green stamens that bring snail tentacles to mind: exquisite alien geometry. I lingered at the spindle now, its racemes of otherworldliness, before I walked to our front door and tugged at the lever of the carillon.

The Schmidts were almost ready to leave. We dealt with keys and practicalities – to my gratitude they had organised information and labelled things meticulously – and then, Herr Schmidt said, there was just one last thing: a lady from the electricity company was coming to read the meter at one-thirty. No problem, I said, I'll be here. Oh no, said Herr Schmidt, we can't leave until the meter has been read. It's no big deal, I said, all I have to do is let her in. No, said Herr Schmidt, I want to watch her take the reading. *But it's not even noon!* Oh. OK.

I went outside, feeling resentful: an hour or two was nothing in the scheme of things, but I wished they would leave. It was my garden, and it wasn't quite. I wandered around, knowing I should enjoy this time before the removal lorry delivered days of work – but I found that I could not begin to make the garden's acquaintance while the Schmidts were still on the premises. Their presence was stifling. I resisted an urge to rip out some variegated periwinkle there and then – to grip the stems at their bases, a handful, and yank them sharply, the soil pattering; Herr Schmidt had lived here for forty years, I could grant him two more hours. The periwinkle cultivar, its green leaves patterned loudly with cream, jarred with the sheer green leaves of the native

Vinca minor that spread through deep shade behind the pond. Variegation is an irregularity of pigmentation. When such mutations occur they are propagated by growers and prized by gardeners for their ornamental qualities: visit almost any garden centre and its aisles will, where there are hostas or *Euonymus fortunei* or hollies or periwinkles, be busy with green-and-gold-, green-and-yellow-, green-and-cream-patterned leaves. The bronzing greens of a *Penstemon digitalis* are a different matter, for like the silvered greens of wormwood and lavender they are intrinsically green. At a visceral level that I cannot explain I want leaves to be green – unless they are deciduous and it is autumn. There is something wrong about a holly, that winter-solstice symbol of evergreen life, that is not absolutely, glossily green. I love the green patterns of green leaves, their shapes and textures and infinite green dealings with light. The dark glinting tapestry of native periwinkle.

In the end I went back to the car, where I ate an unusual lunch of things I had found when emptying the fridge that morning – I remember some browning blue cheese and limp coriander – and waited until a cheerful lady arrived to read the meter. I went into the garden again, giving the Schmidts space to take their leave of the house.

I waited and waited, and then they were done. They came outside to say goodbye: Herr Schmidt seemed angry but I think he was sad, and that was sad to see. As we were wishing each other well, Frau Schmidt paused and pointed at the ground: *AMEISEN!* she exclaimed, ANTS! There were ants in the lawn! So there are, I said, I do hope you make it to Bern before the rush hour. *Ich muss spritzen,* I have to spray them. *Not my idea of organic gardening.* Please don't worry, there's really no need. *Aber ich muss spritzen!* NO! Sorry, no – I don't want you to spray the ants. But you cannot have ants in the lawn! Sure I can, I said. The Schmidts went on their way.

I thought about another moving day long past, a woodpecker drilling the lawn for ants. I wondered whether green woodpeckers visited this garden too, or would when the ant populations had recovered. I crouched down and peered into the grass, its other world of matted stems. The ants were busy, and two or three carried translucent larvae in their mandibles. Maybe they too were moving home, as ants do from time to time: I hoped they were not uprooting their colony because we had disturbed them. As if on cue, the removal lorry rumbled up the lane.

At last, when the men had left, I walked around the garden. Late sun pooled through the trees and I breathed the garden in. Shaun would be home before long. Home: I'd soon get used to the word again.

The gnome had gone from the front garden but the blue hedgehog remained, its smirk now bordering on insolence. I tested keys and poked around in outbuildings. The Schmidts had left us many things, including a basket for the dog we didn't have and several pairs of old shoes. There was a huge old kitchen cupboard in the shed, and I opened its double doors. I'd had my doubts about the organic garden, but nothing had prepared me for the grim farcicality of what the cupboard contained. The shelves were packed with bottles and cartons of chemicals, arranged by genre and excruciatingly detailed in the forms of life against which they were marshalled. Ants, of course, and wasps, and aphids of both specified and unspecified colour or woolliness. Slugs. Two kinds of fungus. Algae. Moss. General vegetation. There were sinister archaic cartons – who knows how long they had been there – some of which may have contained substances now banned for horticultural use. Three different types of rodenticide. A chemical arsenal that, Shaun later said, would suffice to take out a small state.

I felt then that the place was not just stifled, but poisoned: a stifled, toxic plot. But the garden was about to start living again, and I could say the same of myself.

That evening Shaun and I dined on pizza and champagne at a rickety table on the little terrace with the improvised steps. The redundant stairwell earned a new designation, the 'death pit', and we resolved to install some lights or get the thing covered over.

We sat out into the night, the mountains dark against the darkening sky. The deep rural darkness that my body knew from childhood, before I went off to live in cities. Dark that you see with open eyes, that absorbs you and mops up thoughts, and shows you new stars in its utterness. That makes you ready for sleep, though you want to stay up all night and watch those new stars, your mind emptying. The garden there, breathing, in the dark. The woods, too. Wildness at the garden's edges, banished but there.

Night sound, its pulsing accumulation, out-lulling quiet. The running stream. Cricket wings rasping, finely tuned. The pure tones of cow bells and the solemn ones of the church clock. And then – listen! – two notes were splashing in air. We knew their perfect pitch from long ago, and the calm song of midwife toads grew into the night. A benediction.

The Garden

Another evening shaded out, the garden waking to dark. Crickets. Rustlings. Toad song. The music of the spheres. A pair of bats, their passing shriek-squeak: winged mammals, liminal things in haste between day and night. Through the treetops and around the house, back and around in a looping pattern, finding their way by the feel of sound, their wondrous cheiropteran sense. When the bat call has faded from earshot it thrums still – you know it – against the house, the trees, the cliff, the garden's sides. It echoes in your own senses, in the viscera and neurons of your memory, and you think of a little girl in a cotton nightdress at an open bedroom window. You have often wondered what became of her. The nightdress had a scratchy trim, you notice now with hindsight and a prickling at the neck.

I am not at a window now, I am in the garden in gathering dark. Shaun is around. The evening seems still, but is not. Scents come and go on warm air, the potency of stocks, the sweet green of drying hay. Farmyard manure. There are currents of freshness too, stirred by the stream or released from the small back patio, the limestone corner where house becomes cliff. Time for dew: it draws something from the earth, the 'vegetal' smell that Shaun, these days, associates with coming home.

I don't know how long I have been sitting here, within an angle of the stone walls, the new terrace giving on to the valley below. The view is a flux of light and atmosphere: there is something musical about its evolutions and modulations. I have watched the late light intensify on the long meadow beyond the village. Earlier, a file of reddest cows threaded slowly through the green, and once they stopped and turned in unison to look back at something I could not see. The birdsong intensified too. Later the valley was in shade, and the western sky behind the trees was bright with a colour I could not name. To the east a single peak held the last sun, ink-dark firs washed with orange. I wonder if you could paint that strange effect: my camera would round it up to brown.

The tree-textured mountain solidified at dusk. Its form dark against the deep-blueing sky. I did not notice when the moon first appeared – a storybook crescent, Venus there too, brightening and dimming – nor when the birdsong ceased but for a flurry or a call here and there, a dash between treetops, unfinished business.

I was up before five this morning, the world, the garden pinkening. The stream running bright and early, the birds sing-ing as though they'd never stopped. A large toad was sitting on the doorstep. I picked it up and it sat calm in my hand, pebble-weighty and pulsing with life. We looked at each other, and then I placed it in shade where there are rocks and alchemilla and too many slugs. It hauled itself off unhurriedly and merged into the shadow and leaf litter. A belated bat hastened for eaves or trees, fleeing dawn.

My feet brushed through dew – the days are hot at present, the nights cool and limestone-moist – and I scrambled up the meadow slope and looked back down on the village, the valley, the atmosphere whitish now, the church tower faint, the church clock whited out. The tall grass was draped and strung with gossamer and the air smelled, as it felt, new. I sat down on the bench, a split section of storm-felled oak, and fingered the hard bark, the ridges and pits of oak topography, and watched the light in the moisture-charged air. A patch of mist shaped like a cloud hovered in the valley bottom, just above the ground. A cloud had gained gravity, I thought, and fallen to earth and bounced, a cloud in the place of mist. When does a cloud become mist and mist cloud? Perhaps I will ask Ed, but I think I know what his answer will be.

A heron crashed into my thoughts with a primal squawk, its great wings flapping slowly, as fast as great wings can, its legs folding down like landing gear. It touched down on an upper branch of one of our towering firs, and the branch shook frantically. I thought the huge bird would lose its balance, but the oscillations steadied and it drew itself up, collected and improbable on its flimsy perch. The poise was short-lived. The heron shifted, the branch tipped and lurched, and the bird clattered off into the wood. Usually the herons fly on a north-south axis, over the garden, out over the valley, their u-bend necks outstretched, their fishing bills primed to kill. There is something about their craggy-gangly forms that makes me think of pterodactyls.

To a non-gardening ear, Eve's morning and evening visitation may smack of routine. That is not the case. Every day takes you a new way through the garden from one plant to another, one vista to another, a stirring of air or nuance in temperature. The smells of earth and vegetation revitalised by night – you absorb them and are renewed by them as though drinking in with all your senses all that is good in the world – or an acrid hit of fox that lingers in your nostrils and mouth. The garden does not have views so much as viewpoints, for what you see changes with wind and light, humidity, the cycles and contingencies of plants.

This morning I looked at a globule of dew in the base of an alchemilla leaf. There is something about this effect, moisture rolled by the texture of a leaf into more-than-crystal clarity, that draws the eye and stills the mind. The lettuce seedlings were fewer, and a huge snail adhered to the galvanised slug barrier, digesting lollo rosso. It resisted like a suction cup when I pulled it off, and I took it to the top of the garden where it could do no harm. The snails in this place are enormous. The limestone rock and walls that shelter them provide them too with calcium to grow those prodigious shells, and birds must pick and work to get at the flesh inside. For all the redwings and blackbirds and thrushes that frequent the garden, I have never come across a bird-smashed snail shell here, only empty ones that you could almost hold to an ear.

I wondered about an aquilegia, nodding and iridescent with earliness. How you might put its intricate shape into words. Whether it had grown from a seed in that precious envelope – I sowed the last of them two years ago, soon after our arrival here, and three or four germinated – or whether it was a self-seeded native. I wondered whether it mattered. It didn't, for the species was the same, and it did, for my father had collected the seed from a plant that he grew in Sussex.

I pinched off a dead head here and there. The *Geranium* x *magnificum* has formed its last buds now, but it flowered lustily through June, its bottomless purple streaked with veins like tributaries to dark rivers. I have divided the pieces that I collected from Frida's garden the autumn before last: the plant thrives in this thin alkaline soil as it did back in England in much richer conditions, and that surprises me. The resilience of plants sometimes does: it could put a person to shame. The geranium has come a long way since my parents planted it in 1960, the house just built, the hedges not yet laid, and called it Burton's Blue. The Irish Blue too is growing like a weed, a native, and its flowers come into their own against the buffs and pales of the limestone. This morning, against the low first sun, their lavender-grey petals were shot with electric rose. Those fine pink veins are a recent discovery, though I have grown Irish Blue for years now, on and off. It must be the light.

The foliage of the Japanese anemones seemed more voluminous today; maybe it was the early hour, the garden living, waking, becoming with all its heart. Their green textures. Frida potted up two plants for me, and in the first year they neither died nor grew, as if they had been dug up so often that they feared to put down roots, or couldn't see the point. But I know now that in a month or so there will be slender stems and tactile buds, and that next year their roots will push out into the soil and send up new shoots. The anemones too have come a long way, for their place in my parents' garden pre-dates mine. I do not intend to dig them up again.

The buzzards cruise and swoop in and out of the frame of things, and they are always here at noon: two or three wheeled overhead today as I ate my lunch on the terrace. Their caw is elemental, hurled into the air, and their shadow, whether you are a person or a mouse, is ineluctable.

Later, as I worked at my desk, the French windows open, a

slow worm tumbled methodically down the garden steps and pulled itself smooth to the threshold, where a ray of sun was warming my foot. A marvellous creature, bronze and fluid, lizard eyes alert. A cricket was splayed on the window in front of me, one foreleg raised above the other, and I thought of Spiderman.

Before Shaun came home I climbed the meadow slope once more and picked an armful of flowers. Wild carrot, ox-eye daisy, scabious, salvia. I picked them as I found them, and put them in a vase as I had picked them: it was as though they had arranged themselves where they grew. It did not occur to me that the cream umbellifers and whitest daisies, the tweedy lavender buttons and purple spikes, were natives. They were neither wild flowers nor garden flowers, but flowers from the garden. They were lovely.

The hornbeam tree twists and flows before my eyes. It grows from the base of the meadow slope, a few feet above the path. Had I not found it, I tell myself, I might have planted a hornbeam here.

Right here. You are drawn to it as to the centre of things.

I have never seen its like. Although it is a fully realised tree it is barely as tall as I, a fraction of the heights to which hornbeam left at large will grow. Shaun says that it resembles a bonsai, and it does, though the curvature of its lovely crown is many times higher than any bonsai I have seen. Bonsai growers achieve their miniature extremes by specialist root pruning; this tree's roots are curtailed too, by limestone, and one day its stunted form will be ancient like a hawthorn on Malham karst. The hornbeam is diminutive, and huge.

Its fluted trunk is already showing signs of age. The special young hornbeam sheen – like slate, slow worms, leather, metal, like all of these and none in particular – has coarsened and is browning. There are bumps, and greyish blotches, and faint vertical striations. There are raised concave scars that I inflicted myself, cutting off small branches that detracted from the trunk. The textured bark may have lost its gleam, but is far from dull: it is lived-in, as human faces are, and it reflects light still, softly, like the light of spring.

When you plant a young tree, you ought to ensure that its formative branches do not cross. You should prune out inter-secting or straggly growth until those branches have formed an open, balanced crown – for chafed bark and poor air circulation catalyse disease, and what is good for a tree is, on the whole, pleasing to the eye.

But some rules have beautiful exceptions. The trunk of this tree forks into branches that fork again, and cross, and cross again, and reach out and up into a rounded crown that I trim lightly from time to time. The hornbeam has taken shape in its own way, hidden inside its twigginess while Herr Schmidt clipped its surfaces to an idea of order.

I discovered the tree towards the end of a mild January day. Months after our arrival I had still done nothing about the horn-beam slab that was neither tree nor hedge. I disliked it intensely: it was incongruous, pointless, but there was always something else to do. Then, on that winter afternoon, admittedly bored with work, I looked up from my laptop and decided that the thing was intolerable. I pulled on my wellingtons – I kept them by the desk, with my trowel and secateurs – and fetched the loppers and wood saw from the shed. It was too warm for a jacket, too warm for January.

The unhappy structure had three main stems, and the old year rustled in curled-up leaves as I cut the two outer stems to the ground. The central stem was thicker and harder to reach, bristling with growth. I cut away the lower twigs, a slender branch or two, clearing space to work with the saw, and as I lopped a taut and lively trunk took shape. I clipped upwards until the trunk branched out. Then, with my trusty secateurs – their weight in my hand, a forged curve cradling and working with the base of my thumb – I clipped tiny shoots from those branches, their Vs and twists and turns and returns. I stood back and looked. The revealed tree twisted upwards, horn-strong and poised, balletic.

The hornbeam tree's spell. A Sussex bluebell wood, its special green light. The animate interior of a garden hedge, and a threading dog rose. A way of being at home, a way to being at home.

The garden was overwhelming. As I root around for words with which to tell of its abundance I am conscious that I might be accused of exaggeration – but I will have to take that risk. From our first July night, whatever the season or weather, the time of day, the garden held me immersed. It laid claim to the senses, opened up dimensions that the outside world passed over. It was life at full throttle, life for its own sake. It piled up impressions in a joyful blur, and it resolved itself into moments of lucid detail, clear and bright as those dewdrops on alchemilla leaves.

There was a bright fluttering at the margins of my vision. I thought it was happiness, and it was, but when I focused on those edges there was always something else as well, a play of light or leaves, or leaves in light, or light in leaves, or butterflies.

So many butterflies, red admirals and peacocks, and great pale things like petals shed on wind. Chalkhill blues, their place in my heart, bluer than harebells, of the Sussex Downs. The harebell family flourished here, from those simple bells of downland blue to a lush, mauve-flowered species that I bought once in Cambridge. Here it is native to the meadow slope, native to the garden.

It was many months before I saw the first slow worm. One morning, towards the end of our first Jura spring, I sat outside the front door with a mug of coffee. The renovation work was under way, the back of the house a building site, and for much of that year I would haunt the ends and edges of the place, rummaging and looking: the meadow, the wood, the pond, the bank where ground elder crept in, the neat little front garden cut from the limestone cliff. It was not so neat now: I had dug out conifers and variegated hostas, and planted alchemilla and aquilegias, Sussex geraniums, amongst the catmint that remained. All those foliage textures of green and blue and zinc. Flowers that would sing a rainbow, its limestone-cool notes: greenish, blue, indigo, violet. I put in a *Geranium* Rozanne as well, its greens and blue-violets preternaturally bright, bright still beyond November, as if the plant were above the seasons; it came onto the market long after my mother had made her list. Green-stemmed dogwoods. A native rose, *Rosa glauca*, named for the muted blue-green of its airy foliage. The glaucous leaves are tinged and veined with reddishness as though colour leached from its purpled arching stems; not for nothing was this shrub once known as *Rosa rubrifolia*, the red-leaved rose.

A pulsatilla for Shaun, hoary purples and lichen tones. The European pasque flower is related to the 'prairie crocus', the emblematic flower of Shaun's native Manitoba. *Pulsatilla vulgaris*, I learned from *Flora Helvetica*, is still to be found in a corner of the eastern Jura not so far from here.

The sun was cool on my face and arms, the air washed by early rain, the coffee dark and bracing as coffee should be. It was good to be alive. Our wrought-iron table was rusting fast in the valley's unique humidity, that medium of greenness and magical light. Native ferns unfurling, a fiddle-head ensemble. A colony of ferns grew higher up where the garden became wood and bright moss sagged loose like fleece, and back in the autumn I had dug some up – their fibrous crowns ripped loudly as I cut and pulled them apart – and planted them here where the rocky border merged with the limestone cliff and the light was always complex.

Something glinted amongst the flickering greens. A slow worm reared up as if to sniff the air, taste the day on its fast lizard tongue. The sheer strength of its musculature. It lunged at a bright dogwood stem, and I wondered if it reached out with phantom limbs, the habit of a distant evolutionary past when slow worms had legs: if I had X-ray vision I would see traces of shoulder and pelvic bones on the creature's now-slithering skeleton.

No doubt there were always slow worms behind the scenes, but this first sighting made my heart sing. Nearly four seasons had passed since the soil was last flecked with metaldehyde, this green place made to be what it was not, strewn and sprayed with substances inimical to life. The garden had been detoxifying. I could feel it relaxing, I was sure, hear it breathing free and deep – or maybe that was me.

Pesticides and fungicides and herbicides are not a matter

of right and wrong: plenty of gardeners choose to use them. That said, I do not understand why you would dump chemicals around your own green space. Why would you poison or eliminate the food supply of creatures whose presence in your garden is a privilege – yours, not theirs – and that, by living and feeding, keep aphids and slugs and snails, more or less, from being your problem? The hoverflies and ladybirds; those redwings and thrushes and blackbirds; the newts and toads and hedgehogs and slow worms that, if you keep your eyes open and are extraordinarily lucky, will bring revelations to your lawn, to your very doorstep? Whether or not there was a connection, I took the slow worm for a sign that our little paradise was discovering some kind of ecological rhythm.

The peridot tracery of the ferns. Sapphires can be orange or yellow as well as sapphire-blue. Peridot, my birthstone, is always green: fern-green, moss-green. Peridot-green.

Moss was spreading amongst the paving bricks, I noted with satisfaction, and over the chunks of limestone that lay around in the border: I'd taken them for concrete when we arrived, for they too had been treated with herbicide and so clean were they that they looked fake. There is nothing like the greens of moss: they glow with innate light. And this moss was too luminously green to be real – unless you were there, in that moment.

Beneath the dogwood a diminutive pair of palmate leaves waved from a plastic pot. There was something unusual about them, though I was looking out for the slow worm and a moment passed before my thoughts caught up. For more than a year the pot had contained, buried in compost, the fragment of my father's hellebore that I'd brought back from Fran's garden more on principle than in hope. The shoot had not surfaced, the surface was covered with bittercress, and when we arrived here a few months later I tucked the pot out of the way.

My gardens have always been littered discreetly with small flowerpots. You plant or sow them with long shots and experiments, or a tiny rooted piece of something dug up with something else, or broken off as you weed and move things around. You set them amongst plants in corners and borders, and then you forget about them: it is an incidental business, and in any case you never carry labels in your pocket, let alone a pencil, and you are sure that if something grows you will identify it by the shape of its leaves. Months, a year later you happen upon a pot when you are rooting about under foliage or cutting something back. It might be barren but for that bittercress – a reproach of a weed that seems to crop up when your cutting or seeds have failed – and you empty the compost into the border. But within the flourishing crown of a hardy geranium you might just find a pot containing clustered dots: you swept up some aquilegia seed from the path last summer after pulling out some brittle old stems. Mallows, a small miracle: I pocketed some ripe seed heads one September day, hiking with Shaun, and pushed the blunt rounded seeds into a pot of compost, and wedged the pot between the stems of a lavender that grew on the retaining wall above the vegetable plot. Later, cutting dead wood from the lavender, bruising its foliage to pungency, I happened upon some leggy seedlings with the mallow's distinctive leaves. I'd collected the seed in the Jura hills, but my mother could just as well have harvested it from the plant in that cherished photograph.

It is worth forgetting these little pots. Aquilegia seeds need a period of stratification – exposure to cold, inducing deep dormancy that they might fully experience spring, wake into germination – so abandoning them to a harsh Jura winter was just the thing. And it is easy to give up on something too soon; just think of that anisodontea twig. I am sure, had it not been so well concealed, that I'd have emptied the hellebore pot around the roots of the dogwood long before those two leaves appeared.

I turned the pot over. Below the surface the hellebore had been very much alive: roots protruded from the drainage holes, and when I squeezed and tapped the pot a stringy ball popped out. I wondered how on earth the plant could grow for so long without leaves to make food by photosynthesis: it must, I thought, have been starving. I fetched a trowel, and held back the loosened soil with my other hand as I scooped amongst the ferns. There was a movement in my palm, something denser than earth and animate, and when I lifted my hand, slowly, it held a small dark toad. The toad had vertical pupils – I was sorry I had unearthed it, hoped the light did not hurt its night-vision eyes – and its hindquarters were encrusted with yellow eggs. A midwife toad, a male, earning its common name. The day was too light for song, but the creature's throat pulsed once and a single note sounded elsewhere.

I planted my father's hellebore there. I would never uproot it from that precious spot: I was sure of that, at the time.

We opened up the house, and the green and the light poured in.

The builders removed the low sloping roof that cut the house off from the garden, that bothered and oppressed you because you knew the garden was there. The house acquired new dimensions, vistas. The first floor grew westward, into the garden, a pitched structure with great sawn beams: I loved the blonde untreated wood that light and time would darken, its suspended weightiness, its stored-up life. The complex interior angles where old and new roofs intersected. Their forest-like vaultings, the house putting on new growth. The end façade that drew you out through glazed folding doors, out into the garden.

At night the house was more than quiet. There were patterings on the roof – raindrops, we thought, or drops shaken by trees after rain, or a cat, rats, a pine marten maybe. Things knocked and creaked, the house shifting, its timbers expanding and tightening. A dormouse stirring in its sleep.

The new terrace was retained by a wall of local limestone. The mason, a Portuguese craftsman of titanic strength, collected rocks from a nearby mountain and bumped them up the lane in his flatbed truck, load after load, a rosary swinging violently from the rear-view mirror. Steps led up from the terrace on the axis of the extended room. If you sat deep inside, your eye would move straight through the vaulted woody space, out through the central glazed door, up across the terrace, up the steps, on up the sloping lawn, to rest at an outsized earthenware urn. The bank where anemones now grew, the upward firs beyond, the wood's edge, the western sky beyond still, bright. Sometimes your feet might follow your eye, or start to, but when you opened the door to a cold damp blast – March, a lively brutal day – and stepped across the terrace, a maple leaf inlaid here and there, old now and tanned, algae greening the textures of stone, things sidetracked you. And one thing would lead to another. You might pull a groundsel seedling or two before they could hit their stride, and prod around where you planted that geranium last year – here, some pink-tipped shoots: good – and before you were aware there was mud on your hands.

I never passed the wall without touching a stone, its soft

facets and grazing roughnesses. The shapes and colours of the rocks (when does a stone become a rock?), their characters. Each its own piece of the hills, the place where the garden was. I felt it through my fingertips.

Sometimes, in summer, the doors folded back, the house wide open, the afternoon heavy and thrumming, a dragonfly would motor into the living room and whirr iridescent through the rafters.

We covered over the deadly stairwell at the foot of the cliff, where a hot day grew hottest and the evening cool began. My study opened onto the new little patio. No white walls crushed me here: my desk, my beloved London kitchen table, faced the garden through glass. A lilac fell away from the slope where the cliff became steep meadow, and when I looked out the tree's malformation gave an arching frame to what I saw.

I ought to have been content. But once I had a taste of the light and green I wanted more, more outdoors indoors. We ordered the biggest skylight that the low roof could sustain, and one day the carpenters sawed a hole directly above my desk. It's a wonder I got any work done. Now, when I was not watching the garden second by second, its movement and light and colour, its comings and goings, its sudden small dramas, I would crane my neck back and watch the framed space above.

Winter-bare field maples, stark and organic as a fabric print. Their greyish forms sun-tinted, the sky blue and solid, far from the sea. The trees' dark forms darkening at dusk, the night sky catching up. Snow: white-out darkening the room. When I was young I knew that it had snowed because my bedroom curtains glowed with a special light that foretold a day of magic. Seen from underneath, though, snow is the colour of lead. If it has fallen in big slow flakes, settled softly on the skylight, light will suggest itself in primrose or dove-grey mottlings. As it thaws and refreezes the layer becomes denser, and shrinks: you can see bits of sky, and a brilliant edge of sunlit snow. Soon, if the milder weather holds, there will be a squeegee-like juddering: the snow will slide from the skylight and crash wet to the ground, and you will think of avalanches and blink at the vividness of the revealed sky.

The field maples crowd into the frame. I'd like to say that I watch them come into leaf, but that watching is really a noticing that something has happened. The happening takes place behind your back – unless you are into time-lapse photography, which has nothing to do with plant time. I certainly watch the trees in spring and summer, the workings of light and air in the textured green canopy, until my neck aches. Autumn is announced quietly, by the fall of a yellowed leaf on glass overhead – it's the woody stem that you hear. Then the maples are charged with butter gold that shines on the greyest day.

The trees seem to lean in: sometimes I think they are falling on me. Maybe, one day, they will. I've had that vertiginous feeling, that bodily thought, before, leaning back to look up at something close and high, a cliff or a mountain face – but when I step outside I remember that the trees really do tilt out from the cliff, in over the house. Who knows how deep and fast their roots are holding? They grow out of the rock, just a few horizontal inches, and then they reach straight up for the light, tall and slender, taller and taller, leaning out as they stretch away from the fulcrum of their roots. I worried about them at first – it is in my nature, like Chicken Licken, to expect the sky to fall in – but Shaun pointed out that the trees had grown there for more than a few decades. An arborist removed the three that troubled me most, and pronounced the others sound. Small branches and debris fell on the roof in gales, but the trees themselves remained rooted. I decided that Shaun and the arborist could not both be wrong, and turned my attention back to what the skylight framed.

Water drops fallen flat. The western sky. A full moon impassive in scudding clouds. The underside of torrential rain: sheets and rivulets. A single bright star, not Venus. Summer green on green. An early-morning moonset, strange yellow skeins, the moon dissolving. Filigree frostwork. A sky rich and deep from sunset, the trees leaning in, black and pure.

A strange thing happened. I looked up from my desk on an afternoon in early spring, up past the lime tree to the top of the garden. Something about the light – the way the sun angled in and pooled intensely on the shaded grass – took me back to London, many years back, to those first moments in our echoing new home, to the window and the woodpecker. As I looked now there was a peripheral flash of red and olive, so brief I must have imagined it, and when I adjusted my focus the garden was still. I got back to work, sent an email or two. When I next looked up a woodpecker was working the grass, its plumage flickering moss tones, its scarlet cap blazing as it hopped through sun. That was a coincidence: we'd never seen a green woodpecker here before, though we often heard the spotteds drumming up in the woods.

If I had thought the woodpecker into being it was heartwarmingly real. It meant that the ants were thriving, that the garden was recovering – that its fractured ecology was knitting back, or knitting in new ways.

*

I ought to have planned the garden while the building work was under way – mapped it all out with sketches and lists, maybe even a scale design, as a proper gardener would have done – but I did not. That said, there are other ways of making plans. Every time you stand at a window or sit at a desk, and look, or turn at the top of a flight of steps, or pause on your way up the meadow slope, and look, you are planning. And scheming: you have agreed with Shaun that there is no need for yet another tree on the lower lawn – but you badly want a quince tree and it will fit right there, just off-centre, where an underground spring rises close to the surface; quinces relish sogginess as grass does not. In the gently sloping grass beyond you will plant bulbs of *Narcissus poeticus* – responsibly sourced, of course – and the bright-eyed native of those otherworldly meadows will glimmer, perfumed, in the tree-filtered light, and when you stop to inhale it all your senses will be possessed. The Schmidts' rudbeckia near the steps is just too much, too yellow: you should rip it out, once and for all. The leaning lilac's inner curve: if you cut out that straggly branch the arch will be perfect, for the time being.

The two firs tower from the shadowy place where woods and garden merge. Their vertical solidity this bright afternoon, their stark shadow across the grass, the dark dimension in between. If you planted a medlar there, on the upper lawn – it is not really a lawn any more, but a green space in which, left to their own devices, ox-eye daisies will shimmer knee-high in May, and grasses will grow tall to seed, and Shaun will mow green paths through their living, humming, stridulating depths – if you should plant a medlar there it will thrive in the afternoon shade, and at a certain point between spring and summer its not-quite-white five-petalled flowers will store up light and release it sparingly, and in autumn its big exotic leaves will flame beacon-bright, salmon and gold and rose and chartreuse, in the darkness of the firs.

I did not spare a thought for the leylandii and old boundary shrubs when the mason razed them like so much derelict concrete: one day we would plant a hornbeam hedge. We resurfaced the garden path with stone; there was only one position for the path itself, hugging the base of the meadow slope. Once the building work had finished I unreeled a hosepipe on the trampled lawn, and curved it to mark out a deep border that was contoured to the path and the slope like the lane that meandered through the valley. As for the lawn, we scattered some grass seed and left the rest to chance. Daisies would show themselves soon enough, tentatively at first, as stars do when the evening is thick and not quite dark. Clover would move in too, and honeybees in on the clover.

I will never finish planting the border: I never really started. It happened, some uprooted, travel-weary plants from England and bits of alchemilla that I saved from the building site. The main thing was to get them into the ground; I could move them later, once I had drawn up a planting scheme. But I knew I would never get around to the latter either, that I'd carry on planting and looking and replanting, finding a rhythm as I dug and scooped, my bare hands in their element, easing each plant into place, the soil back around its roots, firming the surface. Maybe, deep down, I could not be bothered – but that was not the whole story. Without consciously considering it, I had to do things the garden's way. A garden is not a blank page, a tabula rasa: something of this garden was here first, and I had to discover it for myself. The garden could only take shape from within.

At last we planted the hornbeam hedge. The trees were three years old, and though they had been grown as upright stems their hornbeamness was irrepressible. They made me think of stick men drawn gesturing or in motion.

The hedge was of this place and it was also of Sussex, the garden and the wood. It bounded the garden in more than one sense: this garden of soil and limestone and green-smelling air, and the garden that I carried with me, in my heart. That garden may be intangible, of no specific shape, but it is always hedged with hornbeam.

I loved the way the hornbeam hedge dipped and rose and flowed with the ground. Its green depths would fill out fast, and we would clip it lightly with hand shears two or three times a year. I'd peer into it as it grew, the light in those lovely pleated leaves, the trees' growing contortions, their conversation with the twisting little tree that I discovered on a January day. If you traced a line to that tree from each end of the hedge, the hornbeam tree would form the apex, the hornbeam hedge the base, of a near-perfect isosceles triangle: the garden's chance design.

'The *Horn-beam*', the writer and diarist John Evelyn told the Royal Society in 1662 – Milton lying low, an exile at home, dictating drafts of *Paradise Lost* – 'makes the noblest and the stateliest *Hedges*'. It 'grows tall, and so sturdy as not to be wronged by the *Winds*', and it 'flourishes with a glossie and polish'd *verdure* which is exceeding delightful'. Evelyn was right, and he should be, for *Sylva* – as his paper was published, the first book on the newly formed society's list – saw great acclaim as a textbook on forestry, and Evelyn was a man who loved trees.

Since I first read *Paradise Lost* in that charmed winter interval all those years ago, I have assumed the 'verdurous wall' of Milton's paradise to be a hornbeam hedge. Sometimes I wonder whether Milton did too.

I met Milton often as I worked my way through undergraduate and postgraduate degrees in literature. Whenever I opened *Paradise Lost* a word, or a relationship between words, or a passage of several hundred lines, led me into complexities of history and theology, a scholarly domain. Sometimes it was exhilarating – but along the way I forgot how to read, and by the time I completed my doctorate I could not pick up any book with an open mind, let a poem or a novel happen to me. The need to have an opinion, to find something to say about everything I read, got in the way.

One bright Jura day – I do not remember exactly when, but the young hornbeam hedge was in full leaf, polished and verdurous – I took down *Paradise Lost* and began to read. Just like that. I own several copies of *Paradise Lost*: my favourite, an anniversary gift from Shaun, has thick old creamy pages and engravings by Gustave Doré, but I have always read the paperback that I bought in Gower Street aged seventeen, thrilled and daunted by its annotated bulk. The volume has bulked up further over the years with strips of torn paper and Post-it notes and pencillings: it is interleaved and marked with bits of me. The corners of its covers have grown blunt and soft, and the spine has loosened such that the book these days, very handily, opens flat.

I carried on reading.

I think the garden led me back into *Paradise Lost*. Not because Milton's poem is 'about' a garden, nor – when it is not presuming into Heaven or dropping down to Hell, or traversing the dark inclement wastes of Chaos – 'set' in that mythic original garden, but because it is the poem of a gardener. One who gardens, who has an affinity for gardens, who thrives on small negotiations with the natural world. Organising, tending, eliciting, pruning: a garden, a poem. You do not need anecdotal claims that Milton always had a garden and 'appears to have amused himself in botanical pursuits' to know that he was a gardener. You just have to read his words on the page, or hear them read aloud.

Milton's words infiltrated the garden in simple ways that, at last, I was free to appreciate. Those multisensory 'airs', melodic and fresh, cool, perfumed, earthy, tuned for every sense but sight. Dewdrops – a visual memory, perhaps – 'which the sun/Impearls on every leaf and every flower', but especially euphorbia and alchemilla. You could close your eyes and lose yourself in the stream's 'liquid lapse'. You could walk to the top of the garden where a wild rose blooms amongst spindle, and close your eyes again, and concentrate, and breathe in that most elusive of '[n]ative perfumes'.

I learned what I had not noticed before, that the forbidden fruit was more suggestive of quince than of apple: it was 'downy', and diffused an 'ambrosial smell'. I knew that smell. Every autumn, back in London, I would pick the first yellow quince from our tree – its skin was leathery, and coated with down that rubbed off onto my hands – and set it in a dish on the living-room window sill. Sun-warmed, it scented the indoor air one suggestion at a time. I thought back, too, to my conversation with Herr Correlli, the kind green-fingered car mechanic, and my idle speculation that the fruit tree I loved above all others was the species that bore the forbidden fruit. No matter that the paradisiacal diet is raw (in paradise there is never 'fear lest dinner cool') and that raw quinces are inedible for all of that ambrosial smell. If you wish to taste paradise in these postlapsarian times you must cook quince long and slow, but maybe things were different before the fall; who knows?

Now that the hedge was planted I could think about getting my quince tree. It would glow with ancient-shaped golden fruits on lightless November afternoons, like fruit trees painted in tempera centuries ago.

I learned something else from *Paradise Lost* this time around. Paradise was not merely surrounded by woods, or enclosed from woods that must be lopped and pruned and kept in check. Paradise contained and was infiltrated by woods: woods that might prove to be 'wild woods', and woods to which Adam and Eve retreat, ashamed, after tasting that quince-like fruit.

Whichever way you looked at it, the garden was of the woods.

You go into the garden, out in, and potter, fiddle about – garden – as that toddler did in mud and space, in her element. One thing will lead to another.

A green-stemmed dogwood against the wall in sun. The stems are not quite olive nor yet quite lime but brilliant, and their bumpy leaf buds have filled out, loosened, while your back was turned. The leaves will unfurl at their certain point in green's infinite range, and you'll marvel once again that things of such softness could be so crisply grooved. The stones coloured by cool spring sun, the sun low in the day. Up the steps. A black squirrel leaping through the overhead trees, its limbs outstretched in bursts of flight from one tree to the next, each pause a pure instant of animal vigilance. Ash to maple, maple to maple, the canopy pushed high from the high-climbing slope. The path's granite glitter dull with winter residue. Another cluster of groundsel seedlings.

The groundsel came in with a consignment of topsoil, and although I try to weed it out before it can spread fungal rust around, or flower to set a thousand drifting seeds, it replicates itself almost overnight. Groundsel (*Senecio vulgaris*) belongs to a plant category known as ephemerals because their growing cycles are brief: unlike an annual, let alone a perennial, this common European native can germinate, and flower, and set seed, and germinate again, several times in one season. In practice a gardener might describe it as the opposite of ephemeral, for the plants themselves may be short-lived but the groundsel is always bloody there. It is the very definition of a weed – a wild plant growing where it is not wanted, the dictionary says, though if I were defining the word I would include unwanted cultivated plants as well, like that cream-patterned periwinkle.

I tugged at the groundsel seedlings now, but the soil was compacted and I went off to find my trowel, its copper point sharp and polished by earth. You try to look after your trowel and secateurs – a well-made tool is a precious thing – but you invariably put things down and find yourself searching in long grass, on the garden's many ledges, amongst foliage and under new heaps of weeds. Today the trowel was on the rug beneath my desk. As I jabbed assertively at the groundsel a smattering of new aquilegias caught my eye, self-seeded from a ripened head or an armful of clippings. With the tip of the trowel I levered up some seedlings on lumps of soil, hoping their roots would not notice, and set them into spaces amongst geraniums and perovskias and young montana divisions. In the coming months their maidenhair leaf forms would lend new rhythm to the border, quiet at first but growing in volume as the weeks went by.

There was a bright alchemilla seedling too, growing in the wrong place – the lawn – but wanted as a weed is not. I could not remove it without disturbing its roots, and would have to pot it up. I used to think alchemilla would grow anywhere, from moist shade to drystone walls, Wealden clay to Jurassic lime, and I've learned that it will, more or less – but only on its own terms. When I first unpotted the Sussex perennials here, slicing a geranium in half as I went, a penstemon into three, and settled the plants into the new border, and looked, and dug up one or two again, and planted them again, and looked, I began to see alchemilla in my mind's eye, mounding and ribboning along the back, bordering the path beneath the high trees where the soil was dry: green upon dew-transmuting green. Alchemilla had spread itself around the garden plentifully. I lifted plants and replanted them along that barren strip, over and again, over time, digging in compost as I went, watering and watering, and not one survived long enough to put down roots.

Toad song, a single note. I did not hear it strike up; I seldom do. It is like the onset of rain: you think you may have heard or felt a drop, but maybe you did not. Toad song drips into your consciousness, one more-than-liquid note at a time, until you are listening. I put down my trowel and went up to the shed to find a pot for the alchemilla seedling. As I crunched onto gravel the song broke off and a brief, frantic scuffling was absorbed by the wall.

There is something enigmatic about the drystone walls that

hold the garden back from downhill collapse. An earthy laby-
rinth runs amongst the huge stones or small rocks, the earth and
rock beyond, a whole realm of teeming life that shows itself in
signs and glimpses. A fresh hole in impacted soil between two
stones. It is perfectly round: a shrew, perhaps, or a slow worm,
or a young adder (shudder). A dull flash across your path, a
small rodent surprised by footfall, hurtling for the wall. That
scuffling, a tiny toad on which you almost trod mid-song, and
thankfully did not. A stone, newly dislodged, that has rolled to a
halt on the path. That would take the strength of a rat or a snake
– or maybe the earth and stones have subsided from a thousand
comings and goings, shiftings and scratchings and burrowings.

I turned to look back down the garden. The day had
dimmed; I'd been outside for longer than I thought. The eastern
sky warming pink and orange, spindle-berry tones: that happens
here sometimes, on special days, as the sun declines to the west.
A charmed moment just before dusk, a brightening surge inside
the garden, neither pink nor grey. The hornbeam hedge glossy
and sinuous. It was suddenly, briefly bare, as bare as hornbeam
can ever be, the last leaves shed as it awakens in bud. And here,
now, the light strange, the hornbeam poised, the waxy blossom
of a *Viburnum* x *bodnantense* rhymed with the amelanchier's
pinkish buds, a shade that I would recognise but cannot name.
The hedge, the blossom, the buds, the here and now. Something
like this has happened before: a perfect, fleeting convergence of
things. I think the garden's life is threaded on such moments.
For the most part they pass unnoticed, but when you chance
on one you are witness to a revelation. In a day or two the viburnum blossom would fade, the amelanchier buds expand, to
different lighter shades.

At close quarters the viburnum's flower heads were complexities of whitish to deepest rose. I breathed in a sweet fresh
draught and headed back to pot up the little alchemilla. My
father's penstemons were very much at home, clumping up pro-
digiously. I dug up two plants there and then, and pulled them
apart and replanted them, five or six now, and watered them
in – and the aquilegias, I almost forgot. One of the penstemons
looked out of place. I dug it up, wet and muddy now, and set it
back in the ground a few inches to the left. My hands and trowel
were sticky with mud, my knees too, somehow, though the grass
seemed dry.

You are in your element. In the garden, in the moment, doing
your own thing. Gardening, whatever that means. A feeling that
you may have known many years ago, a way of feeling connected with things: it has little to do with innocence, and much to
do with a dog rose and a hornbeam hedge. Drenched cobwebs
at first light. Being at home in the garden. The little girl grew up,
but she never disappeared. These days, when she goes to sleep,
the garden is on her mind as it is on Eve's, '[w]orks of day past,
or morrow's next design'. Cherished perennials multiplied, the
border's rhythms strengthening. Ground elder to weed out of
the bank – it has crept back and is stifling the montanas – and
Euphorbia amygdaloides to move down from the wood, its lovely
green forms acid on dark. That quince tree to order: it's a little
late to plant one, but you cannot wait until next year.

There is the meadow slope to climb at first light.

'Now as I was young and easy', Dylan Thomas began his
own enduring poem of paradise lost. You are not young now, of
course – but here, in the garden, you are easy.

The church clock strikes the hour, one chime too many. You

have been on garden time, which knows no hours – but it has gone 'shut of evening flowers' and your eyes have adjusted to the darkening. The two streets below smudged with halogen, the church tower vague in thickened light. The forms blending in the valley, field with tree with roof. A fine reclining crescent moon. A hunting owl, its haunting call in tow. Toad song, naturally.

A cool moist rush of air. Tomorrow the garden will glister with dew.

When it rained the pond was stirred to a milky, muddy suspension. Once though, on a day after torrential spring rain, the land sodden, the damp air gentle on my face, the pond was pellucid; utterly still. I had never seen such clarity, I thought then. The bottom was hyperreal, as though the silt and reed shoots, the twigs and fallen maple leaves, had acquired new dimensions or were seen through spectacles that were fractionally too strong.

Shaun loves the pond: he loves the garden, its place amongst the hills, the valley; the light and the green; the air, its fresh vegetal quality that, he says, you will never smell anywhere but here. As soon as he comes home from work, weather permitting, Shaun puts on his old shoes and walks up to the top of the garden. I can see him there now, in my mind's eye, half obscured by reeds in the fir-dark shade, inspecting something – the arrivals and sudden disappearances of frog or newt spawn, the creatures taking shape in those little jellied globes; reeds flattened by a heron's crash landing; wild strawberries ripening at the edge, perfume-flavoured. Kingcups that are huge and more than yellow, and lovelier than water lilies. Maybe he returns the gaze of the languid, predatory newts: they hang watchful from the water's surface and then they flip and swim, their small limbs working purposefully, their bellies flashing orange, down to where leaves layer in their patterns of decay. Maybe he is lost in thought, or no thought at all, as the garden brings him back from his working day, its clamour and its claims, and there is something contented in the way he stands. And that makes me happy, too.

'Flowers worthy of Paradise'. That was it, exactly. I must have read those words in *Paradise Lost* on many occasions – but now I noticed them for the very first time, the phrase and the lines that made it meaningful. They merged with my thinking, my gardening.

When we first look into Milton's garden, with Satan, we see:

> *Flowers worthy of Paradise which not nice art*
> *In beds and curious knots, but nature boon*
> *Poured forth profuse on hill and dale and plain . . .*

These lines take a passing swipe at the 'niceness' or precious-ness of seventeenth-century garden fashions: at intricate knot gardens and parterres, over-bred tulips with crazy price tags, flowers complicated out of themselves, dianthus pinks grown 'double' (another poet, Andrew Marvell, quipped brilliantly) as the aspirational gardener's 'mind'. But Milton's words said more than this to me; I recognised my garden in them. They voiced something that the garden had been telling me in its own word-less ways, at which stray bluebells and a germinated acorn had hinted many years before – not that I was listening then nor, had I listened, could have understood. Something had happened, it dawned on me, since our arrival here: I had ceased altogether to distinguish between 'wild' and 'garden' plants. In this garden the only plants were plants worthy of paradise.

The aquilegias. The montanas planted in London suburbia, at home in the Alps and the Jura hills and edging back into the garden that was made from those hills. I dig up clumps from the foot of the bank, the boundary with the track, and tease them apart into many small plants. Each is a neat assemblage of tongue-like leaves, a tuft of roots gathered at its base as in a woodcut from Gerard's *Herball*. The roots are almost transparent, and so short that you wonder how they could take hold readily, as they will, the little plants clump up again without delay, doing what montanas do. Then again, the montana is of this soil, of this hilly or mountainous limestone place – though it grew happily enough, too happily some would say, in our London clay. I thread some into the border, two quick trowel scoops at a time: their patinated leaves will grow softly and their florets whirl motionless, blue through purple, pivoting on that roseate glow. Others I replant on the bank, further up where the variegated periwinkle used to be and ground elder is advancing fast. I hope the montanas will establish here, with some stinking hellebores – their sea-deep evergreen leaves, their chalky green flower heads – that I found amongst rocks behind the pond. I hope that grasses and ox-eye daisies and campanulae will make their way down the bank from the humming, buzzing, flowering swathe that used to be the upper lawn.

I should not complain about the ground elder, though I do of course. I don't have a leg to stand on, for the tawdry periwinkle kept the elder at bay. *Aegopodium podagraria*, the gardener's nemesis, grows freely in the margins of the woods and the fields.

It belongs here, whether you like it or not, and mostly it does no harm. But where you decide it's not wanted ground elder is an execrable weed, colonising the soil by underground stealth, giving roots a bad name. Even if you resorted to glyphosate, which is unthinkable, you would never gain the upper hand. Every so often I hack it out from the bank and hope the hellebores and montanas will one day hold their own. Perhaps I should not have ripped out the periwinkle, but I did: I hated those patterned leaves. Elsewhere I do not mind the ground elder, its massed green foliage. Down near the track, up beyond the pond in a patch that I have never explored.

By accident I learned to watch and wait. One May we looked on helplessly as the garden grew ungardened through long weeks of rain, and a spotted orchid appeared in the thriving lawn. Shaun left that patch to run wild too, when he finally got the mower out, and the following spring three orchids bloomed in endorsement.

I dug out the Schmidts' rudbeckia in chunks – I thought it jarred with the reds and pinks, the earthy sedums and muted anemones, hot echinaceas, Michaelmas daisies – but fresh shoots grew back like weeds, and I left them to it when the building work began. And on a charmed December morning, bright and sharp, the garden all the colours of frost, the earth's breath on the air, I walked up the path towards the steps and a surge of red and black and white and gold rose from the darkened seed heads of the rudbeckia. A charm – that aptest collective noun – of feasting goldfinches. I loved the rudbeckia then. I would come to like it too, the following year, the massed clear-cut flower heads, their dark eyes, their colour that, when I gave it a chance, was so much more than yellow.

Once you have cleared or enclosed or acquired a green space, begun to organise or reorganise what is there – to garden it – you have to carry on. You cannot stop gardening, for the woods have a prior claim on this place and they will inch back at the slightest opportunity. So will the ground elder, and the young wild boar that prospected one night for roots and beetles in the lawn. To lop and prune, as any gardener knows, as Milton knew, is to enter into a circular relationship with the natural world. The very practice of cutting back stimulates new growth: the more she and Adam 'labour', Eve complains on the morning of the fall, the more their 'work . . . grows':

> . . . *what we by day*
> *Lop overgrown, or prune, or prop, or bind,*
> *One night or two with wanton growth derides*
> *Tending to wild.*

This is why you trim the hornbeam hedge. If you clip off the growing tips, especially the top or leader shoots, the trees of which the hedge is made will branch out along the length of their trunks and the hedge will grow dense as a hedge should be. If you do not the hedge will grow leggy, and there will be gaps for prying eyes all along the base. The hermit Gall would have discovered this too as he cut back and trimmed and negotiated with what was there: a lovely paradox, gardening.

Sometimes nature solves your gardening problems of its own accord. It will deal with aphids itself, if you'll only lay off the pesticides, and in so doing it will populate your green place with chattering, humming, singing, pollinating, interconnected life. Then there was my failed attempt to grow alchemilla where the border adjoined the path; only something strong and green would do, but if a hearty, adaptable plant like alchemilla would not grow there I'd no idea what would. One day I happened upon small clusters of leaves – spikes, rosettes – here and there in the bare dry soil. Euphorbias were moving in. Not the glossy spurges that grew up in the wood, but inhabitants of more arid parts: *Euphorbia cyparissias*, the needle-leaved cypress spurge, and *Euphorbia verrucosa*, the warty spurge, so called for its bizarre, knobbled seed heads and lovely as its name is not. They turned up suddenly, self-seeded, all over the place. I pulled them out of walls, dug them out of the vegetable plot, and added them to the arrivals at the edge of the path. Their roots were tiny and shallow; on one occasion I forgot to water them in, and still they grew. They spread throughout the border, and I let them be so that they flowed along the edge of the path and in amongst the perovskias and geraniums, the green-stemmed dogwoods and metallic sea hollies. Their forms were vigorous and abstract; their green repertoire touched on blue and ran to phosphoric. They were perfectly of the place.

I bent to pull a sow thistle from the base of a retaining wall, the sun heavy at my back: mid-afternoon, late July. There was a small upheaval as the thistle snapped off, and my stomach told me that what was there was rather more than plant. The basking adder, exposed, held momentarily still, its head raised alert from the centre of its slack knot.

I care very much about snakes, their fragile place in the order of things, but I have always feared them. Inexplicably so, for I have seen few in the course of my life and none of those encounters was especially adverse. We disturbed a grass snake in a field when I was very young; I don't think I saw the snake itself, but the grass moved in a disconcerting way that I still remember with trepidation. Another grass snake in the lane: its snaky length affected me though it was dead, crushed, and for days I tiptoed past it as car tyres ground its poor form slowly out of sight. There was the adder sleepy with September sun, arranged on a Cornish hedge amongst the thrift and baking slate, its slate-green back flashed with dark diamonds. I came upon it as I climbed a stile, and froze before I knew what I had seen, the seagulls low overhead, the snake indifferent to my presence and my fear, minding its own business. I cannot explain that reflex. It lurches in my stomach, before thought, and it does not make sense, for slow worms are snake-shaped and they captivate me, their shiny-smooth forms and lidded lizard eyes.

This adder was a slender juvenile, blackish and dull: I had to crouch down to make out its telltale black zigzag, and when you look at something closely you are too involved to feel fear. The pupils of its eyes were vertical, like those of a midwife toad. It began to move, its dry scales flickering rhythmically. I watched as the adder towed itself back into the wall, pulling its knotted body loose as a bow might be untied, and I forgot to shudder. And why should I have shuddered, I thought afterwards and think now, ashamed of myself, my presumptuousness: it was I who had startled the snake, frightened it away.

The next afternoon, the day's heat gathered at the foot of the wall, I tiptoed over to see if the adder was back. It was, looped relaxed amongst the sow-thistle stems, and the following day it was not.

*

A glow worm lambent in the terrace wall one summer dusk. Scarlet hips tumbling through leafless scrub, a dog rose discovered by fall. A four-legged tadpole finding its feet on a reed below the pond's surface. Euphorbias in the border, wild. Grass blades turned by frost to fern. The colour of a geranium shoot. Three toads at the door in March.

The garden pulses with life. I organise it loosely, lop and prune, weed and plant and replant, negotiate with its wilder tendencies. I tend it with all my heart.

In my element, in my garden. When I say 'my garden', I am not thinking of ownership – it is Shaun's garden as much as mine – but feeling a visceral, living connection. I could not look for this connection, only discover it. Enracination. The garden is its own place and reveals things on its own terms. It teaches me how little I know, and it teaches me about belonging. It is not that the garden belongs to me, for this green place was here first, the woods and rocks and adders and toads and flowers worthy of paradise. It is, rather, that I belong to the garden.

One evening, late, I looked up from my desk and met the bright calm eyes of a dormouse. It was perched outside the glazed door, where the eaves met the wall that held back the cliff and indoor light shone softly out. The dormouse craned down towards the glass and was peering in as though it found me interesting. I wondered how long it had been watching me. I got up slowly and stepped over to the door, and the mouse edged closer too, fearless, and we looked at one another through the glass just inches apart. Then the creature turned unhurriedly, and its furry tail receded into the dark. A patter on the ceiling above my head, the dormouse returning to its nest in the roof. I felt that I had been blessed.

I opened the door and stood in the plane of light, the darkness absolute beyond. The garden there, alive with night.
A smell between earth and leaf.

The Limits of Paradise

I drove home through the gorge on a late-spring afternoon, the windows rolled down, the air green. The river poured in and out of earshot as the engine decelerated into sharp bends, groceries shifting on the back seat. Birds loud above and around, a heron hunched on one yellow leg in bumpy shallows. Aquilegias crowded the verge to my right, purple struck to pewter by sun, their shapes merging in multitude. I drank it all in.

A flutter of apprehension as I turned into the narrow lane that ended at our house – there had been one or two problems – but the way was clear, and I felt an immense lightness as I parked the car with a smooth three-point turn. Home, safe. It was a glorious afternoon.

At what point, I wonder, can you say that a garden is established? My garden had no beginning, and it will never quite end: even if the woods should one day reclaim this place, the trees will remember it. Some of them, at least – the quince, the medlar perhaps. A hornbeam or two, remnants of the hedge, or the specimen that one gardener clipped to a block and another to the shape of a little tree two removes from its natural habit. Aquilegias, running wild, may harbour vegetative memories of a garden elsewhere. The ramsons will seem always to have grown here, and only they will know in a plant's unknowing way that once, down by the river, picking garlicky leaves for an omelette, I pulled five small translucent bulbs by accident and planted them up near the pond. They have naturalised in recent years, and they ripple silken in spring.

The fields were like silk too, when I turned off for the gorge that afternoon: ribboning skeins, the fir-dense mountain cresting round above, the garden there on the other side, out of sight. Shaun loves this view, the colours and contours smoothed by light as pastel is smoothed through paper. When you see it, you are coming home.

The garden was certainly establishing. The poet's narcissus bright in unmown grass. The Irish Blues would soon be in bloom again and spill over the terrace walls, touch the border with their quiet grey-lavender light. They flourished too on the sunny levels above the vegetable plot, and down in the front garden amongst nepeta and alchemilla, and in pots beneath the kitchen window. When I dug one up and cut it into roots the pieces grew back with gusto. They colonised spaces along with other geraniums from my mother's list, bright heaped leaves and flowers that saw you into autumn if you deadheaded regularly. Brookside, pale of eye and close to indigo; Spinners, a solid colour all of its own, a rich purple hinting at pink. The Striatum never made it to Switzerland. Though my father tended it carefully, the maverick geranium with blue-blotched flowers disappeared a year or two after we tracked it down in a hot Kent field and were moved by a stranger's generosity. The important thing, we agreed, was that we had found it for my mother, the last plant on her last list, and planted it in her garden.

The hornbeam hedge was dense now, verdurous: it wrapped

us in green. Leafcutter bees sawed rounds from the leaves to build their sequestered nests: were I to make a home of leaves, I would choose hornbeam too.

My father's hellebore grew amongst the ferns and limestone chunks. It had paused for a while – that fibrous root ball taking stock, putting out feelers – and then, one autumn day, I noticed a great mass of leaves. I let the plant be for one more season, and then I hacked it into two. In March this year both plants had flowered abundantly, and there were blooms for my father's birthday and for Shaun's a little later. I floated them on water in the pottery dish, and the living room centred on their viridescent forms and wine-coloured intricacies.

It amazed me, and does still, that every single species that I dug out of the Sussex clay grew more or less readily in this limestone place. Yes, I'd have planted the geraniums and anemones come what may, the astilbes and aquilegias, a fiery euphorbia, the hellebore. But now, a few years on, you might think that they had grown here forever. They were vigorous and at home amongst the native plants that, banished by the Schmidts, had made their way back into the garden where they too belonged. I reflected, not for the first time, that plants can be quite staggeringly adaptable. I was not so sure that I could say the same of myself.

Everything was green, lit by sun through trees. Even the fir shadows were green that afternoon. The shiftings of young leaves, the maples' bright rattle, the lime stirring softly. The sheer hum of life: the air and the trees, the running stream, the warp and weft of birdsong, crickets out there – celestial noise. A woodpecker drumming in the trees above the house. A loud splash up in the pond, and a fainter splashing. Two tractors down below, a motorbike accelerating out in the gorge, the world outside. A car door slammed nearby, and the sound tightened in my shoulders.

I had cloistered myself in the garden, our paradise, busy with things of the soil, putting down roots. But the world was there too, pressing at the boundary, and its claims differed from the green encroachments of ground elder and maple saplings. I did not notice at first, tending and attending to the garden. After those lonely, bruising years in Zurich this living place made me alive in ways for which I had longed and ways of which I could not have dreamed – but if I'd hoped the garden would solve a problem that mainly concerned people, I was in cloud cuckoo land. It is hard to solve human problems unilaterally.

Of late, I had been feeling vaguely exposed whenever I stepped outside the front door. We had lived in the village for a few years now, kept smiling, chatted to anyone who would chat to us, engaged local tradespeople. My French had improved – a kindly cashier at the supermarket told me so almost every week – and I used it whenever I could. I hit it off with the electrician, M. Jeanneret, who saw beauty in life and told me that the valley and the hills gave him joy, which buoyed my heart as well. We'd found friends, a warm Swiss-German couple, Max and Anna, who laughed fearlessly and in whose company a meal took hours. M. Froidevaux, a retired farmer who managed the recycling point, had been cordial since the day we stopped to admire his magnificent dahlias; he still scrutinised us when we drove past, but in the rear-view mirror his hand would be raised in a delayed regal wave. We ought by now to be finding our way into the community. If anything, though, I was less

at ease than I'd felt on the day we arrived, for back then I was
high on optimism – the garden, home at last – and the happy
assumption that everything would fall into place, we into ours,
if we only made the effort. Of course it would, because of the
garden. And people are people, aren't they?

As it was, we started out with a handicap. In Zurich we were
foreigners – but here it mattered, additionally and minutely,
that we were not of the village. 'Where are you from?', *vous êtes
d'où?*, is a common and anodyne question – it is one of the first
things you ask when making small talk in any language. The
question carries additional weight in Switzerland, where your
Heimatort or *place d'origine* means so much more than the place
of birth specified on your passport: it is bound up with how
you identify yourself, and how others identify you. Then there
was that worldwide phenomenon, the collective mindset of the
small community – and this one was very small, its population
around 300 and declining year on year. Either you were of the
village, or you were not of the village. Our next-door neighbour
Mathilde, at loggerheads with a local farmer, was keen to point
out, as though it explained everything, that the farmer was not
from the village: he was from central Switzerland. How long had
he farmed here? Oh, twenty-seven, twenty-eight years. One day
Anna said quite suddenly, as we walked up through the woods,
that she did not always feel *wohl* here – well, at ease, at home.
Seriously? How come? She and Max had lived in the village for
over twenty years. They both spoke excellent French, did their
bit for the fundraisers: hell, they were Swiss! I haven't really got
to know anyone, she said. Anna came from a village not so far
up the road, just the other side of the *Röstigraben*. And Max,
who was from eastern Switzerland, how did he feel? He loved

the countryside, she said, and he knew people in the town where he worked. They were both foreigners in the village, Max would tell us later.

Shaun and I were foreigners squared; cubed, for all we knew.

We went out and about in the village, introduced ourselves whenever we could: we'd moved into the little house up there on the hill. *Oui, je sais*, said some people, yes I know, *l'Anglaise et le Canadien. Bonne journée*, have a nice day. *Vous êtes d'où?* others asked. Small politics rumbled. There were disputes and alliances, and the village had a proper feud that had raged for many years between two farming families. No one appeared to know the grounds, only that the families had hated one another for at least two generations. We kept our heads down, hoping to find out for ourselves what people were like, hoping that they in turn would judge us as they found us.

M. Froidevaux called over one day when I was crushing tins and posting them through an aperture at the recycling point. The dahlias were not yet in bloom. I want to have a word with you, he said: *c'est grave*, it's serious. I laughed. No, he said, it's serious. You left a bag of garbage by the bottle bank. I laughed again: of course I didn't. Yes you did. No I did not. I would never have done that: I know the rules, I added, my sarcasm neutralised on the spot. That's as may be, M. Froidevaux responded gravely, but who else could it have been?

Our next-door neighbours, the Duponts, quizzed us from time to time – who we spoke to in the village, who we knew. They cultivated us when we moved in, and told us the way of things, who were the good people and who the bad. We were left in no doubt as to how they felt about our predecessors. The Schmidts had complained about the Duponts' motorbikes and the stuff that they hoarded at the edges of the lane. They had even insisted – would you believe it, *incroyable!* – that the lane should be kept clear at all times, but Philippe had built a shed on their parking space, and it was not so convenient to walk to and from the communal lot below. *But it's a public lane*, we should have said then and did not, *it was the access to their house. It's the access* – the thought juddered – *to* our *house*. The Schmidts were always there, Mathilde went on. It was so much nicer when the Duponts had the lane to themselves. What did Shaun do for a living? She didn't like professional types, by the way. And why did we not have children?

We would not under any circumstances fall out with them, we resolved. We'd meet them halfway. Everything would be fine. Nobody could possibly block a public lane unless they were load-ing or unloading – and who cared about twenty minutes, half an hour now and then? But one evening the car, unloaded, stayed put in the lane. It was still there in the morning, condensation thick on the windscreen, when I had an early appointment. I rang the front doorbell, the back doorbell, the front again. I called, I shouted. In the end I sounded the horn. An upstairs window opened after a further wait. I'm terribly sorry to disturb you, I said, but I have to go out. Would you mind moving your car? Thank you so much. It happened again, and then again. I was well and truly on the back foot, and that was my fault. Shaun would have dealt with things more robustly – but he was often away, and I was always there. I was an outsider: I had to make myself accepted, get on with everyone. And I needed to keep things friendly at all costs.

Over the months the car turned up in the lane more fre-quently and for longer. Often it was joined by other cars; for people who appeared to dislike so many other people, the Duponts received a great many visitors. Several times a week I found myself ringing at one door and then another: please could you possibly move your car/cars? Thank you so much, I said, kicking myself, when someone sauntered out, and fine-tuned a roll-up, and paused again to inspect the sky. It was irritating, but I supposed it was not the end of the world: if this was the price of goodwill, so be it. Give and take. The village was watching us, we couldn't afford to have trouble. And up there beyond the walls and shrubs, and in due course the hornbeam hedge, we were in paradise.

Suddenly it had become the norm, and the little white car acquired a personality. When I saw it in the lane it had an air of pettiness; on occasion it was malevolent. I had only myself to blame. A Canadian friend agreed, and recommended a book titled *The Tyranny of Niceness*. Call the police, said Lars, a Swiss person would have done that ages ago. That was true: in Switzerland the police will respond to lesser incidents than obstruction of a public right of way – the starting of a lawnmower on a Sunday, for example. But we were not Swiss. Then Lars pointed out that both our insurance and our safety would be compromised if vehicular access to our home were blocked: what if there were a fire? We hadn't thought of that. We were terribly sorry, I told Philippe, but we really couldn't negotiate with them every time we wanted to go out or come home. Of course they needed to load and unload from time to time, but could they please be just a little more mindful? And the lane really had to be kept clear overnight: what if there should be an emergency, a fire? Philippe shrugged: the firemen could run the hose up past his car, and they could always ring the doorbell if they wanted him to move it. Shaun was away, I was tired.

We had paid a high price for goodwill that didn't exist. We got on with our life. There was the garden to tend, there were montanas to divide, euphorbias to move around; ground-elder roots to grub out of the hellebore bank, newts to watch as they watched us. There was grass to mow and grass to leave rough for orchids and butterflies. The hornbeam hedge to cherish and to clip.

The hornbeam hedge. Our carillon jangled one morning, violently. When I went downstairs Mathilde was at the kitchen window, peering in, her hands big against the glass. I had arranged large pots outside in a polite effort to break her habit – they were earthenware, and spilled with Irish Blues – but Mathilde simply clambered over them. It's almost eleven, she said when I opened the door, and you are not dressed. That was true: I was still in my bathrobe, as sometimes happens when you are alone in the house and you open your laptop at breakfast time. Philippe, Mathilde continued, had reason to believe that we had poisoned their cat. The cat was not dead, but it was unwell. *Tu plaisantes,* I said, you're joking, though I was sorry the cat was out of sorts; what were we supposed to have done? It was that fancy new hedge of ours. According to Philippe we had treated the roots with rodenticide, and a mouse had eaten a root, and the cat had eaten the mouse. It showed imagination, Shaun said later on the phone: not even Herr Schmidt would have dreamed that one up as he surveyed his chemical arsenal.

This is the leaf, I thought later, dressed at last and holding a green serrated form to the light, that hung in the hedge that grew from the root that killed the mouse that poisoned the cat that . . .

A few euphorbias had seeded themselves under the hedge. They belonged in the border, and there was deadheading to be done. I wandered off to find my trowel and secateurs, back on garden time.

The garden had a life of its own.

Clearing leaves from a drain, we discovered two young fire salamanders. They were black and yellow, shiny as wetsuits, and their tiny bodies trailed like comma tails from huge-eyed heads. We tucked them in again, beneath the leaves. Adders in the cellar walls, dormice and field mice and who knows what else in the roof. Bats, I hoped. The woodpeckers on the lawn, a pair now, and the herons that crashed around the pond. The newts, their bright gaze giving nothing away. Toads and slow worms at the threshold. Our garden and our house were habitats, like a forest or a tumble of rocks.

The creatures had their own ways. So did the vegetation, the flowers worthy of paradise: plants that I and others had planted here, and wild arrivals that found their own way around, nature teaching me how to garden this place. My parents' perennials were doing their own thing too, becoming more than Sussex plants. Vegetal origins had grown indistinct, the aquilegias mingled with their wild selves, the sedums with sedums planted by the Schmidts. And their histories were blurring in other ways.

One September day, as I climbed the steps to the shed, the slope jostled and shimmered with Japanese anemones. Downy buds promised more, some tight as full stops, others slashed with pink. They needed their own collective noun, I thought, as goldfinches have. There was something else about them, too: a feeling that I had known them all my life.

As I said goodbye to the gardens, first in Sussex and then in London, I dug up a precious and weighty thing. It did not have mere significance: it was a living connection that I had to keep alive. The responsibility was huge, and at times it was overwhelming.

The plants: what about the plants?

I had dug them up and replanted them, and dug them up again, and split them, and pressed them on to friends with a burdensome exhortation: please don't let them die. I drove from Switzerland to England to dig them up once more and slice a section from each. I drove the pieces back to Switzerland, and the pots leaked into the spare-wheel recess. I tucked them into temporary places while the building work took place, and when I unpotted them again and planted them out – here, at last – I worried on: what if the soil were too alkaline, the winters too harsh?

But here I was, and here they were. Something of my parents lived here in the garden.

I cannot pinpoint the change: it happened imperceptibly, between days and over years, like the roots of that hellebore cutting. Though I did not notice it at the time, I began to see the Sussex plants differently. When I saw a geranium pure with first light, the ghost bells of penstemons at dusk, a plenitude of anemones reaching for the sun, I no longer saw my parents' plants – or rather, not always first and foremost. They had grown to be part of the garden in more than vegetative terms. The weight of my responsibility for the plants was lightening. I carried it still, but as time went by it needed less attention.

The plants belonged to the garden, and they were lovely, and they were plants from my parents' garden. My dealings with them had grown less devout, for the connection was there, alive and green. Maybe I am talking about grief. It never leaves, nor would you want it to, for grief is love, but in time it assimilates itself to who you are. The memory does not fade away, it fades into your life, a positive thing. There is less commemorating and more remembering. You are not consumed with guilt when an anniversary slips your mind. You live your life and the memories are there, in your heart, and the plants are there, in the garden. Growing.

Without people, there would be no paradise.

Without a gardener to prune and lop and tend – the verbs are woven into *Paradise Lost* – the garden would not be a garden. Arbours, allées, paths would grow 'unsightly and unsmooth' with those fallen blossoms and honeydew gums: the browning mush, the stickiness (have you ever cleared up after an ornamental cherry, or walked beneath lime trees at aphid time?). With 'branches overgrown' they would become impassable, impenetrable. The God of Genesis, after all, put man in the garden of Eden 'to dress it and to keep it'.

Paradise depends on people in other, emotional and visceral ways. At the tragic climax of the story of the fall, there is a juncture at which Eve has eaten the forbidden fruit and Adam has not. '[S]he took of the fruit thereof, and did eat, and gave also unto her husband with her; and he did eat': the Authorised Version of the Bible dispatches this moment in twenty-one words. Milton lingers in it, considering Adam's apparent choice between obedience to God, with its reward of immortality, and mortal life with Eve. In practice he has no choice: Adam must eat the fruit because he is human. 'How can I live without thee', he agonises inwardly,

> *how forgo*
> *Thy sweet converse and love so dearly joined,*
> *To live again in these wild woods forlorn?*

We know that paradise abounds in wanton growth and thickets, that Adam and Eve are hard-pressed to keep it all under control, 'keep' it 'from wilderness' – to maintain the garden in the literal sense of ensuring its continued existence. But the 'wild woods' give me a jolt every time I read the words, for I do not expect to find them here, in paradise. They hint at something more than those tendencies 'to wild' that a gardener keeps in check, at something else altogether: desolation, darkness, loneliness, fear. Without Eve, Adam seems to be saying, this is what paradise would be.

What makes paradise paradise, for Adam, is Eve's 'sweet converse and love' – but in the end paradise is not enough. Conversation, that word exquisitely defined as having one's being in a place or amongst persons, is on Adam's lips when, newly created, he is led into the garden. A social animal alone in paradise: an excruciating thought. He tells God that he is lonely; he has 'all things' here, he says, except for someone with whom to share them – and what 'happiness' is there in 'solitude'? He speaks of 'conversation' and, inter alia, of 'society', 'fellowship', '[s]ocial communication', a whole lexicon of words, in fact, for having one's being amongst persons. Adam needs Eve to be created. And the words in which he expresses that need slide between intimate conversation with one other and social conversation with people, the world of men. This is why, even with one another for society, paradise is not enough for Adam and Eve.

Paradise is not enough for anyone.

*

A conical object spins through the air on a slow diagonal trajectory. Its motion is deliberate, as if some hand had given it a vigorous twist and sent it on its way. A winged maple fruit, a season on the turn.

There is something dignified about the sun in late October, its heatless intensity. This afternoon it has organised the garden into dark and bright. I have climbed the meadow slope to the greying oak bench, and the brightness on my face is like warmth itself. The village down below, flung where the valley and gorge intersect. The panoramic fields beyond, the red cows scattered on their length of green. The church poised and upward.

I pull my focus back inside the hornbeam hedge. Its leaves are dull, draining to yellow. The foliage of one plant is browned and curling: the same tree turns early every year, a good month before the rest. The first autumn I thought that it had died, though the leaves did not fall – and when they dropped the following spring, all at once, its branches were flexible and charged with green. Maybe this tree lives harder and wears itself out sooner.

The garden grows into its surroundings, its walls and cliffs of limestone, its edges blurred with maple and ash, ground elder, hornbeam. The stinking hellebores, a colony now, have burst into life as other plants are returning to the earth. The sedums collect autumn in their earth-red flowers, and Irish Blues have opened their last few buds at the ends of straggling stems; I ought to have cut them back by now. Spindle berries tumbling out of scrub, redder than Sussex spindle pink, their orange seeds long since dispersed. The medlar flaming. The border contoured to the meadow slope, the hedge to the dipping ground. The grass that Shaun has sculpted to sweeping forms, to mown spaces and rough volumes in order that orchids might grow here too. The garden has settled into itself: it has shape and rhythm, and is thriving. I want to tend it until my dying day. And this afternoon, looking down on it all, feeling the split oak with my fingertips – its roughness, its solidity – I know that I cannot. A decision that I have been avoiding has somehow made itself: we have to leave the garden, our little paradise. It is the loveliest place on earth, but it is in the wrong place.

Unlike, say, anger or joy, unease does not draw attention to itself. But in the last year or so I have come to be less easy as I go about my business in the garden, or watch leaves in the sky-light above my desk, the small abrupt movements of a foraging wren, a bumblebee in the doorway with dangling legs and laden pollen baskets. There is a weighing in my stomach: I notice it from time to time and then it goes away, or I stop noticing. Sometimes I am conscious of the boundaries in a way that is not wholly comfortable, and at such times I cannot say whether they close in too much or do not enclose the garden enough. Maybe both. It has to do with nothing specific: not with the people next door, nor with our sense that we are scrutinised – Max sometimes feeds us third-hand information about our life – nor with a way people have, though they always say *bonjour*, of watching us with a gaze that, as it watches, pushes us back. It has to do with all of these things, and more. In the garden, I am in my element. Outside it too, in many respects, walking the hills or mountains with Shaun, attuned to the rock and the habits of plants, the ways of the trees and the light, what the garden is of. But with the passing years I feel ever lonelier, more foreign amongst people. I have known that feeling before, in

Zurich, in the grey city a world away from this green valley with its white church and red roofs and redder cows. We have not even begun to integrate here, and we are not so sure that the village wants us to.

There have been signs that all is not as perfect as I wanted it to be. Those spells of grey non-weather have been affecting me again: they find their way into my head as they didn't when we first came here, when everything seemed green because so much was green and because of how I felt. When we said we would stay here forever (I'm leaving this place feet first, I told anyone and everyone then).

Back in June, flying into London for a string of appointments, I felt a strange sensation of lightness when the plane touched down at Heathrow in rain. And the following day, as I made my way through rush-hour crowds on Villiers Street, I caught myself thinking, I am comfortable here. I'd never really noticed being comfortable before: either you are comfortable, or you notice that you are uncomfortable. Maybe I have got used to not being at ease: it hits me when I am.

Later in the summer, when the aquilegias ripened, I shook some glossy seeds from their paper-brown vessels into an envelope and posted them to a friend in Cambridge. Mary has never set foot in the garden, but I know that she understands it. I'd been meaning to send her some seeds from this place for quite some time, and something made me do it then: a feeling, perhaps, that we might move on.

I want to go home. That is an odd thing to want when you are in your home, as I have been for nearly five years now.

Then, just last week, the joyful M. Jeanneret came to investigate an electrical fault; a kitchen socket had stopped working and the lights were behaving oddly. We talked about the glorious autumn, the colours of the leaves and the sky, the crisp morning air, the berries, how it has been an exceptional year for spindle, *le fusain* (the tree named in French for another of its uses, charcoal). M. Jeanneret said that my French has improved tremendously. I told him that plant names fascinate me, and I showed him my copy of *Flora Helvetica*. *Ah oui*, he had one himself, though the text of his was in French of course. *Merde!* The socket wasn't earthed! Nor had it tripped the circuit breaker, there could have been a fire. I laughed. No, really, he said. Our predecessor had done the wiring himself, I told him, and was proud of it. *Merde! Piccolo bello*, he added as the socket tester beeped. What we'd made here, he went on, was *un véritable petit paradis*. It had been a few years now, we must be well and truly at home. And I heard myself saying, I don't know. I love it here so much, but I don't know any more. My own words shocked me, but M. Jeanneret nodded. *En tout cas, ç'a été une belle étappe, n'est-ce pas?* In any case, it's been a beautiful life phase.

Yes.

Being lonely is not a thing you care to admit to yourself, let alone to somebody else; it is as if you have failed in something. But I am lonely here, in Switzerland. Not just alone, insofar as I am alone today in the garden, as I often am when Shaun is away: I can be happily, wholly engrossed in solitary pursuits, my gardening and writing, for hours, a day, two days at a stretch, knowing that Shaun is there at the core of my life. Lonely: lacking 'conversation', a being amongst people. Maybe you are truly, terribly alone, not amongst people at all; maybe you are alone with some fact or loss while others carry on as though the world has not changed utterly. Maybe you are amongst people with whom you have no connection, from or by whom you are excluded. Whatever the case, you are not quite so sure of your being.

Your sense of who you are is shaped and nurtured and tested and battered in relation to other people. And you may not learn this until you find yourself amongst people, a people, with whose ways and values your own are incommensurate. You may have started out with good intentions, in good faith, and done your best – so far as you know – to be acceptable. You may have made friends here and there – but a few friends cannot solve a cultural disconnect, and in time you must acknowledge that you have failed to integrate, for this society is at odds with who you are. And this means that you should leave, for it is someone else's country, someone else's way of life. It's a pity, and it is nobody's fault.

Outside the yellowing hornbeam hedge, nothing has changed; why would it have done? Down the lane, beyond the village, on the roads, in the cities, out at the borders, in Swiss German and in French. In our mailbox. There are so many things to which I have not adjusted, nor wish to. The casual and not-so-casual xenophobia, and the comments and complicated attitudes that I encounter because I am a woman. The populism. A lack of the thing that Milton calls conversation. That palpable closedness – I feel it, anyway – and a readiness, which I find confusing, to engage with strangers by physical force when you might say excuse me, or await your turn. The reluctance to smile that wrong-foots and bemuses me, for if someone smiles upon catching your eye your reflexes respond before you can think. The anger: the normality of road rage, and the sudden flare-ups in shops and car parks, on doorsteps, pavements, trams. I wonder whether Swiss people find these things negative too; I suppose I will never find out. But I do not want to live like this.

It seems that I am not the only one to feel uncomfortable here. Ahmed is going back to his own country too, back to Morocco. He's given notice on his lease. We went to his restaurant a few weeks ago, when we were in Zurich. I've had enough, he said, something is wrong, there's no joy, so much anger: everyone around here seems depressed. I need to move on.

So do I.

Because globalisation has shrunk the world in many ways, it is easy to believe that you can take yourself anywhere. I've learned that you cannot, for people are local, of places (*locus* is the Latin word for 'place'), and some do not take readily to those who are not of their kind. We moved a thousand kilometres within Europe, a stone's throw in this day and age, and could get by in two of Switzerland's written languages. I assumed that we would integrate through the sheer will to do so, and I was naive, maybe complacent, certainly wrong. I have learned that you cannot set up a life elsewhere without putting yourself on the line.

Would things have turned out differently had life taken us to France or Germany instead of to Switzerland? Yes, I think, and no. There would have been different people, different rules and notions of rules. Different, undoubtedly more liberal, social attitudes. We would not have bumped up against certain models of national and local identity – the self-enclosure in the middle of Europe, the layers of introversion, the whole business of dialect – though there would have been others to negotiate. Living in a single standard language – French or High German – we might have achieved a level of communication that is out of the question here, where dialect often still excludes us and so many conversations are linguistic patchworks, a getting by. But I have also come to wonder whether it is possible to be yourself in a language that is not your own, however great your competence. And I expect I am wrong to wonder this, for who you are is surely an adaptable thing, and many people set up lives in other languages. For my part, though, I have felt diminished, not quite myself, trying to live for so long in foreign tongues. Maybe I simply love my own language too much.

My double life was always going to catch up with me. The garden was my way of making home when I found myself out of place amongst the people of Switzerland. That I might find home in a corner of the natural world alone was a simplistic assumption, but it came naturally to an erstwhile toddler who, given 'mud & large spaces', could be 'quite self-sufficient', a child who rummaged in hedgerows and felt safer in woods than she did at school, an adult who will disappear on garden time for as long as the world permits. It was not so far-fetched, for those who know me well, to believe that with a space to plant and tend, to garden, I could put down roots. Shaun's wish for me, inscribed in my *Flora Helvetica*, was 'many happy years of gardening in Switzerland': I've had a good few.

This place of green magic is beyond any space or corner or bit of ground that I could imagine: it is a place of perpetual revelation. It has brought me back to life – I do not say that lightly – and deepened the dimensions of my life. It has taught me things about myself and about gardening, that delicate collaboration with the natural world, that I did not know were there to be learned. It has made me aware of how little I know, made me humbler. It is the loveliest place in the world – in our world, at least, for Shaun and I will never know its like again. It breaks my heart that we must leave, for Shaun loves the garden, the valley so much – and we came here, after all, because he wanted me to be happy. I was, I think, to begin with.

I truly believed that we had come home, that we would be here forever, the garden our own green place, our paradise. I have found connection here, a sense of profound belonging. But even this healing, life-giving place cannot solve a problem of sheer cultural misplacement, the special loneliness of being out of synch, at odds, with how other people are and live. I am not as self-sufficient as I once assumed. We are not: Shaun feels the isolation too – though, working in a busy office, he has discovered it in a different way and at a different pace. He says that he misses feeling part of something.

We need to have our being amongst people again, and that means leaving Switzerland. If we stay here, the hedge may start to close in and our paradise turn into something else. Paradise is an ephemeral place, so fragile that it makes you hold your breath. If you happen upon it you must live every moment there to the full, notice everything that is offered you – a cowslip floret, that earth-green smell that Shaun adores – for paradise is but a feeling or a circumstance away from wild woods. Not woods of beech and maple, but an intangible wilderness.

I will take the garden with me, and find it somewhere else – somewhere back in England. The anemones and Burton's Blues, the aquilegias, the hellebore belong here in the Jura now, but when we leave I will take a cutting or two, an envelope of seed. The Sussex plants grow in many gardens these days, a lovely consequence of our own uprootings, all this moving around, all this leaving and looking for home. They bear witness to my life, to our life together.

A stirring and a pattering like the first drops of rain. The movement does not subside but intensifies to steady air raining leaves, rushing the firs to a high-pitched sough. The weather is on the turn. Tomorrow will be cold – the temperature is dropping now – and there will be rain, and wood smoke in the village.

The dead heads of the anemones are little balls on sapped, contorted stems: they look like abstract sculptures of themselves. I will leave the other seed heads into winter too, the sedums and echinaceas, rudbeckia and grasses: I won't cut them back until the birds have stripped out all the food they can. The season will touch their elegiac forms with light and dark, frost and mist, the valley's exhalation. Perhaps the goldfinches will return.

I wonder when I will say goodbye to this place. Maybe I will not. Maybe I'll leave without looking back, and take the garden with me in my heart. I think that might be better.

The sun gone, the wind cold. I make my way down the dropping path. The air stills briefly: that clear cold green smell tinged, now, with humus. I left my trowel on the terrace wall. I dig up a penstemon, of a piece with a plant that my father grew from seed many years ago, and tease it into rooted sections. I plant three pieces back in the border, and two on the slope by the shed. I am instantly absorbed, back on garden time, a plant in one hand, my copper trowel in the other, easing soil back around the roots. Here and now in the garden, in the near-dark, planting for the future, whatever it may hold.

Oui, ça a été une belle étappe.

The hornbeam hedge will turn quickly now, and its leaves will rustle through winter while the new buds form. Khaki curls holding on to the end, or the beginning.

Epilogue: Going Back

London, a new day. After breakfast I walked west through the still-cool streets, and at Charing Cross I bought a ticket and a takeout coffee. The train pulled out through suburbia, out into Kent, the bramble-thick cuttings, on out into Sussex. The landscape widening, the fields, the hedges, the station names in order to the place where I grew up. I had not been back for many years.

We were at a turning point, soon to leave our place in the little old mountains, unsure where to look for home.

Things had moved on without me. There was a café in the village now, busy with local people whom I did not recognise. Someone asked me where I came from. Here, I said. I drank my coffee slowly. When I got up to leave, a man shook my hand: I was a stranger now, but I'd been welcome.

I walked out of the village and up the lane. It was not as steep as it used to be; maybe I was fitter. The countryside was managed differently, too: hedges had grown to ranks of trees, and there were fewer species on the banks and verges beneath. The hay field where we tobogganed in precious times of snow was rough with scrub and willow. The birch wrecked by lightning when I was very small had sent out leaves at the tip of one jagged branch, like the tree in *Waiting for Godot*. All these decades on, the tree's sheer will to live.

I walked on up the hill, past the house with the front lawn that the Tanners used to weed obsessively. And they were there, snowy-haired as my parents ought to be, examining something in the grass. I wanted to stop and talk to them about weeds and daisies, to tell Mrs Tanner how I was a stranger in her country as she once was in mine, but I kept on walking: it had been too long. I hope she is at home here now.

I walked on up and around the wooded corner, slowly now, the hornbeam luminous. There was the house, the garden that my parents made from a field. It was August: the anemones would be in bloom. My stomach dropped. The high hedges had been replaced by a fence, the garden grubbed out and grassed over. I'd seen it something like this in a photograph taken long before I was born, when the house was just built and the garden not begun – but this time the house looked old, and sad. It was a house without a garden, and yet not quite a house in a field. Maybe, one day, it will be a field again.

I walked away, down the hill, out amongst the hedgerows. Hazel, hornbeam. A spindle hinting at pink. The verges brimmed with meadowsweet. Its perfume hung between almonds and vanilla.

Acknowledgements

If the writing of this book has sometimes seemed a solitary endeavour, that is only part of the story. I have been sustained, and the book nurtured and infinitely enhanced, by the help, support, generosity and professionalism of many others.

Heartfelt thanks to my editor Jenny Lord, as subtle a reader as a writer could wish for and under whose influence the book has become ever more itself. She has provided enthusiasm and perspicacity in equal measure, and wielded her pruning knife delicately. I am so very grateful, too, to Holly Harley for her phenomenal patience and superlative editorial support. Special thanks to Steve Marking and Pauline Teunissen for transposing the garden so exquisitely from the text of *Where the Hornbeam Grows* to its covers.

I owe a great debt of gratitude to my agent Jessica Woollard, another marvellous reader, who saw before I did what the book might be. She has championed it, and guided me, with wisdom and good humour, and an instinct for getting to the point of things.

A huge thank you to Cheryl Clements, who gave up time that she could ill afford to comment on an early draft in detail and with unflinching candour: that was invaluable.

ACKNOWLEDGEMENTS

Robert Macfarlane believed, on the scantest written evidence, that I had a book in me. I am simply indebted to him for setting the ball rolling.

To Shaun, I owe everything. He has lived this book with me, and supported me endlessly. I thank him here simply for his love, and for believing in what I do, and for making sense of the wild woods.

Notes

Abbreviations used in the notes

AV   *The Bible: Authorized King James Version with Apocrypha* (1611), ed. by Robert Carroll and Stephen Prickett (Oxford: Oxford University Press, 1997). References are given by chapter and verse.

DJG Derek Jarman, *Derek Jarman's Garden* with photographs by Howard Sooley (London: Thames and Hudson, 1995)

DTP Dylan Thomas, *The Collected Poems of Dylan Thomas: Centenary Edition*, ed. by John Goodby (London: Weidenfeld & Nicolson, 2014)

ELM Helen Darbishire, ed., *The Early Lives of Milton* (London: Constable, 1932)

FH   Konrad Lauber and Gerhart Wagner, *Flora Helvetica* (1996; Bern: Haupt Verlag, 2009)

MW John Milton, *The Major Works*, ed. by Stephen Orgel and Jonathan Goldberg (1991; Oxford: Oxford University Press, 2003)

PL   John Milton, *Paradise Lost* (1667, 1674), ed. by Alastair Fowler (1968; Harlow: Longman, 1986). References are given by book and line number.

Epigraph

Page

ix 'comment . . . "coin du monde"': Gaston Bachelard, *La poétique de l'espace* (1972; Paris: Presses Universitaires de France, 1957), p. 24. Trans. by Maria Jolas, *The Poetics of Space* (1964; Boston: Beacon Press, 1994), p. 4.

Growing

Page

4 Édouard Manet (1832–83), *A Bar at the Folies-Bergère* (*Un Bar aux Folies-Bergère*), 1882: The Samuel Courtauld Trust, The Courtauld Gallery, London.

8 'enclosure green . . . verdurous wall': *PL*, IV. 133–43.

13 'with branches overgrown'; 'With thicket overgrown'; 'lop . . . tread with ease': *PL*, IV. 627; 136; 629–32.

21 'force . . . drives the flower': 'The force that through the green fuse drives the flower' (comp. 1933), *DTP*, pp. 43–44, l. 1, title. 'Lop. . . bind'; 'direct . . . climb': *PL*, IX. 210; 216–17.

Uprooted

Page

47 The Italian draughtsman and printmaker Piranesi (1720–78) first published his etchings of imaginary prisons or 'Carceri d'invenzione' in the late 1740s, with a second series in 1760–61. Giovanni Battista Piranesi, *Le Carceri*, intro. by Mario Praz (Milan: Biblioteca Universale Rizzoli, 1975).

54 Driven by a compulsive need to tell his long and 'ghastly tale', the protagonist of Coleridge's 'The Rime of the Ancient Mariner' has a become a shorthand for the buttonholer. The Mariner holds a passing man captive with his 'skinny hand' and 'glittering eye':

The wedding-guest sat on a stone:
He cannot choose but hear;
And thus spake on that ancient man,
The bright-eyed Mariner.

'The Rime of the Ancient Mariner' (1797-98, 1817) in H.J. Jackson, ed., *Samuel Taylor Coleridge* (Oxford: Oxford University Press, 1985), pp. 46–65, ll. 584; 9; 13; 17–20.

55 *'like . . . back'*: 'Fern Hill' (comp. 1945), *DTP*, pp. 177–79, ll. 28–29.

'sea-mews'. PL, XI. 835.

56 *'platan'*: *PL*, IV. 478.

57 *'to give thee . . . my side'*: *PL*, IV. 483–85.

61 Franz Kafka, *The Trial* (*Der Prozess*, published posthumously in 1925), trans. by Idris Parry (London: Penguin Books Ltd, 1994); *The Metamorphosis* (*Die Verwandlung*, 1915) in *Metamorphosis and Other Stories*, trans. by Michael Hofmann (London: Penguin Books Ltd, 2007).

65 *'O flowers . . . water'*: *PL*, XI. 273–79.

'native soil'; *'from . . . forth'*: *PL*, XI. 270; 261.

66 *'nursery'*: *PL*, VIII. 46.

'bred . . . hand . . . rank . . . water': *PL*, XI. 276–79.

67 *'wanton ringlets'*; *'wanton growth'*: *PL*, IV. 306; 629 & IX. 211. The serpent also coils in 'many a wanton wreath' as he sets about tempting Eve: IX. 517.

Who will garden paradise now is a doubly poignant question, for the paradise of Milton's poem will, in due course, cease to be. When the retributive flood of Genesis 7 rises

Above the highest hills: then shall this mount
Of Paradise by might of waves be moved
Out of his place, pushed by the horned flood,

With all his verdure spoiled, and trees adrift
Down the great river to the opening gulf,
And there take root an island salt and bare,
The haunt of seals and orcs, and sea-mews' clang.

PL, XI. 829–35.

Flora Helvetica

Page
78 Lorna Price's *The Plan of St Gall in Brief* (Berkeley: University of California Press, 1982) provides excellent reproductions and an overview of the manuscript.

The chief source for the life and legend of St Gall is the *Vita sancti Galli* by Walahfrid Strabo, who died in 849. An English translation is included in Maud Joynt, *The Life of St. Gall* (London: Society for Promoting Christian Knowledge, 1927).

83 '*Transparent . . . air*': PL, VII. 265.

84 '*Zum . . . da*'; '*möglichst*': FH, p. 8; p. 7.

85 '*Carpinus . . . comune*': FH, p. 170.
'*sehr . . . giftig*': FH, back paste-down.

86 '*light-blue-lilac*'; ('*hell-blaulila*'): FH, p. 990.
'*sylvaticum . . . guaud*': FH, p. 728.

87 The sinister Madame Beck is a central character in Charlotte Brontë's novel *Villette* (1853), ed. by Margaret Smith and Herbert Rosengarten (1984; Oxford: Oxford University Press, 1990).

91 '*Thy going . . . native soil*': PL, XI. 290–92.
'*meet . . . marriage*': *The Doctrine and Discipline of Divorce* (1643), MW, pp. 182–226 (p.186).

92 '*Must . . . soil?*': PL, XI. 269–70.

92–93 '*whole . . . Switzerland*': Patrick Leigh Fermor, *A Time of Gifts* (1977; London: John Murray, 2004), p.80.

93 *'the mountains . . . sky'*: *PL*, VII. 285–87.

94–95 *'Greater Blue . . . readily'*: William Curtis, *The Botanical Magazine; or, Flower-Garden Displayed*, Vol. 3 (London: printed by Couchman and Fry for W. Curtis, 1790), p. 77. This exquisitely designed publication was intended, the title page states, 'for the Use of such Ladies, Gentlemen, and Gardeners, as wish to become scientifically acquainted with the Plants they cultivate'. The entry for each plant comprises a page of text and, on the facing page, a hand-coloured illustration.

100 Milton's controversial treatise on regicide was *The Tenure of Kings and Magistrates* (1649), *MW*, pp. 273–307.

'fallen . . . solitude': *PL*, VII. 25–28.

As fellow republicans of a gardening bent, Milton and Nicholas Culpeper (1616–54) might well have had much to say to one another. There is no record that their paths crossed, and they must have just missed each other at Cambridge; Culpeper matriculated in the year that Milton left after taking his MA. The numerous expanded, embellished and illustrated editions of Culpeper's so-called 'Herbal' that were published in the years and centuries following his death – not to mention the branding of the Culpeper name – belie the sheer radicalism of the book that he published in 1652. *The English Physician or An Astrologo-physical Discourse of the vulgar Herbs of this Nation* (London: 'Printed for the benefit of the Commonwealth of *England*', 1652) was printed densely in a small format without illustrations, which would have minimised its cost. In describing the characteristics, properties and medicinal applications of common native plants – 'such things', the title page continues, 'onely as grow in *England*, they being most fit for English Bodies' – Culpeper set out to bring a 'compleat Method of Physick', in plain English and for the threepence price of his book, to those who could not afford doctors' fees. He had already, in 1649, antagonised the Royal College of Physicians by translating the College's standard pharmaceutical text from Latin into English, thus making its exclusive knowledge available to all literate Englishmen.

'*from . . . off*': *PL*, III. 46-47.

101 '*Seasons . . . sweet approach . . . ever-during dark*': *PL*, III. 41–45.

'*Sat . . . of it*': Jonathan Richardson, 'Life of [Milton], and a Discourse on [*Paradise Lost*]' (1734), *ELM* pp. 199–330 (p. 291).

102 '*justify . . . men*': *PL*, I. 26.

'*alwayes . . . lived*': John Aubrey, 'Minutes of the Life of Mr John Milton' (1681), *ELM*, pp. 1–15 (p. 6).

'*early . . . even*': *PL* XI. 275-76.

108 '*Tending . . . wild*': *PL*, IX. 212.

109 '*fragrant . . . earth*'; '*odorous . . . shrub*'; '*beauteous . . . all hues*': *PL*, IV. 645; 696; 697–98.

110 'a heaven':

> To see a World in a Grain of Sand
> And a Heaven in a Wild Flower,
> Hold Infinity in the palm of your hand
> And Eternity in an hour:

'Auguries of Innocence' (comp. *c.*1803) in William Blake, *Complete Writings*, ed. by Geoffrey Keynes (1957; Oxford: Oxford University Press, 1985), pp. 431–34, ll. 1–4.

114 Odilon Redon (1840–1916), *Mystical Boat* (*La Barque Mystique*), 1890s: Ian Woodner Family Collection, New York.

115 *'plentifully'*; *'perfect blew'*: John Gerard, *The Herball or Generall Historie of Plantes* (London: printed by John Norton, 1597), p. 354; p. 353.

'perfect . . . Gorhambury': Nicholas Culpeper, *The English Physitian Enlarged* (London: printed and sold by Peter Cole, 1653), p. 112.

To the Wooded Hill

Page

119 *'and . . . shade'*: *PL*, IV. 137–38.

120 *'high-climbing hill'*: *PL*, III. 546. Milton is referring here to 'some' hypothetical hill, not to the one on which Paradise is situated.

121–22 *'It is a . . . restrained'*: John Ruskin, 'The Lamp of Memory', *The Seven Lamps of Architecture* (London: Smith, Elder, and Co., 1849), pp. 162–82 (p. 162).

123 *'So it . . . praise'*: 'Fern Hill', *DTP*, p. 178, ll. 33–36.

134 C. S. Lewis, *The Lion, the Witch and the Wardrobe*, illustrated by Pauline Baynes (1950; Harmondsworth: Penguin Books Ltd, 1959), p. 14.

137 *'accidentally'*: *DJG*, p. 5.

'holey': *DJG*, p. 12.

138 *'plonked . . . chances'*: *DJG*, p. 14.

'I can . . . peace': *DJG*, p. 57.

146 *'hoary . . . white'*: Ebenezer Sibly, Appendix to *Culpeper's English Physician; and Complete Herbal* (1789; London: for the Author, [*c.*1794]), p. 26. On paper, Sibly (1751–*c.*1799) cuts a colourful figure: astrologer, doctor, freemason and white supremacist.

148 *'angels dancing'*: *DJG*, p. 102.

151 Caspar David Friedrich (1774–1840), the German master of craggy, misty, sublime landscapes. His much-reproduced *Wanderer above the Sea of Fog* (*Wanderer über dem Nebelmeer*, 1817: Kunsthalle, Hamburg), is the epitome of Romanticism. For cliffs and crags see especially *Uttewalder Grund* (*c.*1825: Lentos Kunstmuseum, Linz) and *Das Felsentor im Uttewalder Grund* (1800: Museum Folkwang, Essen).

Where the Hornbeam Grows

Page

159 '*enclosure green*': *PL*, IV. 133.

164 '*airs . . . airs*': *PL*, IV. 264.

170 '*Have nothing in your houses that you do not know to be useful, or believe to be beautiful*': William Morris, 'The Beauty of Life' (lecture delivered 1880) in *Hopes and Fears for Art* (1882). *Collected Works of William Morris*, 24 vols (London: Longmans Green and Company, 1910–15), Vol. 22, pp. 51–80 (p. 76).

175 '*pastoral mountain*', '*restrained*', '*long . . . hills*': Ruskin, 'The Lamp of Memory', p. 162.

176 '*fower square*': Gerard, *Herball*, p. 1284.
'*Pfaffenhütchen . . . prers*': *FH*, p. 704.
Thomas Wolsey (1470/71–1530) is wearing his red biretta in the portrait that hangs in the National Portrait Gallery, London (artist unknown, 1589–95, based on a work of *c.*1520).

179 '*variety . . . dale*': *PL*, VI. 640–41.
'*Tending . . . wild*': *PL*, IX. 212.

179–80 '*hairy sides*', '*steep wilderness*': *PL*, IV. 135.

180 '*wisdom . . . out*': *PL*, III. 50.

'*humble . . . implicit*': *PL*, VII. 322–23.

182 '*other . . . Hornbeam*': Culpeper, *English Physician* (1652), p. 26.

The Garden

204 The story of Chicken Licken, a catastrophic thinker who becomes convinced that the sky is falling in when an acorn drops on his head, is as old as the hills. I grew up with Vera Southgate's version, *Chicken Licken* (Loughborough: Ladybird Books Ltd, 1969).

208 '*The* Horn-beam . . . *delightful*': John Evelyn, *Sylva, or A Discourse of Forest-Trees, and the Propagation of Timber in His Majesties Dominions* (London: printed by John Martyn and James Allestry, 1664), p. 29.

209 '*verdurous wall*': *PL*, IV. 143.

210 '*appears . . . pursuits*': Henry Todd, 'Some Account of the Life and Writings of Milton' in *The Poetical Works of John Milton*, second edn, 7 vols (London: Joseph Johnson et al., 1809), Vol. 1, pp. 1–164 (p. 148).
'*airs*': *PL*, IV. 264.
'*which . . . flower*': *PL*, V. 746–47.
'*liquid lapse*': *PL*, VIII. 263.
'*Native perfumes*': *PL*, IV. 158.
'*downy . . . smell diffused*': *PL*, IX. 851–52.

211 '*fear . . . cool*': *PL*, V. 396.
'*wild woods*': *PL*, IX. 910.

215 '*Works . . . design*': *PL*, V. 33.
'*Now . . . easy*': 'Fern Hill', *DTP*, p. 177, l. 1.

216 '*shut . . . flowers*': *PL*, IX. 278.

217 '*Flowers . . . plain*': *PL*, IV. 241–43.

'*double . . . mind*': Andrew Marvell's satirical take on these artifices, in the persona of a rural labourer, deserves to be quoted at length. 'Luxurious man', the mower or reaper rants exquisitely,

> *to bring his vice in use,*
> *Did after him the world seduce:*
> *And from the fields the flowers and plants allure,*
> *Where Nature was most plain and pure.*
> *He first enclosed within the gardens square*
> *A dead and standing pool of air:*
> *And a more luscious earth for them did knead,*
> *Which stupefied them while it fed.*
> *The pink grew then as double as his mind;*
> *The nutriment did change the kind.*

Andrew Marvell, 'The Mower against Gardens' (comp. 1650–52), *The Poems of Andrew Marvell*, ed. by Nigel Smith (Harlow: Pearson Education Limited, 2003), pp. 133–34, ll. 1–10 (l. 9).

220 '*labour*', '*work . . . grows*', '*what . . . wild*': *PL*, IX. 208–12.

The Limits of Paradise

236 'prune': *PL*, IV. 438 & IX. 210.

'lop': *PL*, IV. 629 & IX. 210.

'tend' ('tendance', 'tended' and, in this sense, 'tender'): *PL*, IV. 438, V. 22, VIII. 47, IX. 206, 419, 801 & XI. 276.

'*unsightly . . . unsmooth*'; '*branches overgrown*': *PL*, IV. 631; 627.

'*to dress . . . keep it*': *AV*, Genesis 2:15.

'*she took . . . did eat*': *AV*, Genesis 3:6.

236–37   *'How can . . . forlorn?'*: *PL*, IX. 908–10.

    237   *'keep from wilderness'*: *PL*, IX. 245.

         'to wild': *PL*, IX. 212.

         'all things', *'happiness'*, *'solitude'*; *'conversation'*; *'society . . . Social communication'*: *PL*, VIII. 363–65; 418; 383–429.

    241   *'fusain'*: *FH*, p. 704. Some artists prize the charcoal of spindle tips above drawing charcoal made from any other wood.